Al's Odyssey
From Catonsville, MD to Japan

Edward Albert Aldridge II's World War II Letters

Edward Albert Aldridge II

Edited, Explained, Annotated by Elwin Carl Penski

Copyright © 2009 by Elwin C. Penski
All rights reserved.
El's Research Studies
Website: www.ElsResearchStudies.com
ISBN-13: 978-0-9841210-0-7
ISBN-10: 0-9841210-0-5

Library of Congress Control Number: 2009906604

Suggested Cataloging Data

Authors:	Aldridge, Edward Albert
Title:	Al's Odyssey, From Catonsville MD to Japan
Subtitle:	Edward Albert Aldridge II, World War II Letters
Edition:	First Edition
Publisher:	Joppa, Maryland, El's Research Studies, 2009
Description:	382 pages, 34 images, 9.5 inch height
Note:	Includes footnotes, index, and references
Language:	English
Subjects:	United States History, World War II,
	United States Army Air Force History
	19th century to 1946, ; Tinian, Japan
	Catonsville, Maryland; Catonsville Manor
	Penski. Neher, & Aldridge families
	Miami, Florida; Amarillo, Texas
	Fort Meyers, Florida; Naples, Florida
	Lincoln, Nebraska; Clovis, New Mexico
	Topeka, Kansas
Format:	Book

Dedicated to the millions of young people killed or injured in our nations wars

and

the young men closely related to Al who died too young.

<u>Men Al Knew Well</u>

Edward Joseph Kampel (1921-1945), Al's Cousin
Herman Penski (1911-1943), Al's Uncle

<u>Men Al Never Knew</u>

Edward Albert Aldridge I (1901-1922), Al's Father
Nicholas E. Aldridge (1984-2003), Al's Grandson
Nelson Aldridge (~1909-~1923), Al's Uncle
James E. Penski (1975-2000), Al's Nephew
Henry L. Penski (1881-1902), Al's Great Uncle

In history books they are just names and statistics, but to their close family members, they were the whole world.

"To be prepared for war, is one of the most effectual means of preserving peace."

From President George Washington's first annual message to Congress, January 8, 1790

Contents

Introduction to Al's Odyssey	1
Al's Name	3
Acknowledgements	4
Background	5
World War II and How It Started	5
Creation of the U.S. Army Air Force (USAAF)	12
Mom, Margaret Elizabeth (Neher Aldridge) Penski	15
Al's Natural Father, Edward Albert Aldridge I	18
Pop, Elwin Penski	21
Al's Life before the War	31
Miami, Florida	46
Amarillo, Texas	87
Fort Meyers, Florida	150
Naples, Florida	175
Lincoln, Nebraska	196
Clovis, New Mexico	203
Topeka, Kansas	228
Mather Field, California	239
Tinian in the Pacific	242
Coming Home: Saipan and Camp Stoneman	362
Back to Baseball	365
Elwin Carl Penski, Al's Little Brother	368
Index	370

"… there is nothing which can better deserve you patronage, than the promotion of science and literature."

From President George Washington's first annual message to Congress, January 8, 1790

Al's Odyssey, from Catonsville to Japan
Edward Albert Aldridge II's World War II Letters

Introduction
By Elwin C. Penski

Many of my friends and academic historians have concentrated on ancient history of distant places, but my studies have taught me that the most important historians are those who capture events close to home and close to the times when they happened. If history is not captured promptly by the people who understand it and the context, it is usually lost forever.

I love to study history, but many books on history are boring with many names, dates, and short descriptions of events. Often one reads about events without understanding what really happened or the why it occurred. The feelings and logic of the persons involved are usually not included. This book is an attempt to include several types of history in one book (biography, local history, world history, family history and analysis) in the hope of making it educational, useful, interesting, and thought provoking. I did not try to publish this book with the usual commercial and academic book publishers because they are in a very competitive industry; they demand formulas that are not helpful — for example: making books harder to read with never-ending pages of endnotes instead of footnotes, right justification, or breaking words with hyphens. Commercial editors might remove a hundred pages or change the title. Their interests are different than the careful reader.

My older brother, Al was a very likeable, quiet young man caught up in the biggest and bloodiest war in history and in the chaos of an enormous explosion and implosion of the United States Army Air Force bureaucracy, which in spite of many mistakes, won the war. All Al wanted to do was come home and play baseball, but he did his duty for his country. Al liked people, and I do not recall anyone who did not like him. This book is based on his substantially unedited letters, his little brother's memories, family records, and

Al's Odyssey, from Catonsville to Japan
Edward Albert Aldridge II's World War II Letters

the well documented history of the times. I wrote the background chapter, the last chapter, the footnotes, and the large "verdana" background comments throughout, except where indicated.

The letters (1942-1946) were saved by Al's mother and father during and after WWII. During the 47 years after the war, they never discussed them. They died in 1992 and 1966. They were found in 2007 and 2009 in my basement. To my knowledge, no one had ever read them after the war until I gave them to Sheila Richards in the summer of 2007 to put in order and to copy for preservation. Executive Center Services, Inc. of Raleigh, North Carolina typed them. When I read them, I realized that they contained much about everyday life in that period that I had forgotten and/or never read about.

Most WWII veterans rarely talked about their war experiences. Some academics have attributed that to some kind of guilt, but from my knowledge when people have long painful experience, they just want move on and forget it. After the war, Al rarely talked about anything but sports, cars, and his children; but in these letters, he has a voice that most people that knew him probably never heard.

Many men in their final years regret not having preserved more of their family history. I have found that working on these was profoundly moving in both joy and sadness. I had vague memories of all of what was happening, but being only six when the war started I really did not understand. To a little child the war was just an exciting game of fun that made adults unhappy and cry. From the exaggerations of the movies, radio, and reading the newspapers at the time, most children thought the enemies were subhuman beings. Al and my parents tried to teach me that there were people like us on both sides who were victims of the war.

Al's Odyssey, from Catonsville to Japan
Edward Albert Aldridge II's World War II Letters

I tried to do the minimum editing possible of Al's letters in order to preserve the human history during that turbulent time. I tried to preserve the original words, spellings, repetitious language, and slang in spite of modern spell checkers and correcting software. Accordingly, I provide footnotes and background in large type to help the reader understand what Al discussed and did not discuss.

His highly emotional parents, Mom and Pop, were very worried about him. Mom was widowed and pregnant at the age of 19, she lost her father when she was 15, and many other close friends and relatives died while she was very young. She never seemed to recover from those early losses. This problem was compounded by the many deaths during WWII of neighborhood boys and people she knew. Thus, Al clearly tried not to frighten her because she consistently overreacted. I believe Al tended to be quiet because he was always surrounded by people who overreacted even to polite, harmless comments. Also, he was under military constraints not to give out information about the war. I recall WWII sayings like "A slip of the lip will sink a ship." From my experience and reading of history, I realize now that most of mankind's and government's problems stem from overreaction.

Al's Name

Al was known to different people by different names: Edward Albert Aldridge, Edward Albert Aldridge II, Albert Penski, Albert, Al, Henry, and Hank. His father was Edward Albert Aldridge, but he died of scarlet fever before Al was born. His mother gave him the same name as his father. In his extended family, there were many Edwards, thus everyone called him Albert. When he was seven, his mother married Pop, Elwin Penski, but in the Great Depression, no one had the time or money to change Al's last name.

Al's Odyssey, from Catonsville to Japan
Edward Albert Aldridge II's World War II Letters

Some of the neighbors called him Albert Penski, and the Army misspelled his name Aldrich.

At the time he went in the Army, there was a popular radio show called *Henry Aldridge,* and a series of Henry Aldridge movies in the forties. Thus, Al was frequently called Henry. Henry apparently evolved into Hank. I recall that when he returned from the war, his duffle bags had been painted with "Hank Aldridge" stencils. When I asked him about it, he just said, "That's what they called me."

Acknowledgements

The Archives staff of the Howard County Historical Society was of great help in researching the Donut Corporation of America. The Catonsville Room staff of the Catonsville Public Library and the Catonsville Public Library staff were very obliging in providing the Yearbooks of Catonsville High School, back issues of the Herald – Argus, and aiding with the research. Al's daughter, Barbara Jean (Aldridge) Dickens, was the first to read a draft of the book and made many helpful detailed comments. Susan K. Wooden, a professional writer, and my son Carl Albert Penski helped with editing. Sheila Richards, Executive Center Services, Inc. of Raleigh, North Carolina and the staff of Lightning Source were very helpful.

While I received much help, I am responsible for all errors.

Al's Odyssey, from Catonsville to Japan
Edward Albert Aldridge II's World War II Letters

Background

World War II and How It Started

While it is not the purpose of this book to delve into the complexities of events leading to World War II (WWII) about which many books[*] have been written. Nevertheless, it is desirable to provide a brief summary of selected events that will be of help to the reader who has not studied the war's history or who has forgotten it. Wars are a very important part of history due to the fact that they bring very significant change. The change may be good or bad, but it is always dramatic and heartbreaking to many people.

In the early 1800s, Germany was not a country, but 38 states, until invaded by Napoleon, Emperor of France. In retaliation and to defend against such invasions, Germany united and started its expansionistic policies which were successful with some setbacks until World War II.

One can make a good argument that World War II was not a separate war, but just a continuation of World War I. One could say that World War I started in 1914 with a pause for rearming during the period 1918 to 1939 and ran until 1945, the end of World War II. After World War I in 1918, the leaders of Russia, Germany, Japan, and Italy got their countries ready for war and were eager for territorial expansion and/or world domination. Meanwhile other world powers, the democracies, England, France, and the United States, and Germany's neighbors were ignoring or ignorant of what was happening in Germany, Russia and Japan.

---

[*] Taylor, A.J.P., The Origins of the Second World War, Simon & Schuster, New York, NY, 1961;
Churchill, W. S., The Second World War, Six Volumes, Mariner Books, Boston, MA, 1986.

Al's Odyssey, from Catonsville to Japan
Edward Albert Aldridge II's World War II Letters

England, France, the United States, and many other countries were blindly devoting their efforts to isolationism, peace and disarmament. So called "pacifist" activists actually fanned the flames of the impending war by disarming the democracies and blocking their efforts to prevent World War II. As a result, the expansionist dictators grew more ambitious and easy opportunities to derail their advance toward militaristic and expansionist polices were passed up. Nearly every American was a pacifist and isolationist, thinking that we should stay out of international affairs as George Washington advised under different circumstances.

Most historians date the start of World War II to 1939 when both Germany and Russia invaded Poland. As a result, France and Britain declared war on Germany but not on Russia. The only reason Joseph Stalin, dictator of Russia, was our ally instead of Hitler's ally was because Hitler double crossed him by invading Russia. Also the Communist influence and infiltration in the West was very effective.[*] I recall teachers and other adults speaking highly of socialism, communism, and Uncle Joe Stalin. Many major leaders thought that the United States could improve our relations with Stalin during the war. Some people thought the Soviets deserved special consideration because they took the brunt of the war in the European theater[†] even though they had helped rearm Germany before they were attacked by Hitler. Also, when I first started to read as a boy and visited the Catonsville Public Library, I noticed a lot of "red" books published by the Canadian Communist Party, but I was interested mainly in the Lone Ranger and in Ted Williams, the fighter pilot and baseball star. Like most people during that period, my parents were never very interested in politics beyond supporting the Democratic Party and the United States.

---

[*] The Manhattan Project, U.S. Department of Energy, Washington D.C., www.doe.gov/about/history.htm, 2007.
[†] While Russia took heavy losses, Poland lost the highest percent of their population of any country in Europe due fighting during WORLD WAR II. Russia's war losses are hard to estimate because of Stalin's purges.

Background

Al's Odyssey, from Catonsville to Japan
Edward Albert Aldridge II's World War II Letters

Actually, the struggle for domination of Europe had gone on for thousands of years, and Hitler admired the Roman Empire's expansionist and cruel practices.

Some historians say World War II in the Pacific theater started in 1931 with the Japanese invasion of Manchuria. Japan had plotted an imperial takeover of Asia and the Pacific for nearly a century. In 1868, Emperor Meiji became the head of state of Japan. In the Sino-Japanese War of 1894-95, Japan defeated China and obtained control of Taiwan. In the Russo-Japanese War in 1904-05, Japan annihilated Russia's Baltic fleet, and Japan annexed Korea completely in 1910.

In July 1937, the second Sino-Japanese War broke out, and the Japanese forces conquered nearly the whole coast of China. They committed severe war atrocities on the Chinese people. This war with China continued through the duration of World War II. In 1940, Japan occupied Vietnam. In December 1941, Japan attacked Pearl Harbor and several other countries all over the Pacific including the border of India in the West and New Guinea in the South. After Pearl Harbor the Japanese conquered Hong Kong, the Philippines, Malaya, Burma, and Borneo.

The war in Africa started in 1935, when Italy invaded Ethiopia.

Many excuses were put forward for Germany's and Japan's aggressive behavior. The Treaty of Versailles after World War I mandated the following:

- Germany was not allowed to have a military;
- German ships used for trading were given to the Allies;
- Germany was forced to give up territories in Africa, the Pacific, and Europe;
- Germany was ordered to pay $33 billion in war damages.

These steps helped put Germany into a huge, chaotic depression.

Background

Al's Odyssey, from Catonsville to Japan
Edward Albert Aldridge II's World War II Letters

The Treaty of Versailles was too punitive, but not as unjust as claimed by the Germans due to the fact that the treaty was never really enforced. The lands taken from Germany were lands that were conquered (Alsace-Lorraine) or partitioned (Lower Silesia, the Polish Corridor) by Germany, Russia, and Austria in the late 1700's. Hitler, the new leader of Germany, started rearming Germany in early 1933 in defiance of the Treaty of Versailles. German troops invaded the Rhineland in 1936 reigniting German's expansion policies that led to the conquest of Austria, Czechoslovakia, Sudetenland, Slovakia, Poland, Denmark, Norway, France, Belgium, Netherlands, Rumania, Greece, Yugoslavia, Ukraine, parts of Russia, Lithuania, Egypt, etc.

My humble interpretation of why there was such an unbelievably savage war in the 20th century attributes to the success, misinterpretation, and misuse of science and technology. It was widely recognized that science and technology had made enormous progress and was of great value to mankind in the decades before the war. Germany was a leader in science and technology, and many Americans completed their scientific studies in Germany.

First, socialists, like the quacks who sold snake oil medicines, pretended that the ancient economic system of socialism was derived from science and was necessary for progress. They also asserted that it must be worldwide to work. Worldwide government and world conquest have been the senseless goals of tyrants throughout history. On the other hand, the Roman Emperor Diocletian found the Roman Empire (which was not nearly worldwide) too large to manage and thus divided it in half.[*] Corporations also frequently spin off divisions, and the U.S. Army spun off the Air Force when it became too large to manage and had an entirely different culture in contrast to the ground forces. Conquest and unification, even if successful, are not always good

---

[*] Barnes, T.D., The New Empire of Diocletian and Constantine, Harvard University Press, 1982.

Background

Al's Odyssey, from Catonsville to Japan
Edward Albert Aldridge II's World War II Letters

ideas. If companies, countries, and government departments have very different cultures, problems, or visions; unification may not be advantageous.

Second, Charles Darwin had shown how species evolved in his book titled On the Origin of Species by Means of Natural Selection, Or the Preservation of Favored Races in the Struggle for Life. As a result of such science, leaders throughout the world, including the West, felt justified in incorporating this "science" into policies, laws, politics, medicine, genetics, and economics even though these applications contradicted ethics, science, law, most constitutions and most of the religions.[*] Instead of the standard being that *all people are created equal and have individual rights* the standard was changed to *for the benefit the all important state, government may use genocide and greater state control of individuals to improve the state and the human race* – whatever that meant. The *state* is usually the ambitious and corrupt people in control of the government, thus *to improve mankind* usually meant making people more *compliant to government orders or dumbing down the people*.[†] Hence, Germany, Russia and Japan used conquest and genocide in furthering the paranoid goals of their leaders. Stalin initiated large scale genocide when he killed 7 million Ukrainians between 1932 and 1933. Western newspapers, in support of the illusion of socialist progressiveness, cooperated with Stalin by denying the genocide.

Nazi[‡] Germany promoted its own scientific analysis showing that some races were subhuman and should be eliminated. This politicalization and misuse of science resulted in the tragic death of

---

[*] Weikart, R., From Darwin to Hitler: Evolutionary Ethics, Eugenics, and Racism in Germany, Palgrave Macmillian, New York, 2005.
[†] In the 20th century, dictators often killed, persecuted, or drove out educated people.
[‡] Nazi was the common name for the National Socialist German Worker's Party or Nationalsozialistische Deutsche Arbeiterpartei in the German language.

Background

Al's Odyssey, from Catonsville to Japan
Edward Albert Aldridge II's World War II Letters

many millions of gifted, innocent, beautiful, brilliant people. As a result, many intelligent and civilized people all over the world were perplexed by their youthful ideals, damaged, and pained for life by the logic of these stupid dictators and cruelty of their wars on innocent people.

A local editorial published in the spring of 1940, titled "It Might Happen Here,"[*] pointed out the pathetic military weaknesses of the U.S. That was about the time Al graduated from high school and about eighteen months before we entered the war. For about a decade, we had a greatly feared terrible war and an economic depression hanging over our heads. The editorial stated that the weak nations were in the greatest danger of attack. The editorial also held, *"The very weapons that made"* the Nazi's *"successful – thousands of airplanes, tanks, mechanized artillery, and other arms – are the weapons we lack. We cannot build them in a hurry because our puny arms industry is not prepared"* to go into mass production. By disarming us, pacifists[†] had assured that we would be attacked and have no choice but to fight a long hard bloody war.

Japanese leaders saw what a pathetic position we were in. They watched democracies falling one after another leaving colonial empires up for grabs. They recalled that during World War I, the Wilson administration had done a poor job of getting military

---

[*] Editorial, It Might Happen Here, *Herald – Argus and Baltimore Countian*, Catonsville, Maryland, May 24, 1940.

[†] While I tend to be a pacifist in most situations, in this case it would be irresponsible not to call a spade a spade. While nearly all Americans were pacifists for good reasons before World War II, in this instance, it proved to be a tragic error. Most people wanted to avoid the horrors of World War I, chemical and trench warfare, so it was an understandable error. Also, many thought the great flu epidemic and the great depression were punishments from God for our fighting. On the other hand, if history is to be of any value to prepare us for the future, I believe it is essential that history be written honestly and inclusive of the hard lessons learned.

Background

Al's Odyssey, from Catonsville to Japan
Edward Albert Aldridge II's World War II Letters

production going, even by the end of the war. During World War II, the United States was putting painful and effective economic pressure on Japan to force negotiations, and Japan had probably bitten off more than it could chew in its efforts dominate the Pacific area. They needed a more compliant United States to provide them with oil and other natural resources. Knocking out the United States Navy of the Pacific at Pearl Harbor seemed to Japanese military leaders like their only and best choice. Thus, they gambled that an attack would result in negotiations favorable to Japan.

Every knowledgeable person knew war was coming. The only question was when and where.

Al's Odyssey, from Catonsville to Japan
Edward Albert Aldridge II's World War II Letters

Creation of the U.S. Army Air Force (USAAF)

In 1898, the U.S. Army Signal Corps contracted with Samuel Pierpont Langley to build an airplane. The plane which he built never flew but made two magnificent dives into the Potomac River on December 8, 1903 to the great amusement of the newspapers. Several days later Wilbur and Orville Wright of Dayton, Ohio actually flew their airplane.[*][†] In January 1905, the Wright brothers offered to provide the War Department with a flying machine that not only could fly but could fly into the wind. The War Department turned down the offer.

After the issuance of a patent to the Wrights in 1906 and with the wise guidance of President Theodore Roosevelt, on August 1, 1907, Captain Charles Chandler became the head of the Aeronautical Division of the Signal Corps. In 1908, the corps ordered a dirigible balloon of the Zeppelin type then in use in Germany and contracted with the Wrights for an airplane. The Wright plane was delivered in 1909, and the Wright brothers then began to train a few young Army pilots.

In 1911 Congress first funded military aviation, and the importance of military aviation was verified in Europe during World War I. Aircraft proved to be vital for artillery spotting, for bombing, and for reconnaissance behind enemy lines. Every nation sought to be in command of the air, and battles between the "knights of the air" became the core of great legends and there was great romance to flying.[‡][§] At the time of America's declaration of war against

---

[*] Mackworth-Praed, B. (editor), Aviation, The Pioneer Years, Studio Editions, Ltd., London, 1990.
[†] Tobin, J., To Conquer The Air—The Wright Brothers and the Great Race for Flight, Free Press, Division of Simon & Shuster, 2003.
[‡] Germany's Jewish Knights of the Air, http://people.sinclair.edu/thomasmartin/knights, Sinclair Community College, Dayton, Ohio, 2008.
[§] Douhet, G., Command of the Air, Arno Press, New York, 1942

Background

Al's Odyssey, from Catonsville to Japan
Edward Albert Aldridge II's World War II Letters

Germany on April 6, 1917, the Army aviation was ill-equipped. At the end of the war, in spite of $640 million from Congress for aviation, the only American accomplishment in the field of aircraft production was the Liberty engine. Of the 740 U.S. aircraft at the front in France at the time of the Armistice on November 11, 1918, almost all were European-made. In general, the Wilson administration did a poor job of supporting the U.S. troops in combat with adequate production. Still, the U.S. Air Service had distinguished itself in battles against the Germans.

After World War I, there was much deliberation about the function, strategy, appropriate targets and organization of the United States Air Force. Despite much disagreement, a doctrine was adopted that stressed precision bombing of industrial targets by heavily armed long-range aircraft. A big step was taken in 1935 with the creation of a combat air force, called the "GHQ Air Force," commanded by an aviator and answering to the Chief of Staff of the Army. Nonetheless, the GHQ Air Force remained undersized compared to air forces in Europe. The Air Corps could only buy a few of the new four-engine B-17 Flying Fortresses, intended for strategic bombing, and in 1938, there were only thirteen on hand.

The only protection the United States had in 1938 was two oceans. An isolationist government had its head in the sand. In 1938 we could train 500 pilots per year. During the World War II, we graduated 224,331 pilots and 282,836 gunners. The building of air fields and bases took place at a torrid pace. Until January 1943, over a year after the War started, most of the War Department was in temporary buildings on the Washington D.C. Mall. In July 1941, a rush plan for the Pentagon was drawn up, and by January 1943 the biggest office building in the world was dedicated.

During World War II, American air power became enormously dominant. Reports from Europe in 1939 and 1940 proved the leading role of the airplane in modern war. The Army Air Force was directly under the orders of the Chief of Staff of the Army,

Background

Al's Odyssey, from Catonsville to Japan
Edward Albert Aldridge II's World War II Letters

General George C. Marshall. In its expansion during World War II, the Army Air Corps became the world's most powerful air force. From the Army Air Corps of 1939, with 20,000 men and 2,400 planes, grew to the nearly autonomous Army Air Force (AAF) of 1944, with almost 2.4 million personnel and 80,000 aircraft. This was a remarkable expansion. Four air forces were created in the continental United States. In the end, twelve more air forces went overseas and served against the Germans and Japanese. When Al enlisted, he was caught up in the chaos of the rapid expansion.

In the war against Japan, General Douglas MacArthur made his advance along New Guinea by leap-frogging his air forces forward, using amphibious forces to open up new bases. The AAF also assisted Admiral Chester Nimitz's carriers in their island-hopping across the Central Pacific and supported Allied forces in Burma and China. The Twentieth Air Force was equipped with the new long-range B-29 Super Fortresses. The B-29s were used for bombing Japan's home islands, first from China and then from the Mariana Islands. In August 1945, the Twentieth Air Force B-29s from Tinian dropped the atomic bombs on Hiroshima and Nagasaki, fire bombed Japan's cities including Tokyo, and depleted Japan's oil supplies, which ended the war. The B-29 bombings convinced Japan's military leaders not to force a bloody kamikaze fight until being overrun by armies as had been necessary in Germany.

Background

Al's Odyssey, from Catonsville to Japan
Edward Albert Aldridge II's World War II Letters

Mom
Margaret Elizabeth (Neher Aldridge) Penski

Mom was born September 18th, 1902 on Freeland Street in Beltzhoover, Pittsburgh, Pennsylvania. Her parents were Marie Penski[*] and Edward Neher, both of whom had migrated from Germany. Edward came to avoid being drafted into the German Army, and Marie came to join her parents in 1891. She came through New York on a ship from Rotterdam named Veendam. They met while singing professionally with a German opera company. Mom had three older sisters named Florence, Rosaline, and Sophie; an older brother, Carl Edward[†] and a younger brother Benjamin. Mom's family lived in Beltzhoover, Baily Plan, Brookline and Edgesbrook, Pennsylvania (Bridgeville, P.O.) in or near Pittsburgh, Pennsylvania.[‡]

Mom went to Beltzhoover School, and graduated 8th grade with high marks. Also, Mom attended one year at South Hills High School and one year at Short Course Business High School.

Mom married Edward Albert Aldridge on April 29, 1922 at the age of 19. He was a traveling life insurance salesman. He worked for National Life Insurance Company's branch in Nashville, Tennessee. Edward, her husband, died August 4, 1922 three months after the marriage. Edward Albert Aldridge II was born in 1923. As a widow, Mom worked at Joseph Horne Company, a large department store in Pittsburgh, as a typist, cashier, posting, filing and was a

---

[*] Grandma, in Al's letters, was born in 1871 in Hohenkirch, Germany and came to the United States with her Brother, August, when she was 20 years old. Her parents had been here for 2 years. (New York, *Passenger Lists, 1820-1957*).
[†] Carl Edward Neher was born April 8, 1895 in Eureka, McPherson County, South Dakota (*South Dakota Births, 1856-1903*). The rest of Grandma's children were born in Pittsburgh.
[‡] Details taken from Mom's writings.

Background

Al's Odyssey, from Catonsville to Japan
Edward Albert Aldridge II's World War II Letters

personal secretary to Mr. Stouffer, head cashier until December 1930.

Mom married Elwin Penski (Pop) from Baltimore, Maryland, on December 8, 1930. They first lived on Fulton Avenue near Baker Street in Baltimore City until January 29, 1931. After that, they moved into a house that Pop had built in Catonsville Manor, Maryland, and her son Albert joined them. Mom lived there for 40 years, until June 26, 1971.

Elwin Carl Penski (Little Elwin) was born to Mom and Pop several years later on June 18, 1935.

Mom's main interest was people: relatives, neighbors, friends, and everyone she met. She corresponded with all of her relatives, old friends, and distant relatives she never saw for many decades. She talked regularly on the phone to closer relatives and neighbors. When family visited, she gave them a report on weddings, funerals, births, and other major events. I think her concentration on reporting gave Al and Little Elwin to a broad prospective on life – a significant part of a liberal education that people pay a great deal of money for today.

Mom's main hobbies were family, teaching Sunday school, tending to the ill, dressmaking, cooking, crocheting, animals, and playing cards.

Al's Odyssey, from Catonsville to Japan
Edward Albert Aldridge II's World War II Letters

Al's natural father, Ed, and Mom, probably in 1922

Background

Al's Odyssey, from Catonsville to Japan
Edward Albert Aldridge II's World War II Letters

Al's Natural Father
Edward Albert Aldridge I

Edward Albert Aldridge I (1901-1922) was Margaret Elizabeth (Neher Aldridge) Penski's first husband, and Edward Albert Aldridge II's, father.

Actually, I know little about him, but I have assembled here what little information that I could find. My mother referred to him as Ed and he called her Peggy and Margaret. Accordingly, hereafter I shall call him Ed.

I can speculate about where Ed's name came from. His parents were born in England, and they were schoolteachers. Victoria, Queen of Great Britain, was a popular ruler of the greatest empire in the world from 1837 until she died in 1901. Her beloved husband and the father of her nine children was Prince Albert. Her eldest son was Albert Edward, who became King Edward VII in 1901, the same year Ed was born. He was a popular King who promoted peace. Since Victoria had been queen for 64 years, her death had a great impact not only in the British Empire but also throughout the entire world.

The first mention of Aldridge is in 1086 AD when "Alrewic" was sparsely inhabited farmland.[*] Alrewic is a Saxon word meaning "Alder village." Alder trees are a member of the Birch family.

The village of Aldridge had a population of 736 in 1801. Aldridge became an industrial village in the early 1800s. Mining caused a population surge to 2478 by 1901. Aldridge has been absorbed into the Walsall Metropolitan Borough, a modern city.

---

[*] Walsall Local History Center, Walsall, U.K.

Background

Al's Odyssey, from Catonsville to Japan
Edward Albert Aldridge II's World War II Letters

Ed was an insurance agent who traveled a lot. He worked for The National Life and Accident Insurance Co. of Nashville, Tennessee. My mother said that he was the nicest man that she ever knew.

My Uncle, Benjamin Henry Neher, wrote me in 1992. He said, "I remember him (Ed) well; tall, fair, blond, very handsome and had a gentle disposition. He talked to me a lot; I was about 14 years old then. Your mother and he lived with us.[*] His death was a very tragic event as he did not even live to see his son. Soon afterwards, his brother, Nelson, who was around my age, also passed away. A third brother, Frank, was burned in a fire, very badly, but survived."

Ed's sisters Annie and Emily, of the Pittsburgh area, visited us several times. His sisters lived to be quite old. I received a letter from Emily in 1992. She was only seven when Ed died and as a result had no memories of him to share. I met a large number of his cousins, nieces, nephews, aunts and uncles right after World War II when I was a child, but I remember very little except trying to play badminton with them on a very steep Pittsburgh hill where they kept falling down.

The information on Ed's death certificate is given below:

>*NAME: Edward Albert Aldridge*
>*BORN: October 24, 1901 in Pittsburgh, PA*
>*DIED: August 4, 1922*
>
>*CAUSE OF DEATH: Typhoid Fever*
>
>*ADDRESS: 88 Beltzhoover Ave., 18th Ward*
>
>*Pittsburgh, Allegheny County*
>
>*FILE NO: 71901*
>
>*REGISTER NO: 5636*

---

[*] They lived with Margaret's mother, Marie Neher, at 88 Beltzhoover Avenue

Background

Al's Odyssey, from Catonsville to Japan
Edward Albert Aldridge II's World War II Letters

FATHER: Samuel Aldridge born in England

MOTHER: Ann Elizabeth Parry born in England

WIFE: Mrs. Edward Aldridge, 88 Beltzhoover Ave.

BURIED in Zimmerman Cemetery[*], Pittsburgh, PA

In the days before antibiotics, typhoid patients became delirious, ran high fevers, and bled a lot. Margaret said that Ed made her promise to never marry again after he died. Mom kept her promise to Ed for eight years.

Al, Edward Albert Aldridge II, (usually called "Albert") was born January 31, 1923 after Ed's death.

---

[*] Since then, the the Zimmerman Cemetery changed its name to Birmingham Congregational Cemetery. In the late 1990s, maps still used a very old name: German United Evangelical Cemetery. As best as the Cemetery attendant and I could determine, the name on the 1997 Rand McNally map had been wrong for 75 years or longer. Mom's parents and Ed are buried in Lot 681 in Sec. H. Perpetual care has been paid for, and I ordered a new stone for Edward Albert Aldridge I's grave some time ago.

Background

Al's Odyssey, from Catonsville to Japan
Edward Albert Aldridge II's World War II Letters

Pop
Elwin Penski

Pop's father was John Penski (Grandpa) and his mother was Martha Griel. There is some confusion about her maiden name, some records show Puschmann and some records show Griel. When I knew them, they lived on Wilkens Avenue a short distance east of Gwynns Falls River in Baltimore. Pop was born in 1895 and had no middle name. Pop went to a German-English school and dropped out after the six grade to go to work in the meat packing industry. There were no child labor laws at that time. Despite little education, he could do trigonometry and read very well. He read the *Baltimore Sun* newspaper several hours daily late at night. He knew a lot about electronics, construction, Baltimore, and the people who lived there. He built one of the first radios in his neighborhood and neighbors came in to listen. He repaired radios, did plumbing, electric wiring, carpentry, made his own tools, and rebuilt cars.

Pop was a very smart man, but like most people who do poorly in school; he had a problem focusing when talking people were around him. Some academically successful people can focus on their work even in the middle of a lot of commotion, but both Mom and Pop usually ended up at the center of any disturbance. When Pop worked alone or with other working people, he focused very well.

Background

Al's Odyssey, from Catonsville to Japan
Edward Albert Aldridge II's World War II Letters

Pop and three of six siblings: left to right: Freda, Pop, Elsie, and Roland
(About 1899) Pop's other siblings were John, Herman, and Lillian

Background

Al's Odyssey, from Catonsville to Japan
Edward Albert Aldridge II's World War II Letters

Pop during World War I

Pop served in the Army Quartermaster Corp during World War I. The deadliest plague in world history began in 1918, during the war. The influenza epidemic is estimated to have killed 100 million people. The military was hit very hard. Efforts by the unprepared

Background

Al's Odyssey, from Catonsville to Japan
Edward Albert Aldridge II's World War II Letters

doctors appeared to inflame the problem.[*] There were so many dead that Pop recounted how in the winter cold he piled up bodies like logs in the pictures that follow. He also told the story that when his sergeant ordered him to go in the clinic to get a shot for the influenza, he went in the front door and out the back door. Like many people of that time, he never trusted doctors. Doctors had no antibiotics and few treatments that worked.

Edward James Neher (Buddy), one of Al's cousins, wrote me in July 2000 that *"I remember your dad, mom, and Albert visiting us in Hiller, Pa when I was in the fifth grade. Albert demonstrated driving the family car. I don't remember if you were yet in the family. I don't think so. After your family left, I was in hysterics the next couple of days until dad showed me how to drive our car."* If Buddy was in the fifth grade, Albert was about 11 years old. Pop started teaching me to drive long before I was 16. He let me drive his old A-Model Ford around by myself on the backcountry, dirt roads long before I had a license, but I never drove on the paved roads until I was licensed. Now that I think about it, I cannot recall ever seeing any policemen on the backcountry dirt roads in those days.

When Pop was a boy, he rode his bicycle over to Washington D.C. to see his aunt Martha who had a seamstress business there. He claimed that about in 1910, the main road, Route 1, between Baltimore and Washington was unpaved and had only a few horse drawn wagons as traffic. Aunt Martha was aunt to Mom also. They had the same Grandfather, Carl August Penski, who was a Baptist Minister in Danzig, East Prussia; Hamburg, Germany; Baltimore, Maryland; and Eureka, South Dakota. Aunt Martha played a role as matchmaker between Mom and Pop. She never had any children so she devoted time to her many nieces and nephews.

---

[*] Barry, J.M., <u>The Great Influenza</u>, Viking Penguin, New York, NY, 2004.

Background

Al's Odyssey, from Catonsville to Japan
Edward Albert Aldridge II's World War II Letters

Aunt Martha

Pop used to tell me about his learning to drive. When he bought his first car, there was no such thing as a driver's license in Maryland. After he bought the car, the salesman showed him how to start the car, release the brake, and start moving in first gear. On the way home, he figured out how to get it into second gear. His parents never owned a car nor learned to drive. Public transportation was adequate in those days, and some people never traveled out of their neighborhood. Most people only built houses near trolley (streetcar) lines and only went where their legs, trolleys, steamboats, and railroads took them.

Background

Al's Odyssey, from Catonsville to Japan
Edward Albert Aldridge II's World War II Letters

Pop also had a motorcycle. He got a motorcycle license in about 1914. He claimed that when he rode up the street, everyone came out of his or her houses to look. He often warned me about the dangers of motorcycles, but the only accident he ever told me about was the time a horse lurched out in front of him and he hit it.

Pop's Wood Business in the Back Yard in the Early 1930s

Pop ran a wood business in the back yard and on several adjoining lots in Catonsville Manor. Before oil and gas became popular, people heated their homes and cooked with wood and coal. Coal fires had to be started with wood. My dad sold a variety of types of wood that he cut from farms on the western side of Baltimore. He usually worked as a carpenter during part of the year.

Early in the morning, he had several trucks running, saws screaming, (powered by truck engines) and loud men working. The noise was vexing. Looking back, I feel sorry for our few neighbors. The business ended in the forties when most homes obtained oil and gas furnaces. The house is still there, but it looks different. An old

Background

Al's Odyssey, from Catonsville to Japan
Edward Albert Aldridge II's World War II Letters

saw mill shed on an adjoining lot is now part of another house. The following is a typical advertisement for the business.

> THE EVENING SUN, Nov. 3, 1931
> CORD Wood sawed, split; blocks or fireplace;
> $3.50 delivered. Phone Gilmor 7566

Pop was building a house in Catonsville Manor when he married Mom. He had a saw mill there, a number of trucks, a garage, a shed, a well with a hand pump, an outhouse and a business. He bought, rented, and borrowed neighboring land. He delivered ice in the summer[*] and sold firewood in the winter, recycled scrap iron for money, made concrete blocks, sawed lumber, and worked as a carpenter, electrician, and other jobs in between. For example, Pop worked on installing electricity in the Baltimore Shot Tower, worked setting up wood forms for big buildings, changed light bulbs on the tops of skyscrapers, and helped with the construction of the Route 40 Bridge over the Patapsco River.

Pop was depression-proof. He knew how to live frugally. He never borrowed money – he never had a mortgage or even any type of credit[†] to my knowledge. Neither did he ever have health insurance or life insurance. Through the Great Depression, he nearly always had some kind of work and sufficient money for food. Pop was proud that he never had to accept charity or welfare. During the Depression he advertised for help in the winter, but found few

---

[*] Ice boxes were used before being replaced by refrigerators. They were usually made of wood and the ice that cooled the food needed to be replaced every few days. Icemen with a truckload of ice traveled the communities yelling "Ice." The ice was in the form of about a cubic foot block and was carried with a rag or ice tongs. Most women did not work outside the home due to the fact that they had to take care of many such matters.

[†] Retail credit goes far back in time and printed credit cards started around the beginnings of the 1900s. Charge plates, the forerunner of the modern plastic credit card, were introduced in the 1930s.

Background

Al's Odyssey, from Catonsville to Japan
Edward Albert Aldridge II's World War II Letters

people except elderly farmers who wanted to do hard work. He worked for Westinghouse on Wilkens Avenue in Baltimore during World War II where he constructed wooden and metal cabinets for experimental electronic devices for the war.

When relatives visited, they got a splendid meal with several types of meat, several vegetables and multiple desserts. I do not know why, but I was very thin through high school although I consumed great quantities of food. Eating and hard work were our main activities. Pop would come into the house after working to around 10 PM, read his newspaper, drink several cups of weak coffee, and eat prodigious quantities of food, like eight large donuts or sweet buns. Al and I made grilled cheese sandwiches in the evenings. We were relatively poor in most other ways, but when you are poor, you learn to manage money very efficiently. Most of our daily clothes were old, worn, patched, and rarely fashionable.

Pop believed in the sayings of Ben Franklin in *Poor Richard's Almanack* such as: "Plow deep while Sluggards sleep . . ." or "God gives all Things to Industry." Baseball was not quite "industry" to Pop, thus he never fully approved when his boys played baseball. On the other hand, we never skipped our chores or caused him much trouble, and he never tried hard to restrict our activities.

Al's Odyssey, from Catonsville to Japan
Edward Albert Aldridge II's World War II Letters

Pop at His Saw and Al on the Wood Pile, About 1932
Notice the saw had no safety features, but Pop amazingly retired with all his fingers.

Background

29

Al's Odyssey, from Catonsville to Japan
Edward Albert Aldridge II's World War II Letters

Left to right: Al, Pop, Little Elwin, and Mom in the year of 1936

Background

Al's Odyssey, from Catonsville to Japan
Edward Albert Aldridge II's World War II Letters

Al's Life before the War

Al was born in 1923. The 1930 census shows Al living with Mom, Grandma, his uncle Benjamin Henry Neher (age 21), and the Kampels: Lawrence (33), Florence, Mom's sister (33), Edward Joseph (9), and Lawrence (Larry, 4) in Washington, Pennsylvania. In Pittsburgh, he must have spent a lot of time with Grandma, his mother's mother. Mom worked throughout his childhood before she remarried. Al was left in Pittsburgh for several weeks after Mom remarried giving Pop and Mom time for a honeymoon and time to finish work on the house and get it furnished.

Al was 8 years old when he left Pittsburgh to move to Maryland. During the Great Depression, after Mom and Al left Pittsburgh, Grandma lost her home. She lived with her children thereafter moving from one family to the next as she was needed. On moving to Maryland, Al lived in Catonsville Manor; Al lived there until he married after the war. Al's home in Catonsville Manor was one house removed from Ingleside Avenue.[*]

---

[*] Ingleside Avenue connects Franklintown to Catonsville just west of Baltimore, Maryland. In those days, Catonsville Manor referred roughly to the area northwest of Ingleside between Johnycake Road and what is now Route 70. In Catonsville Manor most of the streets were named after Maryland counties.

Background

Al's Odyssey, from Catonsville to Japan
Edward Albert Aldridge II's World War II Letters

Cousin Edward Joseph Kampel "Edward Joseph" and Al (right) in Pittsburgh
Edward Joseph was killed in World War II.

Below, Little Elwin relates his recollections to give a description of what life was like in Catonsville Manor. Life was probably more primitive for Al who was 12 years older.

It was basically a rural area then with small and large farms all around. Today's, Meadows Industrial Park, Social Security Administration, Ingleside Shopping Center, Walden Circle, Westview Park, and Brigadoon were farms. Edmondson Heights

Background

Al's Odyssey, from Catonsville to Japan
Edward Albert Aldridge II's World War II Letters

Park, West Edmondale, and Westview Shopping Center were wooded. We used to sled down Saint Agnes Lane, and, as I recall, it was wooded on both sides all the way and there was little if any traffic.

Most of Baltimore County was agricultural. There were no interstate highways or beltways. Some time later, after World War II, in muddy weather, I recall playing touch football on the new Route 40 and rarely having to move off the road for an occasional car. There were no nearby libraries. The free library in Catonsville opened July 1, 1941 with mostly old donated books.[*] Most of children's reading in those days was the newspaper, the *Baltimore Sun*, specifically the comics, news, sports, and magazine sections. I recall reading the war news at age nine. I had a child's American history book with pictures that I must have read dozens of times. Sometimes, teachers were amazed at my knowledge of history.

Most of the few neighbors and Pop had poultry. I recall chickens, turkeys, ducks, geese, guinea hens, pigeons, and pheasants. Some neighbors had horses, hogs and cattle. A few neighbors grew grapes and had stills in their basements left over from the days of prohibition. Most people had vegetable gardens and fruit trees.

In between the houses, there were fields or wooded areas. Many of the fields had a thick plume grass that burned quickly and furiously, endangering houses that did not keep the tall grass away from the house. The fire departments were not much help because there were no water hydrants or supplies in the neighborhood. Most of the wells were 10 or 15 feet deep and had little water.

My first memories of plumbing were that there was only one cold water faucet in the kitchen. We used an outhouse outside with a cold wooden seat. Baths were taken in the kitchen or pantry in a steel tub with one kettle of hot water. Baths had to be taken quickly

---

[*] History of the Catonsville Library, www.bcplonline.org, 2008.

Background

Al's Odyssey, from Catonsville to Japan
Edward Albert Aldridge II's World War II Letters

as the tub and the water got cold fast. We usually washed off outside at the pump before we came in the house. I recall a kerosene stove in the pantry that was used to heat water. There was a electric stove and oven in the kitchen. Since Mom usually had the oven and five burners going at the same time, she used both simultaneously to prepare dinner. The kerosene stove was smelly, greasy, and dirty; and was replaced by a more pleasant wood stove that not only was used for cooking but heating the kitchen. Pop installed a modern bathroom and kitchen as soon as rationing was over and he could buy the components after WWII.

This is Al's home in Catonsville Manor in about 1930 when Al moved in. Pop built this house in his spare time, and Mom lived there for over 40 years.

Al's Odyssey, from Catonsville to Japan
Edward Albert Aldridge II's World War II Letters

There was a riding academy near the end of a jerkwater[*] streetcar line that ended about a half mile from nearby Franklintown where people rented horses and rode through the surrounding woods, fields and dirt roads. There were horse trails and dirt roads everywhere. The only paved road was Ingleside Avenue.[†] Rarely but sometimes, the County or somebody rolled and oiled a few of the side roads. Occasionally, Pop dumped cinders and stone in the ruts on our street so we could walk to Ingleside without going through the mud.

The streetcar that we used most was the line that ran along Edmondson Avenue. We walked through Judic's field which was mostly woods and emerged from the woods near Saint Agnes Church . We took Old Frederick Road to Orpington Road and followed Orpington Road to Edmondson Avenue where the North Bend loop for turning around was located. From there, streetcars went to downtown Baltimore, Catonsville and Ellicott City. Also on

---

[*] A jerkwater line was a trolley or streetcar line that ran on a single set of tracks. At the end of the line, on Dogwood Road, there was no loop to turn cars around. The jerkwater cars could be driven from either end. Thus, at the end of the line, the motormen just took off the control lever and moved to the other end of the car and drove off in the direction that had been backwards. The seats could be switched in either direction. The line went through Gwynns Falls Park, through Kernan Hospital grounds, along the river, through Dickeyville, an old, beautifully preserved village, and ended at Dogwood Road. My friends and I used to ride it just for fun. It was a better trip than most amusement park rides. Streetcars were a pleasant form of transportation, and if I recall correctly, the fare was only a nickel.

[†] Ingleside Avenue was shown as Shell Road on a 1915 map. (Bromley, G.W. and Bromley, W.S., Atlas of Baltimore County, Maryland, From Actual Surveys and Official Plans, G.W. Bromley and Co., Philadelphia, PA, 1915.)

Background

Al's Odyssey, from Catonsville to Japan
Edward Albert Aldridge II's World War II Letters

Edmondson Avenue nearby was the Westway Theater[*] where we went to see movies and newsreels. The walk was about a mile.

There were a few people who seemed to be wealthy in Catonsville Manor. On the other hand, a few families lived in chicken coops or garages during World War II when house building had stopped. If there was a building code, it was not enforced. After the war, some of those garages and chicken coop grew into large attractive ranch type homes. Some of the children were restricted to their homes and were rarely seen except when going to school. I often wondered what they did inside all the time since I was usually exploding with energy and had to get out and run wild.

Hawkers with horse drawn wagons shouting a loud but unintelligible message visited the neighborhood occasionally selling household items, cloths, ice, fruit and vegetables. Rice's Bakery bread man, delivering baked goods, came twice a week in a small truck. Also a milkman, delivering dairy products, came twice a week. Dry cleaners, insurance salesmen, Fuller Brush Men, ministers, encyclopedia salesmen, and peddlers of all types stopped by intermittently. Those who traveled by foot probably had slim profits and tired feet. The newspaper was usually delivered by a boy on bicycle. The mail was all delivered to a mailbox on the far side of Ingleside Avenue. There was no garbage pickup. We used the combustible garbage to start fires in the kitchen wood stove and the furnace in cold weather. In hot weather, we burned some of it outside. Metals and glass were all recycled. We sporadically picked up soft drink bottles off the sides of the roads and returned them to the stores for money which was usually sufficient to buy a few candy bars and a soft drink.

---

[*] The Westway Theater was located at the intersection of Edmondson Avenue and Aldershot Road. The Alpha Theater was located in Catonsville on Frederick Road across the street and a little east from the fire station. The was a little duckpin bowling alley in the basement of the Alpha Theater.

Background

Al's Odyssey, from Catonsville to Japan
Edward Albert Aldridge II's World War II Letters

Mom was kept very busy doing laundry by hand, ironing, carrying water from the well, boiling water for drinking, cleaning, canning, pulling weeds, feeding wood into the furnace and kitchen stove, reading to children, caring for and plucking chickens, mending clothes, making clothes, taking phone orders for Pop's businesses, shopping, and cooking. She made at least two hot meals a day and packed lunches for everyone on week days. If we ate in the evening, we did our own cooking. Pop usually stopped work at about 10 PM and made some coffee, read the newspaper, and ate various delicacies: limburger cheese, chicken necks, gizzards, pigs' feet, baked goods, smoked fish, and normal foods. We all read the paper before Pop, but we were required to keep in the same shape and order as it was delivered.

Family rules for children at our home were few and simple. Activities like running, playing and visiting with friends remained outside the house even in the winter. When it rained we played in sheds, barns, or garages. We could wander as far as we wanted, but we had to be home at mealtime, chore time, and at sunset. There were no sports programs for children in Catonsville or Catonsville Manor that I knew about. Children found or built their own ball fields on small lawns, pastures or fields and set up ball games as best and where they could. Baseball rules were modified for small fields. Hitting a house was an automatic out. Many games were played with first and third close together to narrow the field due to small fields and few players. A rock usually substituted for a base, and a log might be a backstop. If we had too few players, we deleted a base so that we never had all of one team on base at the same time and no batter. Sometimes, if we lost our baseball, we substituted a tennis ball, rubber ball, or rock. Occasionally, we burned off a field when the weeds got too high to play. Once a park ranger from Patapsco State Park came to insist that we put out our fire, but we never lost control of a fire. We were used to fighting field fires which were usually ignited by careless smokers flicking cigarettes out their car windows.

Background

Al's Odyssey, from Catonsville to Japan
Edward Albert Aldridge II's World War II Letters

A very pretty young woman, who was a neighbor, had a thoughtful boyfriend in his 20s who took a little interest in our difficulties playing sports and had the following card printed which he circulated around the neighborhood and put in local stores. It did nothing to help. Apparently, there were no parents in the neighborhood with experience, time, energy, or interest in sports.

> ● ATTENTION NEIGHBORS!
>
> We are proud to announce that the youngsters of this vicinity have organized their own ball team. This is the start of what we hope to be a permanent youth club.
>
> The boys of the club have voted that the name of their team be "Charley's Milk Bar" because of the generous help and donations made by him.
>
> The games will be played on Charley's field at Ingleside Avenue and Johnnycake Road. Look for schedule of games at Charley's Milk Bar.
>
> This is YOUR team and YOUR youngsters. It is YOUR duty to come to the the games to encourage these youths in their fight for cleaner sports and better recreation.
>
> DON'T LET THEM DOWN!
>
> JOHN WIEDENHOEFT, Manager,
> Catonsville Manor Sports Club.

When we played unsupervised softball at elementary school, we still used rocks for bases; and the fields were like cow pastures except they were more worn. We were usually allowed outside of the school before and after school, at recesses, and lunch time, unsupervised. In elementary school starting in the 4th grade, I brought a ball and bat and organized games and played nearly every day. lunch. On the other hand, at the Catonsville High School, the dedicated physical education teachers organized intramural league sports before school for everybody from the 8th grade on. We were watched and coached more carefully at the High School than at the Elementary School. Team sports were considered part of the education process: learning to work with people.

Background

Al's Odyssey, from Catonsville to Japan
Edward Albert Aldridge II's World War II Letters

Sometimes in elementary school we slipped off the school property to buy gum, candy, or model airplane kits.[*] Some children walked home for lunch. Most children enjoyed team sports even if they were not very good at them.

Fighting among boys was common. Mostly a few bullies picked on younger and weaker boys as a form of amusement. The range of ages of children in a school class was much larger than today – like 7 to 13. The rules of fighting were like modern boxing: no biting, no scratching, no hitting someone who was down, no kicking, no knives, no guns or sticks. The rules were always followed. The boys behaved almost like the heroes in the movies of the period. Many boys owned knives and guns, but I never saw the boys use them. I never saw a fight among girls or women.

Religion was a constant theme in Mom and Pop's conversations, but it did not transfer excessively to their children although Pop required that we read the Bible aloud at home. He was skeptical about most of the Bible except for Christ's teachings. Pop was very religious and always searching for a serious religion. He complained a lot about the sacrilegious language that people used. At the same time, Pop felt that church members and ministers were consistently ignoring the teachings of Christ, and according to his strict religious beliefs, most churches were Satan's hangouts. Pop's grandfather was a Baptist minister, but he died before Pop was born. Pop never found what he was searching for. In looking back, I realize that Bible reading was a useful activity. Many early immigrants to

---

[*] Model airplane kits at that time came in two types. One was a box with one page of plans and a few blocks of balsa wood. Sometimes the box included a lead propeller and wheels, and a few insignia decals. Eight year boys had to be a good carver with a very sharp knife to make anything that looked like the picture on the box. The second kind of model airplane was made from flimsy balsa wood sticks and tissue paper. While they were advertised to fly with rubber band motors, they were usually demolished on their first landing or even when one wound the rubber band too tight. With those one usually accepted the 10 hour task of building a beautiful airplane, showed it around, and threw in the stove when you were finished. All the excitement was in the building of it.

Background

Al's Odyssey, from Catonsville to Japan
Edward Albert Aldridge II's World War II Letters

America had no other book than the Bible, and the Bible provided a basis for education, law, government, customs, and changes in English law and customs. The Bible goes back about 3000 years, is one the main foundations of Western culture, and is the most widely read book in the world. It is a great help in understanding your neighbors and history.

Like Grandma, Mom thought of herself as a Baptist and went to church regularly. She usually attended Baptist churches but often went to churches of other denominations. Before and during World War II, she went to West Baltimore Baptist Church, a church that then held services in both German and English. The German services were mostly for the elderly, and during the war, the minister held services for German prisoners of war at Edgewood Arsenal. Al probably went to church regularly with Mom when he was a boy. My earliest memories were of him playing baseball on Sundays. A few of our relatives called themselves atheists. Discussions among men often involved religion and politics which women found distasteful at the time.

Al probably adopted some of Pop's views, but Al never talked about religion, that I recall, so I am not sure. Also, I think Al studied German in high school, and he was exposed to a lot of German from Grandma and elderly relatives in Pittsburgh and Baltimore, but I never heard him speak a word of German. Mom and Pop frequently spoke to their older relatives in German.

It seemed that everyone we knew supported the Democratic Party. Mom worked as an officer in the Catonsville Democratic Club for years. I cannot recall meeting a Republican until I went to college.

Background

Al's Odyssey, from Catonsville to Japan
Edward Albert Aldridge II's World War II Letters

While a teenager, Al worked at a golf driving range near our home picking up golf balls. The driving range was in Judik's Field[*] which was just on the southeast side of Ingleside Avenue and is now Edmondson Heights and West Edmondale. The balls were driven downhill from a location that is now roughly Newfield Road toward Harwall Road.

Al's main interest was sports, especially baseball. Baseball was by far the most important professional sport before World War II. I conjecture that Al's uncles took him to see the Pirates when he lived in Pittsburgh. They took me once when we were in Pittsburgh. Pop had no interest at all in baseball. Al went to Catonsville schools and graduated from Catonsville High School in 1940.[†] He liked mathematics. The comment about him in his yearbook was,

"When it comes to basketball scores and ping-pong, "Al" has something to talk about. But he lets his friends do all the talking."[‡]

His friends were interested in baseball and most seemed to live in or around Ellicott City. Many of the people he mentions in his letters were baseball friends. He also had friends from Arbutus, Lansdowne, and Catonsville Manor. I vaguely recall Al playing ping-pong on the dining room table.

---

[*] Judik's Field belonged to Mrs. Henry J. Judik. It had been Maidens Dairy farm. It was 120 acres. Now it is Westview Park. (Bromley, G.W. and Bromley, W.S., <u>Atlas of Baltimore County, Maryland, From Actual Surveys and Official Plans</u>, G.W. Bromley and Co., Philadelephia, PA, 1915.)
[†] In those days, graduation was after 11 years of school.
[‡] <u>Spectrum</u>, Catonsville High School, June 1940.

Background

Al's Odyssey, from Catonsville to Japan
Edward Albert Aldridge II's World War II Letters

Al in a Baseball Uniform
Is it the Tricounty League (Ann Arundel, Baltimore, and Carroll Counties)?

Background

Al's Odyssey, from Catonsville to Japan
Edward Albert Aldridge II's World War II Letters

Left to Right: Al, Cousin Larry Kampel, Little Elwin, Cousin Edward Joseph Kampel, and Grandma
On the porch was one many nice homeless cats that decided to move in with us. The picture probably was taken in 1940.

Background

Al's Odyssey, from Catonsville to Japan
Edward Albert Aldridge II's World War II Letters

Al's first job after graduating from high school was with a finance company in Hamilton, Northeast Baltimore where his duties included being a repossession agent. He did not like that job. Next, Al worked for the Donut Corporation of America (DCA),[*] in Ellicott City, Maryland before going into the Army. He worked in the office in the George Ellicott House which was later moved a short distance out of the flood plain and restored. They made 100 pound bags and wooden barrels of dry donut mixes that were dumped into big and small DCA automatic donut machines around the United States, England and Canada. The main ingredients were wheat flour, powdered egg yolk, powdered milk, and sugar. The DCA Ellicott City plant was the largest of its kind in the world. In the Ellicott City plant they also made the donut and other machines. The plant was located on the site of the Ellicott brother's first mill in 1774, a very historic area. It is the site of one of the oldest mills in the country. The Ellicott grain mill was initially powered by the Patapsco River.

Across the Patapsco River from the mill is the Station for the first passenger railroad in the United States.[†] In 1830, the first rail service hauled passengers between Baltimore and Ellicott Mills. For a while Ellicott City was a resort town.

While working at DCA, Al worked as an electroplater, duplicating machine operator, key punch machine operator, and punch card tabulating machine operator.[‡] Punch card tabulating machines were the forerunner of the office computer, and they were used for all of

---

[*] Many Countians Employed at the Doughnut Mill, *The Ellicott City Times,* Centennial Edition of March 1941 Section G, Pages 1-3, March 1941, courtesy of Howard County Historical Society.

[†] Historic Ellicott City, Inc., Ellicott City, MD, www.historicec.com, 2008.

[‡] *U.S. World War II Army Enlistment Records*, National Archives and Records Administration, 1938-1946, Provo, UT, USA.

Background

Al's Odyssey, from Catonsville to Japan
Edward Albert Aldridge II's World War II Letters

the 20th century until the 1980s. They were used for accounting, time-keeping, and payroll, and were programmed by hard wiring boards which were like telephone pluggable switchboards. Changing boards changed programs. The data was entered with punched cards and outputted with printers or card punches. Also, Al must have helped with the plating of the donut machines with chrome.

Speaking of donuts, when Grandma came to our house and cooked dinners, the main thing I recall was that she always made great crispy crullers, not to be confused with French crullers which are made with a lighter batter. Crullers, which could not easily be made by machines, were probably a forerunner of the easily automated donut. They were made with a cake type batter that was rolled flat and cut into strips. A hole was cut in the middle and then one end was twisted through the hole, and they were deep fried. Dunkin Donuts and Krispy Crème, the current donut shops, occasionally still make simpler and sweeter versions of crullers. Since Grandma's crullers were not as sweet as today's donuts, you could taste the delightful, fresh, cooked dough flavor.

Background

Al's Odyssey, from Catonsville to Japan
Edward Albert Aldridge II's World War II Letters

Miami, Florida

In 1941, The Great Depression was slowly ending and President Franklin D. Roosevelt had won an unprecedented third term in 1940. Roosevelt had promised to keep the country out of World War II which was raging in Europe and Asia. His Vice-President was Henry Wallace. A job that paid $1.00 per hour would support a family, buy a house, and a car. Gas was only 12 cents a gallon, a new house $4000.00, and rent $32.00 a month. Music by Glenn Miller and Jimmy Dorsey was very popular, and the New York Yankees had won the World Series.

The business men of Miami expected a very profitable winter, but these hopes were devastated on Sunday morning, December 7, 1941 when Japan attacked Pearl Harbor. The Japanese attack was a surprise attempt to knock out the U.S. Pacific Fleet. This was part of a Japanese plan to quickly create an unassailable Pacific and Asian empire. The surprise attack was very effective. "Most of the planes on Hickam and Wheeler" Air Fields "were destroyed, the Navy lost three-fourths of its planes on the ground, also."[*] Japanese spies had done a effective job of determining our vulnerabilities. Immediately the Hawaiian Governor declared martial law, military government assumed control, rationing preparations started, enemy aliens were rounded up, and schools

---

[*] Your Victory, Mid Pacific Command and Pacific Ocean Areas (MIDPAC), about 1946.

Al's Odyssey, from Catonsville to Japan
Edward Albert Aldridge II's World War II Letters

became hospitals and military posts. The next day, Wake Island was attacked by the Japanese.

So it was, the United States was forced to enter World War II. The nation became near totally committed to the War effort. Suddenly, newspaper editorials begged that we must forget our personal interests, and everyone must contribute to the war effort. We were in what the Nazi called "total war." Ninety two percent of the people on our planet were directly or indirectly involved.[*] Most healthy young men enlisted or were drafted, and many women helped by enlisting or taking what were traditionally "men's" jobs in factories. Nearly all factories were converted to military production. Production for civilian needs only included necessities. Catonsville High School students and staff started National Defense work and training for war. They did things like filling Christmas stockings for the Red Cross to give to servicemen, collected books for military camps, bomb proofing windows, practiced for air raids, sold and bought National Defense stamps and bonds, studied First Aid, donated blood, and collected money for the Red Cross.[†]

The ages of men eligible for the draft were from 20 to 45. Pop, who was 47, registered for the draft in 1942.[‡] When Al was eligible for the draft and a little over a year after the war started, on January 23,

---

[*] Editorial, This Is Total War, *Herald – Argus and Baltimore Countian*, Catonsville, Maryland, December 12, 1941.
[†] C.H.S. and the War, *Spectrum*, Catonsville High School, Maryland, June, 1942
[‡] U.S. World War II Draft Registration Cards, 1942

Miami, Florida

Al's Odyssey, from Catonsville to Japan
Edward Albert Aldridge II's World War II Letters

1943, Al enlisted "for the duration of the war or other emergency, plus six months."[*] The first place Al was stationed was Miami Beach.

German submarines were numerous in the Atlantic between the United States and Europe. Many waited off our east coast to sink our merchant ships in U.S. waters. On May 19, 1942, the Portero del Llano was torpedoed by a German submarine. This brought the violence of war within sight of Miami Beach. Debris from many ships began washing up on Miami's beaches as ships were sunk all around Florida's coasts. The closeness of war's violence plus blackouts, rationing of food and gasoline, restrictions on railroads, and rumors of the possibility that Germans might be landing in Florida ended South Florida's 1941-1942 vacation season.[†]

The businessmen of Miami were thankful to the Army and Navy when they decided to rent their hotel rooms and apartments for $20 a month. The Military used the hotels for barracks; restaurants for mess halls; colleges and theaters for classrooms; and beaches, racetracks, and golf courses for training fields and obstacle courses. At the training peak, the military population of Miami reached 82,000.[‡]

---

[*] *U.S. World War II Army Enlistment Records*, National Archives and Records Administration, 1938-1946, Provo, UT, USA.

[†] Miami 1941-1945, Historical Museum of Southern Florida, www.historical-museum.org, 2007.

[‡] Osburne, R.E., World War Sites in the United States, Riebel-Roque Publishing Company, Indianapolis, Indiana, 2007.

Al's Odyssey, from Catonsville to Japan
Edward Albert Aldridge II's World War II Letters

Pvt. E.A. Aldridge
1142 T.S.S. (T.S.) BTC #9
STU Flight 463
Miami Beach, Fla

February 10, 1943

Mom:

    We have been quite busy down here at the present time and I haven't much time to write. We have been taking tests for the last few days to determine what branch of the Air Corp we are to be placed in. I took three tests yesterday – radio aptitude test consisting of signals from a speaker, the same thing as dots and dashes. We were given two sets from which we where to tell if they similar or

Miami, Florida

Al's Odyssey, from Catonsville to Japan
Edward Albert Aldridge II's World War II Letters

not. One called a mechanical aptitude test consisted mainly on wheels and pulleys. The third was of general work including grammar, definition of words, physics; also one more consisting of purely mathematics.

Today we had an interview to decide our definite classification, however, I have to take another test tomorrow at 7:30, kind of early, but we have to get up every morning at 4:45 except Sunday, which is about six o'clock. The test I am going to take will decide, as far as I can find out, whether I go to AST School, for several months. This school is somewhere in Colorado -- the one Gene Hooper went to -- the boy who worked at D.C.A.[*] in the traffic department. The school is for clerical work of different kinds also supplies, etc.

I'm waiting for a chance to go into town so I can buy a pair of dress shoes – any low cut ones that have a plain toe and are brown.[†] The Army gave me two pair of shoes; however they are not so very light in weight or very good for dress.

To tell the truth I like it okay. The food is very good and there is plenty of it. We got ice cream twice in the last four days, with cake for every meal, and fruit for breakfast every day.

We have done some marching, but are still in the process stage, as they call it here.

---

[*] D.C.A. is Donut Corporation of America, Ellicott City, MD, -- where Albert worked before going in the Army.
[†] Shoes were rationed.

Miami, Florida

Al's Odyssey, from Catonsville to Japan
Edward Albert Aldridge II's World War II Letters

There's a lot more to say, but I want to go to the movies tonight. Give my love to Pop and Elwin, and tell Elwin he'll have to get better than S's on his next report.[*]

Love to all

Al

See if you can get me Joe's[†] address.

---

[*] S was satisfactory.
[†] Joe was Joseph Shearer, Al's first cousin from Pittsburgh.

Miami, Florida

Al's Odyssey, from Catonsville to Japan
Edward Albert Aldridge II's World War II Letters

2/14/43

Mom –

    I got your letter this evening that you sent Air Mail, however it might have gotten here this morning, because I missed the first mail call about noon. Today seventy-five out of the one hundred in our flight got K.P. today. Pop will know what that means. We had to get up at 3 o'clock this morning and did not get in until about seven at night. I sure did get plenty to eat, had double portions of everything that I liked, except milk, ice cream and cake, which I had all I could eat or drink. I don't think I ever ate so much ice cream in one day.

    I'm getting used to falling out early, for we have to get up at 4:45 every day except Sunday – it's not so bad if you go to bed early. They turn out the lights at nine thirty; however, you do not have to be in bed until 10:30.

    We finished our first five days of processing Friday, so now we are supposed to start drilling, which is all we do at Miami Beach, and this is supposed to take about 20 more days. So as far as I know after the twenty days, I go to AST School, as I stated before, for clerical work.

    The amount of time I spend here, however, could be more or less dependent upon how soon there are vacancies at the different schools.

    I'm not in the same hotel as I was last time I wrote you, but the address is the same. I am now sleeping in what used to be the club room. It's a large room, and ten fellows at present are sleeping here. We expect to move out of this room very shortly though.

    Ferel is here, but I don't know where he sleeps, but it is in the same hotel. I don't know how he got in the Air Corp, except that

Miami, Florida

Al's Odyssey, from Catonsville to Japan
Edward Albert Aldridge II's World War II Letters

Fort George Meade had a long quota to fill. I had to take about five tests at Fort Meade to get here and about ten since I have been here.

At night and all day Sunday, we can go any place on Miami Beach we want. The beach is about nine miles long with hotels along one side, and lots of places on both. There are several business sections, with four movies, and almost every kind of store.

The prices here are a lot higher here than in Baltimore, and if you try to buy a souvenir they charge just about any price they want.

I'm finishing this letter in the morning, since I didn't get much time last night.

Every body complained about it being cold this morning the temperature was about sixty with a slight breeze from the North.

As to the letter you received from Collector of Internal Revenue let me know what kind of a letter it is, and what it says, or if it just an income tax form. If you get a chance find call the Doughnut* and find out how much I made during the time I worked there. Did you ever get the insurance blank that I sent home in my first letter?

Everybody's getting ready to go out now so I better be signing off.

Give my love to Pop and Elwin and tell Pop I waiting for a letter from him and also one from Elwin, tell him to make it a little longer and to draw some pictures.

Love to All

Al

---

* Doughnut Corporation of America

Miami, Florida

Al's Odyssey, from Catonsville to Japan
Edward Albert Aldridge II's World War II Letters

2/17/43

Mom:

Just got back from noon chow. We had chicken; I was lucky and got two halves of breast, mashed potatoes, cabbage, red beats, lettuce, olives, and ice cream and cake. All in all it wasn't so bad. Lately the meals haven't been bad at all, the only thing I miss is milk, we only get it for breakfast and then we only get a small glass. Sometimes we get fruit flavored drinks, but most of the time coffee is the drink, I still don't drink it, because it's too strong.

We are starting seriously our basic drilling, which is supposed to be for eighteen days. Every day, for about two hours we get P.T., physical training. It's not so bad but it sure makes your muscles tired. We have to drill every day now in the morning and afternoon.

I read in the paper that there was a cold wave in Washington, and New York, however it didn't mention Baltimore. During that period the temperature dropped {here} to thirty eight and in several places whole fields of different crops were ruined.

I heard about the shoe rationing, but couldn't get much of the details. I want to buy a pair of brown shoes, but I don't know whether I can or not, how about letting me know the details.

Army life sure is different than at home, there is so many things to do that most of your spare time is occupied doing something. It's so dusty around here that we have to polish our shoes twice a day. And it always seems as if you have something to wash, such as socks, handkerchiefs, or underwear. I don't know if I have any more plain white handkerchiefs or not, if I have any monogrammed or not, will you send them to me, along with several white undershirts. I still have one that I didn't wear at Ft. Meade and also the ones the army gave me, but it won't hurt if I had some more.

Miami, Florida

Al's Odyssey, from Catonsville to Japan
Edward Albert Aldridge II's World War II Letters

I finished the candy you sent me today with the help of several other fellows. The cakes you sent were kind of stale when I got them; however, they all were eaten. Most of the sea foam was broken too, but that didn't make much difference it tasted good anyway. I've been waiting for the watch you said you were going to send, however, I guess I am a little impatient, or maybe the time passes a little slower here than it does at home. We get mail call here twice a day at noon and just before supper, and you would be surprised at the number of fellows that are present each time even though they know there is little chance of them getting mail.

Lots of the fellows have been getting their pictures taken down town. As yet, I haven't had much time, but I will get mine taken as soon as possible.

They really rob you when they take, for they charge a dollar for three small pictures like you can have taken at the {amusement} parks for a dime, and then most of them are faded. The larger pictures cost anywhere from two dollars up.

I think its time to close as there's not much more to say.

Love to Pop and Elwin and also you too.

Al

Miami, Florida

Al's Odyssey, from Catonsville to Japan
Edward Albert Aldridge II's World War II Letters

Pvt. E.A. Aldridge
1142 T.S.S. (T.S.) BTC #9
STU Flight 463
Miami Beach, Fla

2/18/43

Mom:

    Received you letter tonight and was very pleased to hear from you. I haven't as yet received the watch, but I suppose it will arrive either tomorrow or Saturday.

    It seems funny that you mention that I get office work because I was called down to headquarter last night about seven thirty. The sergeant asked me if I would like to stay here as permanent party and work in the payroll department or go to clerical school after I finished my basic training here. I didn't know what to do at the moment. What would you have done?

    I don't know if I did the wisest thing or not, but I told him that I would stay here, so the next day – which is today – I stopped my training and started to work. The work, so far as I know after one day's experience, consists of typing, posting and some calculating. I don't have to start to work until about eight o'clock and get an hour and one half lunch period, and quit at five. I'll have to move from the hotel I'm staying at now and move down town about forty nine blocks from here. I'll then be in about the heart of the business section of Miami Beach with any kind of store you want. I will live about 100 ft. from the hotel I will work in, just across the street, with the mess hall across on the other corner.

    I think I'll like it here so I might just as well try to. I will be called a permanent party, but from what I can make out any person here at Miami that is not classified as limited service may be moved at any time.

Miami, Florida

Al's Odyssey, from Catonsville to Japan
Edward Albert Aldridge II's World War II Letters

The sergeant told me that if I didn't want to stay after I had been here several weeks it would be no use taking the job, because after I learned the job I would have to stay for several months.

In the Army every person you see tells you something different and about 99 out of a hundred don't know half what their talking about most of the time.

I'll let you know any further developments that take place so far as the Army life is concerned.

Let me know if you and Pop have been using my car[*] and keeping the battery charged. I don't care how much you use it so don't worry about wearing it out, because as long as the motor runs you can drive it.

I saw on the *Road to Morocco* before I went to the army at the Edgewood.

Did you ever hear anything from the ration board about my pleasure driving before I left?

I found a store today during lunch time, where I can buy a Baltimore paper. The News only, anyway its better then none at all.

I think its time to sign off so love to all.

                                        Your son,

                                                Albert

---

[*] His car was a Ford Coupe with a rumble seat, about 1936.

Miami, Florida

Al's Odyssey, from Catonsville to Japan
Edward Albert Aldridge II's World War II Letters

2/22/43

Dear Pop

I've been quite busy lately; it seems as if there is always something to do around here, especially after we get finished in the evenings. We don't eat chow at night until seven o'clock, so when you get finished most of the evening is over. I usually try to get to bed around nine so I can a nights sleep, otherwise you don't feel so hot the next day.

At the present, the weather here is just about perfect, in every way. It doesn't get too hot in the day, because lately there has been a cool breeze off the ocean. At night its even better -- all you need is one blanket, and you feel comfortable all night.

Believe it or not, I will be here three weeks this Thursday, and I haven't been swimming yet. The water is not cold by any means, for some people are swimming all the time.

The government has really taken this place over in a big way. There are very few hotels that are still occupied by civilians, and most of them are in the heart of the business sections. There are quite a few private homes, however, where civilians live. A person coming here has a hard time finding a place to live, for all hotels are filled to capacity. The only places to rent are private homes, and they want a fortune for a weeks rent.

I received the watch you sent me Sunday mourning about nine o'clock. It arrived in good condition, as the way it was wrapped; it couldn't very easily be broken. At first when I received the package, I didn't know what was in the box. I want to thank you very much for sending it to me as it is just what I wanted. Down here you can't buy a watch, unless you pay an unreasonable price.

I'm starting this letter tonight again. When I got to the hotel tonight, I was told by some of the fellows that I am supposed to be on

Miami, Florida

Al's Odyssey, from Catonsville to Japan
Edward Albert Aldridge II's World War II Letters

shipment. I haven't as yet been told officially about it, as I was down at the Cadillac Hotel working as I told in a letter before.

I really don't know what's going to happen for sure, so as soon as I find out, I will let you know.

I have to go to chow now so I will write you again.

Love to all

                                                Your loving son
                                                      Albert

Pvt E. A. Aldridge
HQ & HQ Sq. STU BTC #9
Miami Beach, Fla.

                                                    February 25, 1943

Mom:

      Just a few lines at present for I only have about ten minutes to write at present. I stated in the letter to Dad that I was on shipment, however as far as I know the shipment is from 89th St. & Collins Ave. to 41st St. & Collins Ave Miami Beach, Florida. I do not want you to worry about me to go abroad, for before I could even prepare for such, I would have to finish my basic training. This training lasts at least three weeks, and I would have to take all of it. I have been working a week now at headquarters, and so far I haven't done very much work of any kind. Although I am learning the general routine, and I think I will like it here O.K.

With regard to the income tax blank and the statement of earnings, kindly send these to me as soon as possible. What I get form the different persons, there are several bills in Congress, relieving men in the service of their taxes, so I don't think it is advisable to pay

Miami, Florida

Al's Odyssey, from Catonsville to Japan
Edward Albert Aldridge II's World War II Letters

them now. Since I am being transferred, even though I am in the payroll Dept., I won't get paid this month, some kind of ruling; therefore I would like you to send me a money order for twenty dollars, as soon as possible. I haven't as yet bought any shoes, for I understand it is necessary to get the Captains signature before this can be done.

The insignias that I mailed are for you, and I was told that anyone could wear them, other than on any uniform. Tell Elwin that I got his pictures and I like them very much, he probably has received the letter I wrote him by today, as Dad too, the one I wrote him. I though Elwin might enjoy it better if I sent his letter separate, as it cost no more.[*]

It's almost time to leave the office for today, so I better close.

Love to all,

Albert.

P.S. Still in Miami, the below is my new address

Lord Tarleton Hotel
Hg & Hq Sq, BTC #9
Miami Beach, Florida

---

[*] Military personnel got free postage.

Miami, Florida

Al's Odyssey, from Catonsville to Japan
Edward Albert Aldridge II's World War II Letters

Wednesday 3/3/43

Mom:

Well all fine, here. I've been getting along fine and feel very good, I had a cold for the first weeks I was here, everybody seemed to have one when we first arrived, but it's gone for good now and I feel better than I have since I have been in the Army.

I getting more sleep now too for I don't have to get up until 5:45 instead of 4:45 as before. I get my meals at better times too and I can take my time to eat. The meals seem to be getting a lot better than they where at first, however I think I'm getting used to the food. The food is all good and tastes fine however, its always flavored and made a little different than what I ate home. No matter how they make it, it still won't taste like a meal at home would. We get plenty of vegetables, and jam, beside meat for every meal and always some kind of desert, cake or jello sometimes, apple sauce, and about once a week ice cream. Just about every Sunday, they have chicken; last Sunday was the best meal since I've eaten away from home -- turkey with all the trimmings. Whenever a General or Colonel visits this place, we always get the best meals.

Most of the fellows that I came down here with, have shipped out during the last week to all parts of the country. I haven't seen Ferel Geer for just about a week, and I don't know if he is still here.

I've got quite a large laundry this week it amounts to about 90 cents, however I won't be able to get it until Tuesday. At present I only have $1.10 so I hope to get your money order tomorrow or Saturday, at the latest.

Pop said he hasn't used my car in his letter; tell him he can use it all he wants. Down here you can get tires recapped, without an order from your ration board.

Miami, Florida

Al's Odyssey, from Catonsville to Japan
Edward Albert Aldridge II's World War II Letters

You said in one of your letters that the insurance had expired, but you didn't say what insurance, I think my automobile insurance is good until May (that is Fire, Theft & comprehensive) however I might be wrong, so if it is that insurance don't worry about it. As far as the other insurance 5,000 & 10,000 liability expires in June I believe. When the tags expire March 31, you might just as well cancel the other insurance as it will be of no use for I don't intend to get new tags.

If you or Pop want to use the car instead of one of Pop's, it is all right with me, for then you can then let the insurance go, as long as the term has to run.

I think you might just as well use it for its not doing any good sitting around. Don't worry about wearing it out because I don't' think you can do it very easy. Pop can drive it to work everyday if he wants.

We keep pretty busy here all of the time for there's always something to do. I work a few nights every week when we get busy and usually a half day Sunday. I don't mind it though because the work is not hard.

The ocean is just in back of this hotel, beside a swimming pool, with several diving boards even closer to the hotel. Yet I haven't been swimming once since I have been here. I don't know why though, I guess, I just never got around to it.

    Tell Elwin I will write him another letter very soon.
    Love to Pop and Elwin.

                      Your loving Son,

                  Abert

Miami, Florida

Al's Odyssey, from Catonsville to Japan
Edward Albert Aldridge II's World War II Letters

Wednesday, March 4, 1943

Mom:

I haven't had much chance to write lately, have been kind of busy getting settled. It's lunch time now, and I had an hour before I had to go back to work but not for long we have to parade today, if it doesn't rain. I'm sending my ration book back because it's of no use of me here. To buy a pair shoes, I have to get the Captain's permission, and they say he don't like the idea of wearing civilian shoes.

Would it be possible for you to buy a pair for me, if you can let me know. I wear size 8 ½ and get them wide, because with the shoes I wear now, they spread out. Brown without any kind of decorations, and plain toes and smooth leather are supposed to be regulation.

I hope you sent me the money order by this time for I would like to get it this week. Everything here is kind of expensive; they get 25¢ for any kind of Sunday sandwich, etc. Since I've been living here, I had to buy, two pair of stockings now I got eight pair which, will be plenty. In fact I don't need all of them now. When I was still drilling I bought two pair, because, we received three pair of sort of heavy ones for work or drilling, and three pair of lighter ones for dress, and we couldn't wear the light ones for drilling. Now I can wear any ones I want any time. I also bought a hat, patches or insignias, for all my shirts and coats, pair of swimming trunks, belt, soap, dish, and a dozen of other things.

My watch has been keeping very good time, and it is very useful. Its time to get back to work so give my love to Pop and Elwin, also yourself.

Your Son

Al

Miami, Florida

Al's Odyssey, from Catonsville to Japan
Edward Albert Aldridge II's World War II Letters

March 7, 1943

Mom:

Received your letter yesterday afternoon, just before lunch. It arrived Okay with the money order inside, which I got cashed at the Post Office. I also received the letter with the two dollars in it, as it happened to arrive the same time as the letter you wrote the same day but, did not send air mail. I also received a letter from, Grandma yesterday; she sent me a dollar, in her letter. I got a letter from Aunt Florence about a week ago, and as yet I haven't answered it, She said, "If I didn't have time to write her, to drop her a card"; and wished me the best of luck and so forth.

There's a baseball game today at Flamingo Park between BTC #4 and BTC#9, the latter is my training unit. The players are mostly professional players from the smaller leagues, however, several played in the major leagues, one with Pittsburgh. I think I will go to see it.

It really seems strange that is could be so cold in Maryland as it is nice and warm down here. We haven't had but one cold day since I've been here, then the temperature only fell to 37 for a short time at night; the rest of the day was warm. I went to the movies last night, and saw *Random Harvest*, wasn't such a bad picture, but there wasn't much action. There wasn't any killing in the picture, but I don't think Elwin or Pop would like it much.

There's not much more to say at present so I am going to close for the time being.

Love to all,
Albert –

Miami, Florida

Al's Odyssey, from Catonsville to Japan
Edward Albert Aldridge II's World War II Letters

Pvt. E. A. Aldridge
HQ & HQ Sq BTC #9
Lord Tarleton Hotel
Miami Beach, Fla.

                                            March 7, 1943
                                            Miami Beach, Fla.

Elwin:

    Just a few lines for my brother. I got you letter the other day, the one with picture of the airplane in the middle, it sure was some plane, with ten guns on it. You must be working hard in school; I understand you got two more "H's. See if you can't keep up the good work, for your brother. It must be cold at home, but that won't last very long for winter is almost over, then you will be able to do all of the playing outside you want.

    Write me often, and send me some more pictures.

                                                      Albert

Miami, Florida

Al's Odyssey, from Catonsville to Japan
Edward Albert Aldridge II's World War II Letters

Tuesday 3/9/43

Mom:

Just received your letter this afternoon, which was mailed March 8 – 6:30 P.M. Air Mail. Air Mail letters do usually arrive here the day before, ordinary letters would, when you send them air Mail.

I'm sorry to hear that Pop is sick again, it seem that when it gets cold and damp he always feels the worse. He ought to be here for the weather fine always with plenty of sunshine, and since I've been here there has only been about two days when it rained. I went swimming for the first time yesterday afternoon. The ocean here is really grand and it isn't quite as salty as it was in Rehoboth Beach. You also can go out much further before it gets too deep. There is also a swimming pool here, where you can go swimming, with several diving boards.

We started a night shift at work it starts at 6:30 p.m. to 12:30 a.m. It isn't at all bad for you don't have to get up in the mornings and get all day off. We only get it for a week at a time so it really breaks the monotony

I got sunburned, somewhat yesterday, but not enough to be too burned.

Regarding the shoes I want low ones, for I have two pair of high ones. I want to get a pair that is lighter than the ones I have at present. I can only use them when I'm off duty, but they still have to be brown, with smooth leather.

Yesterday I bought another Class A uniform for $6.00. Its sort of light brown or tan, the only kind where permitted to wear here. Now I have four suits, but the trouble is they get dirty so easily. When I had three suits, two were in the laundry all the time,

Miami, Florida

Al's Odyssey, from Catonsville to Japan
Edward Albert Aldridge II's World War II Letters

that left me only one which I was wearing. It takes over a week sometimes to get our laundry so if anything happened to the uniform you were wearing you were just out of luck

Another fellow and I went over to Miami this afternoon to go bowling, but we ended up in a movies. We also saw a double feature, *Trail of the Vigilante & You Can't Take It With You*. Both pictures were pretty good. Believe it or not I saw Dick Healy, the oldest one, in the newsreel in Australia sitting on the side of a boat. I'm sure it was him for his address is now San Francisco, Calif. Therefore, the battleship he is on must be in the Pacific Ocean somewhere.

I received the package with the handkerchiefs and undershirts, sometime ago. I guess I just forgot to tell you I received them.

I'm sorry to hear that it is still snowing and sleeting in Baltimore. It must be about time for some good weather, for all I can remember about this winter is bad weather.

I hope Pop gets better real soon. Tell him not to do so much work outside.

Love to all.

Albert

Miami, Florida

Al's Odyssey, from Catonsville to Japan
Edward Albert Aldridge II's World War II Letters

Pvt. E. A. Aldridge
HQ & HQ Sq BTC #9
Lord Tarleton Hotel
Miami Beach, Fla.

March 21, 1943

Mom:

Just a few lines this morning, too let you know all is fine. It's Sunday morning, about 11:15 A.M., just about time to go to chow. I understand we are to have turkey today. I guess I will spend most of the afternoon on the beach, since I do not have anything to do all afternoon.

I am going to start night work starting Monday night until Saturday. I like night work a lot better than day, because, I have a lot more time off. We only work from 6:30 A.M. to 12:00 midnight, and have the rest of the day off, except for a half hour drill.

The telephone call I made yesterday didn't cost me anything, actually. The telephone booth in which I made the call gives back all the money that is put in it. It must be broken. Only a few in the hotel knows this, and I was told not to say anything about it over the phone. I put $5.50 in the slot, but it all came back.

I just received the shoes, when I went for dinner. There just the kind I wanted, and fit perfect. It really seemed funny when I put them on, for they felt so light and comfortable.

Tell Pop and Elwin that I was sorry they were not there when I called, but I will try to call early some morning this week if I get a chance.

                                          Love to All

                                          Al

Miami, Florida

Al's Odyssey, from Catonsville to Japan
Edward Albert Aldridge II's World War II Letters

Pvt. E. A. Aldridge
HQ & HQ Sq BTC #9
Lord Tarleton Hotel
Miami Beach, Fla.

Master Elwin Penski

March 25, 1943

Elwin:

How's my brother getting along now in school? I hope you will make the A class very soon. I received several letters from you, with lots of pictures. I really do like to get letters from you, so keep writing to me, and don't forget the pictures.

The weather at home seems always to be bad, so I guess that you don't get much chance to get outside. However, winter is over, and the nice weather is just around the corner, then you will have plenty of chances to play outside in the sun. It has been sort of bad weather here all this week. It has been windy and cloudy most of the time, so I have only been swimming once this week, so far.

Every day I see boats pass here on the ocean, all kinds, coast guard, tankers, freighters, sailboats, and often whole convoys that take most of the day to pass.

Large airplanes, as well as smaller ones fly over the shore near the edge of the water. Sometimes they fly as low as fifty feet from the water, even lower than the fourth floor of the hotel where I work. A dirigible flies over the ocean almost every day and sometime it flies real low.[*]

---

[*] German submarines still were sinking ships off the coast of Florida in 1943.

Miami, Florida

Al's Odyssey, from Catonsville to Japan
Edward Albert Aldridge II's World War II Letters

I live in the highest hotel on the whole beach; it has about sixteen floors, although I live on the sixth.

In your last letter you asked me how to make an R as far as I know this kind is right "R," but it doesn't make much difference which way you make them just as long as they are neat.[*]

I'm closing now, so write me soon

Your loving brother
Al

---

[*] Elwin only remembers that teachers seemed to get agitated when he was at the blackboard because if he wrote several of the same numbers or letters he wrote them different ways by habit. He would start some at bottom, top, right, or left. When the teacher asked him to rewrite it, he would write it another way because he did not recall how he wrote the previous time.

Miami, Florida

Al's Odyssey, from Catonsville to Japan
Edward Albert Aldridge II's World War II Letters

March 29/43

Mom:

Well, all's well and fine. Haven't had much time to write as I have been quite busy for the past week. I received the cookies you sent the day before yesterday or Saturday. However, they didn't last long enough.

It's getting a little warmer here this week, compared with last, when it rained, and was chilly all week. I couldn't even go on the beach once, although I had the whole daytime off all week. Now that it's nice again, I'm on day work again. We are quite busy at present; however, we are supposed to get more help about the end of the week, as they started a three day course in Pay Roll work today. It's something new that our sergeant started so we won't have the trouble of breaking each new person in individually.

Two fellows working in the department are getting their discharges first of next month, because of their age, around forty.

The sergeant is also going to Officers Candidate School, soon.

There's not much more to say at present, so Love to all

Albert

Miami, Florida

Al's Odyssey, from Catonsville to Japan
Edward Albert Aldridge II's World War II Letters

In March of 1943, Paul Warfield Tibbets, Jr. was assigned as test pilot for the development of the Boeing's new Super Fortress, the B-29. The B-29 was being designed to fly so fast and at such high altitudes the enemy aircraft would have difficulty intercepting it. Tibbets had a long history of flying bombers. He flew the first American Flying Fortress mission against Nazi targets.

The B-29 was so new that Tibbets had to teach himself how to fly the airplane. The B-29s were having many problems with engine fires and production delays. The engine fire problem could cause catastrophic failure of the wing and the whole airplane. While the problem was worked on, it was never completely solved during World War II[*]

---

[*] Birdsall,S., <u>Saga of the Superfortress: the Dramatic Story of the B-29 and the 20th Air Force</u>, Seggewick and Jackson Limited, London, 1991.

Miami, Florida

Al's Odyssey, from Catonsville to Japan
Edward Albert Aldridge II's World War II Letters

Army Air Forces
Technical Training Command
Miami Beach, Florida

April 14, 1943

Mom:

Just a few lines to let you know that I am fine and everything is well.

I haven't written to you for a little over a week, however, it was impossible for me to do so.

I just got out of the hospital this morning; believe it or not, I had the measles. I don't know where I got them, but I had them for almost a week.

It was really good in the hospital, though for, we got the best of food and had nothing to do but read

Miami, Florida

73

Al's Odyssey, from Catonsville to Japan
Edward Albert Aldridge II's World War II Letters

That's all over now, and I am back at work again.

                         Your Loving Son

                         Albert

P.S.
Tell Dad I started to answer his letter but discovered I had the measles while I was writing so I'll have to start over.

Miami, Florida

Al's Odyssey, from Catonsville to Japan
Edward Albert Aldridge II's World War II Letters

Pvt. E. A. Aldridge
HQ & HQ Sq BTC #9
Lord Tarleton Hotel
Miami Beach, Fla.

                    Army Air Forces
               Technical Training Command
                  Miami Beach, Florida

                                    April 16, 1943

Dear Mom & Pop:

    Received your letter today and was very glad to receive it. Several of your letters seem to have been lost since I have been in the hospital.

    You mentioned that my fire & theft insurance has been in force although it's expired. I don't think it would be worth while to keep it since the car is not being used.

    I received a letter from Joe[*], today. He is going to school in the Signal Corp. where he was made a Corporal, when he entered. He also had the measles, and now he has scarlet fever. It seems he has all of the bad luck, at present.

    I received your cookies when I got out of the hospital, but they had been at the Hotel for the arrived the day I left, so when I got them they were not very fresh.

    I just received a letter from Bud Deller this afternoon and from what he says he is a long way from home.

---

[*] Joe is Joseph W. Shearer, Jr, Al's close first cousin from Pittsburgh, PA.

Miami, Florida

Al's Odyssey, from Catonsville to Japan
Edward Albert Aldridge II's World War II Letters

April 19/43

Mom & Pop:

Received your letter today am sorry to hear that Grandfather[*] died. But I suppose he had lived his scheduled time and everybody must die sometime, although no matter who the person may be they want to always live a little longer.

I don't want you to think that I have forgotten about home for that would be the last thing I would ever do. I suppose that you have received the letter, by the time I am writing this one, about being in the hospital.

I have been very busy, for the last week and have had hardly enough time to sleep and eat, but, now, I think it will be a little easier. Our department just was set up again, and is starting a different system.

I was supposed to be up for a Corporals rating, however, the amount of ratings for our department was cut, so now I am up for a "Pfc", a little better than at present.

There has been quite a bit of shipping {out} of the men in Headquarters Squadron, for the past several weeks, however I don't think I will leave here very soon. There are supposed to be several Companies of WAAC's[†] coming to take the place of the permanent party in June. So you never can tell what's going to happen.

---

[*] The grandfather was John Penski of 2607 Wilkens Avenue, Baltimore, MD.
[†] WAACs were the Women's Army Auxiliary Corp

Miami, Florida

Al's Odyssey, from Catonsville to Japan
Edward Albert Aldridge II's World War II Letters

I am living in the Lord Tarleton Hotel, in a room with three other fellows, we also have a private bathroom, and it is our responsibility to keep it and the room clean. I live on the sixth floor, of a seventeen floor hotel. Room 607 – I work in the Cadillac Hotel, which is right beside the Tarleton. These two hotels are just about the two largest, and best on the whole Beach. Clark Gable was supposed to spend every summer on the fourth floor of the Lord Tarleton.

I better close now. Much love to Everybody

                              Your Loving Son
                              Albert

P.S. Tell Elwin I like his pictures.

Don't mind the green writing paper for the Sq ON gave it away free of charge; however, I don't have much more left.

I guess I'll have to close for the present

                              Love to All

                              Al

Miami, Florida

Al's Odyssey, from Catonsville to Japan
Edward Albert Aldridge II's World War II Letters

Pfc. E. A. Aldridge
HQ & HQ Sq BTC #9
Miami Beach, Fla.

Army Air Forces
Technical Training Command
Miami Beach, Florida

4/27/43

Dear Mom & Pop

    Received your package the later part of last week and boy was I glad to get it. I cut the chocolate bar last night and it sure was swell. I just got finished eating another piece of it before I started writing this letter. I had all day yesterday off so several fellows and I went to Hialeah, over to the race track and the airport. Elwin would have liked to see the airport. There were many large transcontinental liners from the Pan American and Eastern Air Lines. Also large and small army planes, including about ten long range bombers.

    We visited the race track, for the Army is going to take it over for a supply station. Although it was not open, the place was really a beautiful picture. It looks more like a large park than a race track. In the center of the track is a flock of Flamingo Birds, a race from South America and Africa. All around the place are flowers of bright colors, and vines climbing over most of the buildings.

    Well I suppose that spring must have arrived in full gala by this time. And I suppose that you are not sorry in the least, for the winter must have been the hardest in several years.

    The weather is still nice around here, not too hot at present. If nothing unexpected happens you can expect a money order from me for ten or fifteen dollars, around the fifth of next month.

Miami, Florida

Al's Odyssey, from Catonsville to Japan
Edward Albert Aldridge II's World War II Letters

At present there isn't much chance of getting a furlough, for we are quite busy and do not have enough office workers.

The garden you are making must be quite a bit in reality now, but I really think it will be a lot better to have your own vegetables.*

I have to close for the present.

        Much Love to All

        Al

---

* During WWII, the government promoted gardens, called "victory gardens", to alleviate food shortages.

Miami, Florida

Al's Odyssey, from Catonsville to Japan
Edward Albert Aldridge II's World War II Letters

Pfc. E. A. Aldridge
HQ & HQ Sq BTC #9
Miami Beach, Fla.

Army Air Forces
Technical Training Command
Miami Beach, Florida

May 1, 1943

Mom & Pop

    Haven't received a letter from you for almost a week, I hope you're not too busy to write. I don't get very much time now, but I think it won't be so bad in a few days.

    Everything here is going along in about the usual manner, with not any thing usual to speak of. I have it easy considering most other Army camps. Time passes so fast I can't seem to keep track of it most of the time. I just put off writing once or twice and before I know it a whole week has passed.

    Is Grandma[*] still at Aunt Kate's[†] or has she came back yet.

    Elwin has only about a month and one half of school left, and I hope he is working hard to get good marks. Tell him I am going to write him a letter very soon.

    Every time I write a letter home, I have to stop and think about how things look at home, for now it seems as if it was all nothing more than a dream. For all I have to depend on is the letters I get from home, and my memories.

---

[*] Maria (Penski) Neher was the mother of Al's mother.
[†] Aunt Kate is Catherine Neher the wife Ben Neher, mom's brother.

Miami, Florida

Al's Odyssey, from Catonsville to Japan
Edward Albert Aldridge II's World War II Letters

I've gained a few pounds recently now I weigh 171 lbs. I get plenty to eat, but once in a while I get tired of eating in the mess hall, so I go over to Miami and buy a meal at a restaurant but I can't afford it very often.

A fellow who used to work at DCA[*] is down here, and I go out with him once in a while.

On the radio now is a blind man operating a circle saw, and it happens he is from Baltimore.

Not much more to write at present.

                                        Love to Everyone

                                        Albert

---

[*] Donut Corporation of America, Ellicott City, MD was where Albert worked before going in the Army.

Miami, Florida

Al's Odyssey, from Catonsville to Japan
Edward Albert Aldridge II's World War II Letters

Pfc. E. A. Aldridge
HQ & HQ Sq BTC #9
Miami Beach, Fla.

May 12, 1943

Mom & Pop

Received your letter today, and am really sorry to hear that Elwin has been sick again. He seems to be sick so often.[*]

Don't think I have forgotten to write, but last night week I had quite a bit of work, and didn't have any time to do anything. However, things are better this week again, so far. We have had so many different systems, in payroll lately, and everyone seems to make more work for us.

Under the present plan, I'm assistant head of all the trainee rolls, and head of all the typing. Its not so bad, however, it leaves me a lot of work to do myself.

I am very fine, and don't worry about me, for I am a healthy as I can be. Every day at noon I go out on the beach and go swimming in the pool.

I am glad that the weather is really nice at last at home. Perhaps now Elwin will be able to keep well, and stop getting colds, which seem to be causing him so much trouble. The sunshine will do him a lot of good just as long as he doesn't go out during the rain and get wet feet.

---

[*] Elwin missed sixty six days of school in the Second Grade. He had every childhood disease: influenza, two types of measles, mumps, whooping cough, bronchitis, colds, chick pox, and probably others. In those days, Elwin only recalls being vaccinated for small pox before entering school. Somehow Elwin managed to be promoted to the second grade.

Miami, Florida

Al's Odyssey, from Catonsville to Japan
Edward Albert Aldridge II's World War II Letters

    For the last two days it has be hot here, however the hot spells usually don't last very long. A breeze from the ocean as a rule keeps it quite cool at night so it is all right sleeping.

    How is the garden marking out, I suppose it is beginning to sprout by this time.

    How are you making out with all of the rationing? I suppose at times it must be difficult to get everything you would like to have.

    Is Pop working much now?* You said in your letter he was working Sunday. I suppose with the garden he must be busy.

    Tell little Elwin that I really like his pictures, and enjoy him sending them to me. Don't forget to tell him to eat a lot of vegetables for they will do more to keep him well than anything else. For when I come home I want him to be strong and healthy like he should be.

    There is an old bomber down Collins Avenue, set up in the park for everybody to see. You can go real close to it and see just what it is like. Elwin would surely like to see it, for it is just like the pictures he draws.

    Its just about time to go to bed, so I say write soon, and Love to Everyone, Mom, Pop & Elwin

                              Your loving Son

                              Albert

---

* Pop worked for a defense contractor called Westinghouse on Wilkens Avenue in Baltimore. He built cabinets for new and experimental electronic devices.

Miami, Florida

Al's Odyssey, from Catonsville to Japan
Edward Albert Aldridge II's World War II Letters

Pfc. E. A. Aldridge
HQ & HQ Sq BTC #9
Miami Beach, Fla.

May 19, 1943

Mom:

Received your letter today, and was surprised to hear that little Elwin had pneumonia.[*] You should have told me when he was very sick, and then perhaps I could have gotten an emergency furlough. I'm glad though the he is getting better for I would rather not come home at all, then when someone is sick. He must have been quite weak for he has been sick off and on all winter.

Tell little Elwin that I want him to get well real soon, and that I pray for him every night. He is good boy and I doesn't deserve to be sick so often.

Thanks a lot for the writing paper, for I am just starting to run out again. I hope it will arrive before the first of next week.

BTC #9 is breaking up and the permanent parties are being shipped out, in three cadres. I am on the first which is to leave here around the twenty fifth of this month. We have been told that our destination would be Amarillo, Texas, however this is not definite. I still will be in P/R dept as far as I know.

As far as getting a furlough is concerned I don't think there will be much chance for some time to come.

---

[*] Little Elwin was treated for pneumonia with sulfa drugs. Sulfa drugs cause vitamin deficiencies which led to rickets which causes bone deformity. When the bones were deforming, Little Elwin complained of chest pains. The doctor interpreted the pain as a heart problem rather than rickets. Years later, the doctor admitted that Elwin never had a heart problem.

Miami, Florida

Al's Odyssey, from Catonsville to Japan
Edward Albert Aldridge II's World War II Letters

I'm not surprised at the raising of the prices of food, for they are quite high here too. Speaking of potatoes we very seldom get them to eat here, and also, get plenty of noodles, spaghetti and rice. We get plenty to eat of almost everything though, except potatoes and meat.

I will write again in a day or two and let you know how things go. Love to all.

Your Loving Son

Albert

Miami, Florida

Al's Odyssey, from Catonsville to Japan
Edward Albert Aldridge II's World War II Letters

Miami, Florida

Al's Odyssey, from Catonsville to Japan
Edward Albert Aldridge II's World War II Letters

Amarillo, Texas

Amarillo, Texas, is located near the center of the Texas Panhandle. It is in a plains region that has a relatively flat surface and little drainage in the soil. Due to the lack of developed drainage, the rainfall evaporates, soaks into the ground, or forms temporary alkaline salt lakes. Amarillo has a history of treacherous tornados and dust storms.

The Army Air Force acquired English Field, a commercial airfield 8 miles east of the center of Amarillo, early in the war. The field was used as a basic training center and to train aircraft mechanics and flight engineers for B-29 bombers. In 1968, English Field became Amarillo Municipal Airport.[*]

Al stayed in payroll work and at Amarillo for a long time. He must have been the only one they could find to run the complex payroll machinery.

---

[*] Osburne, R.E., World War Sites in the United States, Riebel-Roque Publishing Company, Indianapolis, IN, 2007

Al's Odyssey, from Catonsville to Japan
Edward Albert Aldridge II's World War II Letters

Amarillo Army Air Field
Amarillo, Texas
6/7/43

Pfc. E. A. Aldridge
Hq & Hq Det BTS
Amarillo AA Fld
Amarillo, Texas

Mom & Pop

    I am very sorry I could not write sooner, but I was not certain of this address, and I have been very busy, since I have been here.

    At least I am at a real Army Camp, and in the long run I really think it is a lot better then at Miami Beach. Here we live in barracks, with about forty in each barrack. There's more fun living this way then in hotel rooms. All of the fellows in my barracks came with me from Miami Beach so most of us knew each other. We don't have to spend so much time each mornings cleaning now, only sleeping and moping around our own bed, which takes about five minutes, where it took four of us about forty-five minutes each day to clean the room and bath. The trainees take care of the latrines so we don't have to bother about them.

    I am still working in pay roll here and as far as I know will continue there for the present. They are starting a Basic Training School here to go along with the mechanic school and airport already here.

Amarillo, Texas

Al's Odyssey, from Catonsville to Japan
Edward Albert Aldridge II's World War II Letters

It would surely interest little Elwin here for while working I can see all kind of airplanes, from little cubes, like over at the airport[*], to large four motored bombers. They are continually running around the field taking off and landing. In some of the hangers you can see the ones the students are working on, half apart.

One of the fellows who works in pay roll and was in the room with me in Miami Beach and slept next to me here fell off a truck Saturday, while we were moving our headquarters. The truck was going about thirty-five miles an hour. He is in the hospital now. When I saw him Sunday afternoon he was told that the end of his back bone was cracked, however they hadn't finished taking x-rays yet, I am going to see him again tomorrow night.

The weather here is not quite as good as Miami, but is not as hot and the nights are cool. We have to use blankets every night.

On the Post there are eight Post Exchanges, where you can buy anything you want from ice cream at fifteen cents a pint, and really good milk shakes for a dime, sundaes, etc., to clothes. There also is a Service Club where you can read, write, play cards, games, and get ice cream milk shakes sandwiches and cake. Besides, there are two restaurants, and two movies which charge fifteen cents to get in.

I also will have more chance to play ball in the evenings for it doesn't get dark here until about ten o'clock.

Amarillo Texas is about ten miles from camp, a town of about 65,000 people with lots of movies several bowling alleys and skating rinks. It doesn't cost anything to get into town for all we have to do is to walk out to the main road, and you can get a ride

---

[*] Probably, he is talking about a little airport in Baltimore County around Security Mall.

Amarillo, Texas

Al's Odyssey, from Catonsville to Japan
Edward Albert Aldridge II's World War II Letters

right in to town. However, it costs fifteen cents to ride back on the bus. The people down here are more friendly and nicer than those I've met any where else. They go miles out of their way to take you to the part of town you want to go to, and often when you walk down the street they say hello, good morning, or good evening or other such remarks.

All of the land around here is flat and dry with very few trees.

The food here is very much better here than it was at the beach. We also get milk for two meals a day, and potatoes which we seldom saw at the beach.

I haven't received but one letter from you since I have arrived here, and that one was one, which was sent to Miami Beach. My address as near as I can get is at the top of the first page. The first letter I wrote from here I mailed in Amarillo, however I suppose you received it.

Let me know how little Elwin is getting along, and I sure hope by this time he is a well and playing around outside, as ever. It's getting quite late so I will close for the present

                              Much Love To All
                              Albert

Amarillo, Texas

Al's Odyssey, from Catonsville to Japan
Edward Albert Aldridge II's World War II Letters

Pfc E. A. Aldridge
904th Training Group BTC
Amarillo AA Fld.
Amarillo, Texas

June 17, 1943

Mom & Pop:

Just a few lines to let you know all is well. I moved into a new barrack and again have a different address, it is at the end of the letter.

Elwin must be just about finished school, and I bet he must be happy to get a vacation. Tell him I have a small present for his birthday, but I don't know how soon I will be able to send it, for I don't go to town very often.

Our set up here is beginning to run regularly again and at the present we are only working six days a week, which is very good.

I received the writing paper and cookies you sent, just in time though, for I had just run out of envelopes. We have a nice walk every morning noon and night to and from work, its about a mile each way.

The weather here is very dry, even when its gets really hot you don't perspire very much. Every night the sleeping is swell, for its good and cool. We use as many as two heavy blankets almost every night, however the next day it gets hot again.

We have to leave the office now, so I will have to close.

Love to All

Albert

Amarillo, Texas

Al's Odyssey, from Catonsville to Japan
Edward Albert Aldridge II's World War II Letters

Pfc. E. A. Aldridge
904th Training Group BTC
Amarillo AA Fld.
Amarillo, Texas

June 27, 1943

Mom & Pop:

    Received your letter today, and was very glad to get it. Also the one from Elwin. I haven't had much time to write to anyone, however, since I have been moving around so much, and I expect to move again, although I don't know just when, but I hope it will be soon, for the barracks where I am at now is too far from where Hq. is.

    I am glad to hear that Elwin passed to the third grade, of course I was sure that he would if there would be any way possible. He must be glad that summer is here and vacation time brings him plenty of time to play outside in the sunshine.

    Every letter you write you mention a furlough. There is not chance to get one before I am in the army six months, which will be July 23. However, there are four ahead of me in payroll and we have to wait until we get more help before anyone can go at all. I have already inquired as to the fare from here to Baltimore, the same as I did from KB to home. It is about forty dollars a round trip from here, for soldiers and takes about fifty six hours traveling time.

    The soldier who was in the hospital is out now and is all right, for he was only bruised. The doctors told him that he was very lucky to get off so easily.

    I guess Pop takes benefit of the light at nights, to do work around the house. He must like daylight saving time by now. Here it is light to ten o'clock every night, because we just at the end of the time belt, a few miles further west the time is one hour later.

Amarillo, Texas

Al's Odyssey, from Catonsville to Japan
Edward Albert Aldridge II's World War II Letters

There is going to be a Rodeo here over the 4th of July at Amarillo, it is supposed to be the real western style. I have seen quite a few cowboys in Amarillo, although almost of the farmers and ranchers near the town wear western clothes, and high heel boots. There are several stores in town that sell nothing but leather goods for the ranchers.

The watch Pop sent me is still keeping good time as usual, and I am very proud of it. I have to get a new strap for it, as it broke yesterday. I have been looking at one in the Post Exchange (PX) which I am going to buy, which is waterproof and only costs thirty-five cents.

I get paid again on the last day of the month, and I am going to sent twenty dollars home so you can be expecting it around the fourth or fifth of July.

We are not allowed to take photographs or any other kind of pictures in this camp, because of the airplanes here. I am going to get a day off during the week after the fourth of July, and then I will have a picture taken in town. There is no place open at night or on Sunday.

There is not much to say at present so I will write again very soon.

Love to all, Mom, Dad and Elwin.

                                        Your loving son:
                                        Albert

Amarillo, Texas

Al's Odyssey, from Catonsville to Japan
Edward Albert Aldridge II's World War II Letters

On July 10, 1943, the Americans and British forces invaded Sicily.

Pf. E. A. Aldridge
904th Training Group
BTC #12
Amarillo AA Fld.
Amarillo, Texas

July 20, 1943

Dear Mom & Pop:

    It has been quite a while since I have written last; however don't think I have forgotten you.

    I received little Elwin's letter today and was glad to hear from him. He must be proud of such a lovely desk, and I bet he works at it all of the time.* I really am sorry that I could not send him the pencil any sooner, so he could have had it for his birthday, but it is so difficult to get paper or boxes or anything like that around here that I had to get him something small.

    I am still working in Payroll here, and have been working quite a lot for the last few weeks; however we got ten new fellows in the office now, so it ought to be a lot easier from now on. I like this work a lot because it is quite different from anything I have ever done.

    I have been promised another stripe for the last two months, but every time I am put in for one by the Lieutenants, it is knocked

---

* Elwin recalls mostly doing homework on the dining room table where it was warmer and there was more table top space.

Amarillo, Texas

Al's Odyssey, from Catonsville to Japan
Edward Albert Aldridge II's World War II Letters

down by the board because of the other fellows that are in this headquarters, who have been in the army longer than I have been. However, I think I will get it this month if nothing else happens. The extra twelve dollars a month will really come in handy, because in my estimation I deserve it a lot more than a lot of other fellows who get higher ratings.

There have been constant rumors around here that we are going to move again, just like it was at Miami Beach before we moved. The most commonly mentioned destination is Hartford, Connecticut, but for certain we really don't know what will happen. They say it is too cold here to have a Basic Training Center in the winter. I hope we do move if we come any closer to the east.

I am still in the best of condition and feel as fine as ever. They say that I am getting fatter; I now weigh one hundred and seventy five pounds. I take Physical Training three times a week, but I never lose any weight.

The question of a furlough doesn't seem to come any closer at present as it ever did. However sooner or later I am bound to get one. Almost every time I talk to the Lt, he says yes I know you want a furlough. I have been trying every way know to get one lined up for some time in the future so I can get the question somewhat settled.

It must be hot in Baltimore now, for it very hot here in the daytime now.

I hate to write and tell you that I lost my watch, especially Pop, for I was so proud of it and appreciated it so much. I left it in my pants pocket one day hanging in the barracks, when I changed my pants, that evening when I got back it was gone. I tired every way possible to find out who took it, but there is so many trainees moving in and out and going through the barracks all day long. Nobody in the barracks seemed to know anything about it. I

Amarillo, Texas

Al's Odyssey, from Catonsville to Japan
Edward Albert Aldridge II's World War II Letters

reported it to the First Sergeant who put up a notice, but nothing has been heard of it since, that was about two weeks ago. That is the main reason I haven't written lately for I hoped it would show up.

I am sending twenty dollars home as soon as possible, and I want you to get me another, you can take any more money you need from what I have.

I didn't want to write any tell that I lost the watch but I thought it would be best thing to do.

Much love to all.

Your loving son

Albert

Amarillo, Texas

Al's Odyssey, from Catonsville to Japan
Edward Albert Aldridge II's World War II Letters

Pfc. E. A. Aldridge
904th Tng. Gp. BTC #12
Amarillo AA Fld.
Amarillo, Texas   August 7, 1943

Mom & Pop:

    Received your letter yesterday evening and was glad to here from home again. I don't get much time off anymore as before, we have three nights of classes each week after work, and usually have to work one or two other nights each week. So you can see that there isn't much time left to do much of anything but sleep.

    It is really hot here now in the daytime, but each night it gets cool and is just right for sleeping, although I feel sleepy each morning, for we have to get up at about five o'clock every morning except Sunday.

    Is Elwin enjoying the summer now that he isn't sick anymore. I'll bet he is outside all day long in the sunshine. Is he still growing as much as ever, I hope he doesn't grow too much before I get home, which will not be very soon, I don't think.

    Everything here is just the same as ever; however it doesn't seem as if we are going to leave here, as I said before.

    Its time to leave the office now so I will have to close this letter.

    Much love to all.

                      Your loving son,

                      Albert

                Amarillo, Texas

Al's Odyssey, from Catonsville to Japan
Edward Albert Aldridge II's World War II Letters

August 18, 1943

Dear Mom & Pop:

Received your letter yesterday afternoon, and was glad to hear from you so soon. Yesterday afternoon, as I was riding the bus into town I met Byron Witt. He is going to go to mechanic school here. I was certainly surprised to see him, for he has been the first person I met here that I knew.

Don't expect me home on a furlough, for I don't think that I can get one very soon, as there are so many here who have been in the army longer than I and have never had one yet. If it would be as easy as just asking for one several times, I would have had one long ago. But here they can only let several go at a time, and they are taking the ones who have been in the army the longest first.

I am going out on the firing range for three day s starting tomorrow morning, and I won't be able to write or get any mail during that time. It is something new that they are starting for the permanent party here. It will be the first that I have done anything that even looked like the army.

You asked me once how I made out with the money I got here. I get fifty-four dollars a month, out of which comes six fifty for insurance and one dollar and fifty cents for laundry, twenty dollars which are sent home each month, and twenty six which I get. I make out all right when I don't go into town very often, for every time I go into town it costs about three or four dollars. Everything here has gone up since we arrived, and it just about like Miami Beach. It costs thirty five cents to go to the movies in the afternoon.

Everything here is just about the same as ever though, and it looks as if we are going to stay here for a while. I am still well, but I have lost most of the sunburn which I got at Miami Beach. It is

Amarillo, Texas

Al's Odyssey, from Catonsville to Japan
Edward Albert Aldridge II's World War II Letters

getting a little cooler here especially in the day time, when it is the hottest.

I am glad to hear that little Elwin is still well, and he takes advantage of all of the sunshine, for it is the best thing in the world for him.

I have been looking for the watch this week, but I guess it is a little too soon to expect it yet.

The classes I have been attending in the evenings to deal with first aid, airplane recognition, chemical warfare, and other such things.

I have too close now, for it is about one thirty and I have to get back to work.

    Love to all.

                                      Your loving son,

                                       Albert.

                Amarillo, Texas

Al's Odyssey, from Catonsville to Japan
Edward Albert Aldridge II's World War II Letters

August 22, 1943

Dear Mom & Pop:

    Received your letter this afternoon before I went to dinner. I also received your watch, Saturday night. I am real pleased with it and will take good care of it. It is almost like the other one, at first I thought it was the same kind. A watch surely comes in handy here, for on the camp there isn't any place to find out the time other than watches. You always need a watch, for everything is run on a time schedule. You have to be at reveille at 5:20 AM and at chow in the morning at 5:30, otherwise you won't get anything to eat. Then at 7:15 AM I have to be dressed, washed, have bed made floor mopped and shoes shined, so I can make the formation to go to work. At 11^{45} AM we quit work and go to lunch, which is exactly at 12^{00}. Then must be back to work at 1^{00} PM again. Then we get through at five for the day, unless we work again at night. Evening chow is at 6^{15} PM and lights go out at 9^{00} PM. Then you start over again. I guess that you wonder why I am writing all of this, but tonight is my night for CQ[*] Training at Headquarters, and I have to stay awake, from 10^{00} PM to 3^{00} AM, however I am off until 1^{00} tomorrow afternoon. So you can see that if you are by yourself or if the persons with you do not have the time it is awful inconvenient sometimes. When I go into town I have to be off the streets at eleven-thirty week days except Saturday, which is two-thirty in the morning.

    I am sorry to hear that Little Elwin has to go to the hospital to have his tonsils taken out, but it is better to have it done now than when he goes to school. It always seems that he is sick, but I surely

---

[*] CQ was an abbreviation for "charge of quarters." As an officer when I pulled "officer of the day" duties, I was told I was in charge of the base till morning. I took emergency phone calls, took calls from crying mothers, read and forwarded incoming messages, and authorized the fire department to go into secure areas. An enlisted man's CQ duties were probably similar, but for a barrack or group of barracks.

Amarillo, Texas

Al's Odyssey, from Catonsville to Japan
Edward Albert Aldridge II's World War II Letters

pray that after he has his tonsils taken out, that he will not get sick for a long time to come. I am also glad to hear that his heart condition is clearing up, for he is too young to have any heart trouble. Little Elwin hasn't written to me for sometime, so tell him to write me real soon. I always show the letters he writes and the pictures he draws to the other fellows, and continually brag about him. I told several of the fellows, that he was sick several times, now they always ask how he is getting along. I'll be he sure enjoys the swing Pop built for him. Let me know as soon as possible how he makes out when he goes to the hospital, for I will be thinking of him all of the time.

I finally made the grade of Corporal, but I am not so surprised, for I have been promised it so many times, since I have been here and as well at Miami Beach. It helps a lot though for now I get sixty-six dollars a month. I think I will increase my allotment to thirty dollars, starting in September.

I also changed my beneficiary on my service record and insurance policy from, Mother and Grandmother, to Mother and Father. I think it will do a lot better this way.

It is alright with me if you want to spread some of the money I send home. I don't want to keep it all here; it's so easy to spend it, in the army. Every time you go into town you want to buy dinner or something of the sort, so if you don't have so much money on you, you don't spend it so freely, for then the rest of the money you won't have any to spend. Here every time you go to town it costs four or five dollars, for every type of entertainment is a lot higher. Even bowling and the movies are a lot higher than at home. Will you let me know how much, I actually have, now that the income taxes and everything else are paid. To tell the truth I don't even remember how much I had when I left. If I can save some every month, I will have some money to spend when I come home. I try to save a little every month out of what I get, that is where I got the twenty dollars I sent home for the watch.

Amarillo, Texas

Al's Odyssey, from Catonsville to Japan
Edward Albert Aldridge II's World War II Letters

I received a letter from Bunk Healy last week. That is the youngest one that joined the Navy, I guess he is about nineteen now. He's stationed near Petersburg, Virginia, only several miles from where we had the wreck with the station wagon, at a Naval Hospital. He said that the right side of his face was paralyzed. That is all he said about it so don't know how it happened or what caused it. He also said that he was getting home often, so it can't be too bad. If I find out any more about it I will let you know how he is getting along.

I haven't heard from the other Healy boys for sometime. I was surprised to hear that Edward* got married, however Grandma wrote me a letter, and told me he was planning to get married. She also said that when he finished school in California he thought that he would be shipped somewhere in action. I hope it won't be for sometime to come.

I got back from the firing range Saturday evening. I spent three days and two nights there. We had to sleep in tents that we carried along -- two in each tent. The weather is really nice, in fact the nights were the warmest that they have been here for several weeks. We didn't do anything there except eat sleep and shoot. I shot an Enfield rifle, a carbine, and a sub machine gun. I am glad it's all over with, though, for all of the permanent parties have to go out for three days, and I got it when the weather was nice. We were lucky for it rained Saturday night, and when it rains here it really rains. There is a large body of water down at the end of the camp, which was formed one night when it rained all night. It is about 400 yards in diameter. The sun hasn't been able to dry it up in over a month, for every time it rains it fills up higher and higher. We call it Lake Jordan. Colonel Jordan is our commanding Officer there.

---

* He is probably referring to Edward Kampel, his first cousin.

Amarillo, Texas

Al's Odyssey, from Catonsville to Japan
Edward Albert Aldridge II's World War II Letters

I really feel fine now, for I am getting a lot of sleep lately, and plenty of exercise, especially walking. I got brown again while on the rifle range. I get plenty of food and milk to drink.

I get a lot of breakfast food, such as corn flakes, puffed wheat, puffed rice, bran, wheaties, shredded wheat, grape nuts, and other varieties. I always take several boxes every morning. Elwin would like this for we always are having a new kind.

Does Pop still work every Sunday, or does he get them off now. I know though that he still works around in the yard when he gets a chance, for he always did like to. I read the writing on the paper the watch was wrapped in, that Pop wrote. Is the garage[*] finished yet, I don't remember if you ever wrote and told me it was or not, but I suppose it is by this time.

It's $12^{\underline{50}}$ AM now, only two more hours and ten minutes then I can go to bed.

How is Spot[†] getting along. Is he still a bad as ever? Did you ever get rid of the other dog and the cat? I don't remember if we had two or three cats when I left and the only one I remember is the stray black one. It seems so long since I have been home that I have to sit down and think before I can remember how everything looks.

How is dad's father getting along now? I hope he is a lot better now. He must be almost eighty years old now. Are all the rest of the folks in Baltimore, still well?

I read in the newspaper that the ban on pleasure driving had been lifted in the East or was going to be lifted. Can you get gasoline now or is it still hard to get? I think that the A rationed

---

[*] Pop, in his spare time, after work, built a second garage facing Ingleside Avenue for Albert's car.
[†] Spot was the family dog, a large beagle. Spot was not a bad dog, but he liked to play rough, he frightened a of lot people.

Amarillo, Texas

Al's Odyssey, from Catonsville to Japan
Edward Albert Aldridge II's World War II Letters

book was to expire sometime in August, did you get new ones yet? The gasoline coupons here have been cut again, although there seems to be quite a bit of gasoline around. It's been so long since I have driven a car that, whenever I ride in one, I seem at home in the back seat looking out of the window.

Almost all of the country around here is flat and dry. But about ten miles out there are rolling hills, and also small valleys and ridges. The land isn't too good for anything. This whole section called the panhandle makes you disgusted with the state of Texas.

An airplane crashed the other night in the rain. It was going to take off, and was going across the field, it never left the ground and crashed into the telephone wires and went right across the highway in a bank. Nobody was hurt. The next day they took the airplane apart and brought it in one large three trailer truck, the largest one I ever saw.

I haven't received any cookies from home in a long while. May be its too hot to bake. But perhaps you could buy some and send them to me. Do you still get that pound cake from Rice's;[*] I could surely eat a lot of it now. If you send some cookies and cake, pack it good, in a strong box, for the last time I got some in a Rice's box, they were broken.

Well, I guess you must be getting tired of reading now, so I will close for the present.

Love to all

Your Loving Son

Albert

---

[*] Rice's was the name of the bakery that delivered to Albert's home.

Amarillo, Texas

Al's Odyssey, from Catonsville to Japan
Edward Albert Aldridge II's World War II Letters

Cpl. E. A. Aldridge
902nd Training Group BTC #12
Amarillo AA Fld
Amarillo, Texas

September 21, 1943

Dear Mom & Pop:

Just a few lines to let you know all is well with me and the army. I haven't had much time to write, because we moved from our headquarters, and payroll was split up into the four Training Groups.

I am now in the 902nd Training Group instead of the 904th as before. My new address will also be the 902nd Training Group Amarillo AA Field Amarillo Texas.

I received your cookies today and was glad to get them. The tasted very good, and reminded me so much of home.

I would like to wish you a Happy Birthday, although it is a little late. I couldn't get any cards on camp, and I haven't been into town for several weeks.

Amarillo, Texas

Al's Odyssey, from Catonsville to Japan
Edward Albert Aldridge II's World War II Letters

Elwin must now have plenty of school work to do since he is in the third grade. Mrs. Porter, his teacher, was teaching when I went to school, and from what I knew of her she was alright.[*]

Well, I finally think that I have a furlough soon. As far as I can find out at present, I am scheduled for one the middle of next month, and I am going to do all I can to get it.

I'll need a little over forty dollars for the train fare home, and also for the meals coming home. So will you send me a money order for Fifty five dollars about the first of month? Love to all.

> Your loving son.
>
> Albert

---

[*] Elwin recalls Mrs. Mary C. Porter's severe public scoldings which were very upsetting. Young boys are used to physical abuse from each other, but such verbal abuse was hard to take. She must have gotten disappointed when Elwin got zeros on some tests and did well on others. There were two boys in his third grade class that were teenagers who tortured Elwin regularly for amusement. Mrs. Porter never corrected them. In the third grade class photo, Elwin was grimacing because they were twisting his arms to get him to make a funny face. That year, Elwin recalls being so preoccupied with his problems that he often had not started to work on tests when it was time to turn them in. He had a lot of problems focusing on school work and missed 46 days of school in the third grade, but he was promoted anyway. Ms. Porter was the only teacher Elwin had any problems with although the problem of focusing reoccurred occasionally. It is difficult to imagine what harder problems children are coping with today with gangs, drug dealers, and broken families. At that time in history, most students rarely were corrected for much more than for violation of the no talking and no gum chewing rules. No one was teaching students to rebel against parents and authority figures, and I never saw any drug use.

Al's Odyssey, from Catonsville to Japan
Edward Albert Aldridge II's World War II Letters

The following letter was among Al's letters, and it shows the problems on the home front during World War II. Al's grandmother, Marie, had six grandchildren in the military during the War. One did not return. Marie lost had her home in Pittsburg during the Great Depression and spent the rest of her life tending to her children and grandchildren.

Marie. E. Neher
714 Fourth Street
New Cumberland, Pa

September 23, 1943

My dear Daughter:

     Got your kind letter this morning and as busy as I am, I will squeeze a little time out to answer it at once! Darling, you talk about visiting you. I almost spent three months with you. I am glad Katie told you that I was here – no doubt she knows when I asked for my things which I was not able to pack in my grip when I left and I wrote to her and Bennie[*] to send them here to me. Now I am telling you some things which you should keep to your self. I was called on the phone to come to New Cumberland as your sister was very ill when I got here, she fell in my arms and cried her heart out; you know this is not her fashion when she is well. I am writing this to you above and <u>I do not want</u> anyone of our families to know this – not even your <u>husband</u> or Ben. I would not even <u>ask you</u> to come here for <u>the next two weeks</u> as much as I would like to see little sweetheart. She has been improving since I am here two weeks yesterday.

---

[*] Benjamin Neher was her youngest child.

Amarillo, Texas

Al's Odyssey, from Catonsville to Japan
Edward Albert Aldridge II's World War II Letters

She has been the private secretary of Major Bowman, she had a fine position but when the Medical Section left for Kansas and she was persuaded to take a stenography position at the depot. Three officers had the place to boss – one to order this – the next one to order that and the third one coming in saying it's all wrong and giving different orders beside a bunch of machinery making enough noise to wake the dead!!! She must be pretty tough to stand it as long as she did. You keep this all to yourself darling as I write this just for you.

The whole Medical Service was transferred to Kansas.

Your sisters in Pittsburgh do not need to know all this. They have enough of their own worries beside Ed A. Kampel coming over crying about his only boy – they sent him overseas three months ago and he does not know where? Mrs. Rasofield is coming in crying about her oldest boy that they sent over to England! You should see Ruthies mother now. I am ready to cry, but I bit my tongue so I would not collapse. You told me two fine things to make me feel good, first of all little honey boy is well and you saw Aunt Martha and she is well! Every time she writes to me she says I'll be with you again in heaven. This makes me feel bad Much love to you and little Honey. If you don't hear from me often, do not wonder.

Much Love

Your Mother, M.E.N.

Amarillo, Texas

Al's Odyssey, from Catonsville to Japan
Edward Albert Aldridge II's World War II Letters

September 30, 1943.

Dear Pop:

Received the letter you mailed to me on the twenty-third, today. It was at my old Training Group. I am sorry that I haven't written sooner, but we have been terrible busy here for the last month.

I suppose that you received the letter I wrote about me getting a furlough, and I think it is all set so I can leave here around the sixteenth or seventeenth of October.

I am well and I haven't lost my watch, although I haven't been able to get too much sleep lately. Tonight will be the first night in a long while that I will be able to get to bed. I only got about three hours sleep last night, since all of the payrolls were paid off then.

I hope little Elwin's cold is all gone by now, for he doesn't deserve to be sick so often. I am glad that he is in the A Class again, for it must make him feel proud.

How is my Ford now? Do you think that I could drive it when I come home? If you would get tags for it, then you would be able to get another gas book, and since the pleasure ban has been lifted, I will be able to do some driving. The * tags will only be for half a year, and you can get any money you need from my wallet.

Tell mom that I received the box of cookies, and I enjoyed them a lot.

           Much love to all. Your loving son: - Albert

           Amarillo, Texas

Al's Odyssey, from Catonsville to Japan
Edward Albert Aldridge II's World War II Letters

October 8, 1943

Dear Mom & Pop

    Just a few lines to let you know that I received your money order yesterday, and also the box of candy from Mrs. Strauss.[*] It tasted very good, and I was pleased to get since it has been the first chocolate candy I have eaten in quite some time.

    I also received your letter today, and I will let you know when I will arrive at Baltimore; however, I don't think it will be before the twentieth (20th) of this month.

    I will be careful coming home. I think it would be better if you sent me ten more dollars for I bought a garrison hat and I don't want to take a chance of running short.

    We have been lucky lately for, we haven't been getting up until around seven o'clock each morning, but we don't know how long it will last.

    Much Love to Everyone

        Your Loving Son

        Albert

---

[*] Mrs. Strauss was neighbor who lived atop the hill on Montgomery Road.

Amarillo, Texas

Al's Odyssey, from Catonsville to Japan
Edward Albert Aldridge II's World War II Letters

October 15, 1943

Dear Mom:

Just a few lines to let you know all is fine. I don't know for sure when I will leave here, but I expect to be home about Tuesday night. Oct. 19/1943.

My furlough starts Tuesday the 19th at 12:01 AM – I may be able to get a head start.
I am gong to try to leave here Sunday Morning.

I will try to let you know the exact time I will arrive.

Love to all – Albert

Cpl. E. A. Aldridge
902nd Training Group BTC #12
Amarillo AA Field
Amarillo, Texas

October 17, 1943

Dear Mom:

Just a few lines, to let you know all is well.

If this letter reaches you before I do I will be home about noon on the twenty first of October. Just the exact time I am not sure of.

I will probably leave here about nine o'clock Tuesday morning. The time is supposed to be about forty-four hours. But I understand that the trains are never on time.

Love to All
Your Loving Son –

Albert

Amarillo, Texas

Al's Odyssey, from Catonsville to Japan
Edward Albert Aldridge II's World War II Letters

Cpl. E. A. Aldridge   33552323
902nd Training Group
Amarillo AA Fld - BTC #12
Amarillo, Texas

November 4, 1943

Dear Mom:

Arrived Wednesday afternoon at four thirty. The trip wasn't so bad, for I got a seat on every train, all of the way through.

I had a hour and a half lay over at Pittsburgh, and I called Aunt Florence. She and Uncle Larry came down to the station and I saw them for about a half hour, before the train left.

The sandwiches you made lasted until Wednesday morning, so I ate the apples, in the afternoon, Aunt Florence also brought me some apples and some fudge, which I also ate on the train.

Two of the fellows in payroll here left while I was gone, so now there is only two of us left. At the present we have about eight trainees helping us out to get caught up in the work. I suppose that I will have to do a lot night work for some time.

Is little Elwin's cold better by this time, I hope it is so he won't have to miss any more school.

It is getting late so I will write you again very soon.

                                          Love to all.

                                          Albert

Amarillo, Texas

Al's Odyssey, from Catonsville to Japan
Edward Albert Aldridge II's World War II Letters

November ?, 1943

Dear Mom & Pop:

Received your letter yesterday afternoon and was glad to hear from home. I have been working constantly since I arrived here. It is now twelve thirty at night, and I am just finishing

I got a nice letter from Aunt Lilly[*] a few days ago, and am going to answer her tomorrow night. I also got a box of cookies candy pop-corn, and chewing gum from Aunt Florence (Turnbull).[†] I will also have to write her a letter thanking her for it as soon as possible.

I don't recall if I told you in my last letter or not that two of the fellows in payroll here shipped while I was on furlough. There are only two of us left now, and with plenty of work to do, although we have some trainees here helping out, but you have to watch everything they do so close.

I got a cold in my head as soon as I got here, I guess that I caught it on the train, it is just going away.

We had a little snow her last week, the first I have seen since I left Maryland last winter, but it didn't get very long.

How is little Elwin's cold, I hope it is better now. And I sure bet he enjoyed the Harvest Festival.

Love to Elwin, Pop and Mom:

Your loving son
Albert

---

[*] Aunt Lilly was Pop's younger sister.
[†] Al's natural father's sister.

Amarillo, Texas

Al's Odyssey, from Catonsville to Japan
Edward Albert Aldridge II's World War II Letters

Cpl. E. A. Aldridge 33552323
902nd Training Group
Amarillo AA Fld - BTC #12
Amarillo, Texas

                                              November 22, 1943

Dear Mom:

    Received your letter today, and was glad to here from you again. But, am sorry to here that Elwin is sick again. It seems that he gets sick almost once every month or more. Take good care of him, and don't let him go out in the rain too much.

    My cold is completely gone now, it didn't last very long. They never do last very long.

    I received Aunt Lilly's box of candy, and it was very good. I will write her a letter thanking her for it when I get time. Don't send any candy to me for Christmas, for I get to much around here, but certainly would like some fruit cake.

    I wrote a letter to Aunt Florence and Uncle John, and thanked them for the package, for I really did enjoy it very much.

    The fellows that left here are at Fort Logan, Colorado, and from the letters that I get from them; I understand that they like it very much there. They say it is a much better camp than this one is.
    Its getting a little cold her now, in the night time. But it usually is nice in the day time, when the wind doesn't blow.

    My watch keeps perfect time since I have been back here it lost only about a half a minute since I left.

    Give little Elwin my love and tell him to get better soon.

                              Love to All
                              Albert

                              Amarillo, Texas

Al's Odyssey, from Catonsville to Japan
Edward Albert Aldridge II's World War II Letters

Cpl. E. A. Aldridge 33552323
902nd Training Group
Amarillo AA Fld BTC #12
Amarillo, Texas

November 24, 1943

Dear Mom:

Well, tomorrow is Thanksgiving. But here it will be just like any other day. We all have to work, and everything else will continue as any other day.

We are going to have a turkey dinner tomorrow afternoon. But I don't think it would taste as good as it would if you cooked it. Are you going to kill one of the ducks for your dinner?

I got a letter form Mrs. Ridgley's[*] several days ago and she said that Dick Healey, that is the oldest one, was in the hospital in California with a nervous breakdown. Mrs. Healey said that when he went back from twenty day furlough, the same day that I got home, that he was very nervous, and did not want to go back. I have received several letters from Bunk, but he didn't mention anything about Dick in any of them.

It's getting pretty cold here now in the evenings, but it is usually nice in the day time. It rained just a little here today for about a half hour. The first we had for several months.

I guess Elwin is already planning for Christmas, but after all, that is the best part about it.

Everything around is just about the same as usual, still very busy. The way things took time not many people on this field

---

[*] Mrs. Ridglely was the mother of one of Al's friends.

Amarillo, Texas

Al's Odyssey, from Catonsville to Japan
Edward Albert Aldridge II's World War II Letters

usually know what they are doing. To tell the truth I think there are going to be a lot of changes made her in the next month.

I wrote a letter to Aunt Lilly tonight and thanked her for the candy. I have been spending most of the time I get off writing letters.

Did Pop get a ration book for the Ford? I don't see any reason why he shouldn't. It will help him out with the gasoline problem.

Don't work too hard, now that Christmas is getting nearer, and don't worry about me for I am well and feeling fine.

Love To All

Albert

Al's Odyssey, from Catonsville to Japan
Edward Albert Aldridge II's World War II Letters

Cpl. E. A. Aldridge 33552323
902nd Training Group
Amarillo AA Fld - BTC #12
Amarillo, Texas

Dec. 8, 1943

Dear Mom & Pop:

Received Pop's letter several days ago, but we have been so busy here I haven't had much time to write.

Tell Elwin I also got his letter, and I was glad to hear from him and that I will write him as soon as possible.

By the way, who said I was going to move any time before Christmas or any other time. As far as I know I am going to stay here.

I don't think there is anything else I want for Christmas but some cake and cookies. I bought Elwin two sport shirts yesterday and I will send them as soon as I get a chance.

Yes, do buy Pop and yourself presents for me for you can't buy a thing in this town.

I am glad that little Elwin is alright now and I hope he doesn't get sick for a long time.

Bunk told me in one of his letters that Dick is back out a sea, although he doesn't know when he got out of the hospital.

I am closing for the present;

Love To All

Albert

Amarillo, Texas

Al's Odyssey, from Catonsville to Japan
Edward Albert Aldridge II's World War II Letters

Cpl. E. A. Aldridge 33552323
902nd Training Group
Amarillo AA Fld - BTC #12
Amarillo, Texas

December 16, 1943

Dear Mom & Pop:

    Received your package this afternoon and was very glad to get the cookies. Tell Little Elwin that I thank him for the present and to be a good little boy. I will write him a letter tomorrow evening.

    It has been quite cold here, for the last week; it snowed about a week ago, and it is still on the ground. Every afternoon its not so cold for the sun manages to come out. But at night time it gets very cold, and all of the snow that melted in the day time freezes into ice, and now the ground is covered by one large sheet of ice.

    I am well, and feel as fine as ever, so don't worry about me. I haven't had a cold since the one when I got back from furlough. I haven't been working so hard lately, since about half of the trainees here shipped out last month. This is the first month, that our payrolls reached finance on time. This is about the only Training Group, that we know of that met the dead line. Not so bad.

    I get to the movies several times a week on the post; the shows on the post are a lot better and newer than the ones in town.

    I hope that Pop is better by this time, and tell him not to work so hard, or to go out in the rain when he can prevent it.

    I will write soon again.

                    Love to Everybody
                    Your loving son;
                       Albert

Amarillo, Texas

Al's Odyssey, from Catonsville to Japan
Edward Albert Aldridge II's World War II Letters

Cpl. E. A. Aldridge 33552323
902nd Training Group
Amarillo AA Fld - BTC #12
Amarillo, Texas   December 27, 1943

Dear Mom & Pop:

Received your letter last night, and was glad to hear from home again. It is snowing here again, and with the wind blowing it drifting all over everything.

We had two days off the twenty fourth and the twenty fifth, last week, it was the first days I got off since I got back from my furlough. The weather here over Christmas was really nice with the sun shining all day; it didn't get cold until last night.

There was nothing to do here Christmas, so most of the fellows just stayed around the camp. Christmas day in the afternoon we went to the movies on the camp.

The meals on Christmas day were very good, we had turkey and everything that goes with it, both for dinner and supper we also got nuts and some candy.

I suppose that Elwin got the package that I mailed by now, I hope he likes the little jerseys.

The mail here is very slow, especially now around Christmas, as yet I haven't received your package, but I guess that it will be here today. Everybody else is still waiting for packages.

We had a Christmas tree in the day room, but it did not look nothing like the one at home. Did little Elwin like his Christmas presents, tell him to write me and tell me what he got. Also tell me what you and Pop bought for yourselves from me.

                                        Love to Al   Al

Amarillo, Texas

Al's Odyssey, from Catonsville to Japan
Edward Albert Aldridge II's World War II Letters

Cpl. E. A. Aldridge 33552323
902nd Training Group
Amarillo AA Fld - BTC #12
Amarillo, Texas

January 8, 1944

Dear Mom & Pop:

Received your letter yesterday morning. I also received the Christmas presents, but not until, about the first of the year. I got the wallet several days latter; the mail was very slow here in camp.

I like the wallet very much, and don't think I could get along without it now. The fruit cake was very good, but it didn't last long enough.

I also got packages from, Aunt Rolly, Uncle Ben, and Aunt Sophie. Altogether I had a lot of candy and cake. Aunt Rolly, sent me as well shoe shine kit, which I really can use.

The weather here was nice between Christmas and about the 4th of January. We had a snow storm about the 4th or 5th, which was the worst that I have ever seen. The wind was blowing along with the snow, and it drifted into huge banks, stalling most of the traffic.

Elwin must be back in school again by now. I bet he really had a nice Christmas. Tell him that I will write him a letter, as soon as possible.

I am well, and everything here is about the same as ever. About the only thing around here to do is to go to the movies. There is not much to do in town anymore.

Amarillo, Texas

Al's Odyssey, from Catonsville to Japan
Edward Albert Aldridge II's World War II Letters

If you ever think of it see if you can get me a few ping pong balls. We have a table and paddles in our Day Room, but we can not get balls anywhere around here.[*] It won't be long and I will be in the army for almost a year. I think I am going to get the good conduct medal in a few days.

I will write soon again.

       Love to All

                 Your loving son,

                 Albert

---

[*] After the war, there were stories that the Army was experimenting with ping pong balls and took the nation's whole supply during the war for a secret project.

Amarillo, Texas

Al's Odyssey, from Catonsville to Japan
Edward Albert Aldridge II's World War II Letters

January 26, 1944

Dear Mom & Pop:

Received Pops letter yesterday and was glad to hear from you. It was certainly a surprise to hear that Herman[*] died. I didn't even know that he was sick.

Everything here is just about the same as ever; there is not much of anything happening now. I am fine and this is one winter so far that I haven't had a cold. The weather here for the last few days, has been very warm, almost like summer time, but it is raining this morning.

I am glad that Elwin is going to school every day now, and that he is not so sick anymore. Tell him that I will write him a letter very soon, and that I enjoy getting letters from him.

If everything stays about the same around here, for the next few weeks, I will get another furlough about the first of March, I have been trying to get one sooner but, it doesn't look as if I will be able too.

Thanks for the ping pong balls, although I haven't received them as yet, I will appreciate them. It is impossible to get any around here or in the town of Amarillo. I do not need the rest of the set, as we have a table net and plenty of paddles in our day room, but no balls.

I got the good conduct medal the first of the year, although it wasn't official until the eleventh. Now all we can get is a red and white ribbon, but you can get the real medal after the war.

---

[*] Herman Penski was Pop's youngest brother.

Amarillo, Texas

Al's Odyssey, from Catonsville to Japan
Edward Albert Aldridge II's World War II Letters

Its almost time for income tax again, will you get for me a statement of what I made at the DCA for 1943 and what victory tax[*] I paid for the same time. It can't be much, but I approximately figure that I made about 750 dollars last year.

Its almost time to start with, so I will have to say goodbye for the present.

                Love to All,

                        Your loving son,

                        Al

---

[*] A 5% "Victory Tax" was imposed in 1942 on people at about the minimum wage. As best as I can understand, for most people, this was their first United States Federal income tax. An excess profit tax of 90% was imposed on some people with higher incomes. Pop, with a six grade education, used to get very upset when he filled out the forms. This tax did not add to the President's popularity.

                Amarillo, Texas

Al's Odyssey, from Catonsville to Japan
Edward Albert Aldridge II's World War II Letters

Sgt. E A. Aldridge 33552323
902nd Training Group
Amarillo AA Fld - BTC #12
Amarillo, Texas

Feb. 6, 1944

Dear Mom & Pop:

Received your letter yesterday morning. Yes, I received all of the presents that you sent to me. I like the birthday present very much, the gloves are very useful.

I had a very nice birthday, although it was on pay day, I also got a present from the Army on Feb. 1, 1944 although I didn't know it officially until the second.

I'm a sergeant now, since the 1st of February.

I increased my Cl E allotment so now you should get forty dollars starting for the month of February. The first check will come about the first of March.

I also took out a Cl B allotment of $6.25 per month starting in March. That is for War Bonds.

I don't know just when I will be able to get a furlough, but if everything remains the same, it should be sometime next month.

I'll get $78.00 month now, not too bad, for a year.

The weather here has been very nice for the last two weeks. The sun has been shining each day; all you need to wear is a light jacket.

                                       Love to all

                                           Al

                                  Amarillo, Texas

Al's Odyssey, from Catonsville to Japan
Edward Albert Aldridge II's World War II Letters

Sgt. E A. Aldridge 33552323
902nd Training Group
Amarillo AA Fld
Amarillo, Texas

Feb 19, 1944

Dear Mom & Pop:

Received your letter yesterday afternoon, and was glad to hear from again.

It really has been a short month so far, time around here passes so fast you can hardly keep track of time.

The weather here has been very good for the last two months, although it's quite chilly every morning.

I will get a longer furlough this time about twenty days. But it won't be before about the twenty eighth of March. The furloughs here were all put back about two weeks, when they were all much longer.

It's time to eat now so I will close for the present.

Love to all

Al

Amarillo, Texas

Al's Odyssey, from Catonsville to Japan
Edward Albert Aldridge II's World War II Letters

Sgt. E A. Aldridge 33552323
902nd Training Group
Amarillo AA Fld
Amarillo, Texas

Tuesday

Dear Mom:

Well everything here is just about the same as usual. I received the check you sent and it came in handy.

I am in Lubbock, Texas now, just on a three day pass with another soldier. We are going to Midland, Texas about 280 miles from Amarillo. We stopped here for the night as it was snowing most of the afternoon.

We are hitch hiking our way down to Midland. I will probably be back in Amarillo before this letter reaches you.

The fellow I am with has a brother in Midland, who we are going to visit.

Yesterday, it was very warm, but overnight it started to snow. The wind also is very bad it is blowing the snow all over the place into drifts.

The check was for bonds I started to take out for the months of February and March, last year. But they were cancelled and a different type of Bond allotment started.

Amarillo, Texas

Al's Odyssey, from Catonsville to Japan
Edward Albert Aldridge II's World War II Letters

Quite a few fellows from our Group were sent to Cp Kearns Utah and Ft Logan in Denver for over seas training. They missed me again.

Everything here goes along as usual, I probably will be home again in the latter part of June, or July, but you can't always look that far in the future.

How is little Elwin making out in school. I bet he won't want to stay home so much when it gets warm.

        Love to All

                Your loving son

                Albert

        Amarillo, Texas

Al's Odyssey, from Catonsville to Japan
Edward Albert Aldridge II's World War II Letters

Sgt. E A. Aldridge 33552323
902nd Training Group
Amarillo AA Fld
Amarillo, Texas

March 2, 1944

Dear Mom & Pop,

Received the money order of ten dollars that you sent.

I had a fine time on my pass, and it was good to get away from camp. We spent a day in Midland, Texas and visited with the brother of the fellow that was with me, and another day in Lubbock, Texas, but the Towns that are in west Texas are so small that there is not much to see.

The scenery in that part of Texas was mostly dry, wasteland, a very few trees and lots of rock formations. All in all, during three days off, we traveled about six hundred miles and it only cost us forty-five cents for actual transportation.

I bought a birthday present for Pop at the PX today, so keep an eye out for it. It is a little early, but I saw a really nice present that was reasonable.

Let me know if my watch is finished yet, for I miss it.

Love to All

Your loving son

Albert

Amarillo, Texas

Al's Odyssey, from Catonsville to Japan
Edward Albert Aldridge II's World War II Letters

March 12, 1944

Dear Mom & Pop,

Received your package the day before yesterday, also your letter yesterday. The cookies were very good, and I enjoyed them.

Well, the time here sure does go fast, and it seems like weeks go by as fast as days.

I was really surprised at the snow in Baltimore this time of year. The weather here has been very nice and sunny, I get plenty of chances to play baseball, in fact I play ball every day.

We are moving again to a new Headquarters on this field so I may be busy again next week, and then I don't know for how long.

Instead of each Training Group, Squadron, Detachment, or Air Base on the field having its own payroll, they will be consolidated into a huge setup. I don't know what my job will be again until it happens.

But from what have heard so far, I probably will be in charge of 902nd Training Group's payroll.

I am enclosing a check for $40 dollars for which I was overpaid. However, I will not get paid next month, so will you send me about twenty dollars the last of this month. I would keep the money around camp, but I don't like to have that much money around.

Amarillo, Texas

Al's Odyssey, from Catonsville to Japan
Edward Albert Aldridge II's World War II Letters

I understand that I have been frozen on this field for ninety days as a lot of other fellows are frozen for the new Headquarters.

There has been quite a few PP* shipments from this field since I have been back. At present one fellow in P/R department is on one of them.

I have been very lucky so far to stay off as many as I did.

Love to All,

Albert

---

* Permanent Party?

Al's Odyssey, from Catonsville to Japan
Edward Albert Aldridge II's World War II Letters

Sgt. E A. Aldridge 33552323
902nd Training Group
Amarillo AA Fld
Amarillo, Texas

Dear Mom & Pop,

    It's Thursday morning, about seven thirty, and there isn't much to do before I start the days work.

    I haven't been doing much lately for we only have about 1300 men in the Training Group now. So there's not too much to do.

    The weather here is not so bad now, although it has been windy the last few days. There were two days the first part of the week that were very hot.

    I am gaining weight again although I get plenty of exercise playing baseball in the afternoon each day. I weigh 186 pounds now.

    I am going to try to get a troop train, and take some of the men someplace in the near future. Maybe, I will be able to see a little of the country.

    How is Pop making out with gasoline now that they cut the A coupons?

    Did you get my watch back from the jeweler yet? I really miss it a lot.

                              Love to all,

                                Albert

            Amarillo, Texas

Al's Odyssey, from Catonsville to Japan
Edward Albert Aldridge II's World War II Letters

Sgt. E A. Aldridge 33552323
370 1sT AMF Base Unit Section T
Amarillo, Texas

April 4, 1944

Dear Mom & Pop:

Received the money order, and it sure came in handy.

Well everything here is still about normal again, the warmer weather is here, and I hope to stay.

We are now working in our new Headquarters and I still have the same job. I got the pictures of Roger Mellor, and am returning them with this letter. I have CQ again for the Headquarters tonight, so I guess I will have a busy night.

I went out to a lake about twenty five miles from here to see a demonstration of bombing last Sunday. The lake is situated in sort of a canyon, with nothing but sand and rocks around it for miles.

Next Sunday I want to go to another canyon called Palo Duro Canyon[*] which is said to be very beautiful.

You can send me the other twenty dollars about the twentieth of this month; I paid several fellows what I owed them so I haven't much of the money order left.

Love to All

Al

P.S. Notice the new address

---

[*] Palo Duro canyon is the second largest canyon in the United States. It is 120 miles long, 20 miles wide, and 800 feet deep. Prairie Dog Town Fork of the Red River formed the Canyon.

Amarillo, Texas

Al's Odyssey, from Catonsville to Japan
Edward Albert Aldridge II's World War II Letters

E. A. Aldridge
3701 AAF Base Unit, Section "T"
Amarillo, Texas

                          3701 AAF Base Unit
                          Section "A" Flight 1
                          Amarillo, Texas

                          May 11, 1944

Dear Mom & Pop:

    Well I moved again, and my new address is on top of this letter. I am still doing the same job, although, I moved to the other side of the field.

    I received your letter with Roger's address and I am going to write him, as soon as possible.

    It rained here all day today, and now the place is nothing but mud, if you get off of the board walk. I do like the climate here except for the dust. It is nice and warm, and always gets cool in the evenings. I haven't had much chance to play ball lately, but I get plenty of exercise walking to work.

    Several fellows and I went out to Buffalo Lake Sunday, and went fishing, but we didn't catch anything. We were kind of late and didn't get very good bait. It's quite a large lake to be surrounded by just rocks and dirt for several hundred miles. It is also used for swimming when the weather is warm.

    Elwin hasn't much more school for this term, and I bet he is glad. Then he will get another vacation.

    I think I will need the money order sooner than the 20th, of the month, Will you send it as soon as you get a chance? And make

                    Amarillo, Texas

Al's Odyssey, from Catonsville to Japan
Edward Albert Aldridge II's World War II Letters

it thirty dollars instead of twenty as I said before. I am going to buy some more shoes, and get my suntan shirts altered.

Since we moved to a new section I don't know when I will be able to get another furlough, but if I stay on this field for the next two months, I am going to try my best to get home around the first of July. You are supposed to get furloughs every six months, but since my last one was only for twelve days, I am going to try to get another sooner. But I am not sure if I can. Will you send some cookies, if you make any in the near future?

If you can get any of that black bread that Grandma used to buy, you can send me a loaf along with some Kraft cheese to go with it. Several fellows in the barracks get it with cheese and it really tastes good. We don't ever get any cheese, except bitter dried box cheese.

Don't mind the typing errors, as I have typed all day today, the most I have typed in months.

Love to all:

Your loving son

Albert

Amarillo, Texas

Al's Odyssey, from Catonsville to Japan
Edward Albert Aldridge II's World War II Letters

Sgt. E. A. Aldridge 33552323
AAF 3701 Base Unit Section A
Flight I
Amarillo, Texas

May 21, 1944

Dear Mom & Pop:

I suppose you have received the package for Pop by this time. It is a very good pen, although, I got it a little cheaper, on the field. The regular price is about fifteen dollars, and is guaranteed for a life time. If anything happens to it you can get it repaired at the address that is on the side of the pen.

The weather here is very nice although today it is very hot; I think it will rain before the day is over.

I received the money order yesterday, and was glad to get it, I won't get a full pay until June 30th so I guess I will probably need some more money before the month is over.

I cancelled my war bond effective 1st of next month so you should receive one bond most anytime after the 1st of June.

I have been working on a furlough but the best I have been able to do is the fifth of August for twenty days, however that time is still pretty far away.

I really don't know how long, we will be able to stay on this field, since the overseas shipments have been so frequent.

So many of the fellows, that were qualified, have left that there are only a few remaining on the whole field. They have lowered the physical standards for overseas, that only a few are now disqualified.

Amarillo, Texas

Al's Odyssey, from Catonsville to Japan
Edward Albert Aldridge II's World War II Letters

The qualifications don't really mean much to me since I have been qualified for overseas and combat ever since I have been in the army.

I haven't told you before, but I have been on several overseas shipments before but always was lucky enough to get off.

The first one was when I had my first furlough in October, however, I didn't know it until I got back after the shipment had left. That is the one that went to England, and had several of my friends on it. The last one was in March, that was the reason my furlough was so short, and I came home before I really was supposed to get my furlough. However I was only a supernumerary[*] so I didn't go.

No, I am not on shipment again, and I hope to stay away from them until I get another furlough, but, no one knows when the next shipment will come

It just started to rain, and it is raining very hard, but it won't last too long as it very seldom does here.

Happy birthday to Pop

        And Love to All
                Your loving Son
                <u>Albert</u>

P.S. Did you get the new address?

AAF 3701 Base Unit
Section A, Flight 1
Amarillo, Texas
A four leaf clover was included in this letter.

---

[*] A soldier who is not in a prescribed position.

Al's Odyssey, from Catonsville to Japan
Edward Albert Aldridge II's World War II Letters

E. A. Aldridge 33552323
3701 AAF Base Unit Flt 1
Amarillo, Texas Section A.

U. S. ARMY

28 May 44

Dear Mom & Pop:

Received the package several days ago, and it sure was good; however didn't last long enough. The bread and cheese were in good condition, as well as the cookies.

Everything here is just about the same as ever, although, there is not too much work to do, for once. But we will start again after payday.

The weather here is fine, always hot, but not too hot. The nights are the best, as it is always cool.

I only get about five dollars this month on the tenth, so I guess that I will probably need another money order, I hope it lasts for I will get paid in full the end of June. Make it $20.00 this month.

I am going to the movies tonight to see *Two Girls and a Sailor*, I suppose this movie hasn't come to Baltimore yet. We usually get the new movies here first.

How is Little Elwin coming with his school? I'll bet he is glad that he will have a vacation coming very soon. I am mailing the pictures, of this Roger that I forgot to put into the other letter.

Love to All

Your loving son:
Albert

Amarillo, Texas

Al's Odyssey, from Catonsville to Japan
Edward Albert Aldridge II's World War II Letters

Sgt. E. A. Aldridge 33552323
AAF 3701 Base Unit
Section A   Flight 1
Amarillo, Texas

June 15, 1944

Dear Mom & Pop:

Wish Elwin a happy birthday for me.

I was in town yesterday afternoon but I couldn't find anything for Elwin for a birthday present so will you please get him a present for me.

I wish I were able to be home for his birthday. But maybe I will be able to make it by the first of August.

Everything here at camp is about the same as usual.

The weather is very nice, but it gets hot very often in the late afternoon, but by dark it is always cool.

It must be time that Elwin is finishing school. However, you said in a letter that it will run longer than usual this year.

I saw a movie last night, *Mark Twain*, which was very good. About the only thing to do here is to go to the movie for every time you go in to town it costs a fortune.

Best wishes to Pop for Fathers Day.

Time passes so fast that I can hardly keep track of it. The days and weeks so unnoticed that at times I forget even what month it is.

Love to All

Your Loving Son
Albert

Amarillo, Texas

Al's Odyssey, from Catonsville to Japan
Edward Albert Aldridge II's World War II Letters

Sgt. E. A. Aldridge 33552323
Section A   Flight 1
AAF 3701 Base Unit
Amarillo, Texas

25 Jun 44

Dear Mom & Pop:

Well today is Sunday again, the end of another week. Everything at camp is about the same as usual.

Elwin must be out of school by now, enjoying his vacation, which will be over all too soon, as it always is. Being nine years old now, he must be quite a boy.

If everything continues same as usual for the next month, I will be home again, about the 8th of August. It should be a twenty day furlough. If I get the furlough, I will be able to consider myself lucky to get three furloughs, in the last ten months. I was talking to the Lieutenant in charge of payroll, yesterday and he said that as far as he was concerned, and as long as we have the present set up, I will be able to stay here for an indefinite time. However, that depends upon the amount of shipment from this field. We have different shipments about every week; however, the Officer in charge of Unit Personnel is given a specific amount of EM[*] to be furnished for each shipment. He therefore is given a choice of EM to choose from; so far as the Lieutenant in charge of payroll stays with me I won't have too much chance to ship.

---

[*] Enlisted Men?

Amarillo, Texas

Al's Odyssey, from Catonsville to Japan
Edward Albert Aldridge II's World War II Letters

I am going on another three day pass over the fourth of July, the 3rd, 4th, and 5th. A fellow who works in payroll with me lives in Vernon, Texas, about one hundred ninety miles from here, and another fellow are going to go to Dallas Texas. Dallas is about four hundred miles from here. So with the pass, the month of July should pass very fast.

I received the pictures that you sent, and was glad to get them. The weather here for the last several weeks has been very good, although it rains here very often. It gets hot every day, but always cools at night. I have to take two showers each day, one at noon and another at night.

If the war continues, well in the European sector, it shouldn't be too long before Germany falls. According to the radio this afternoon, Cherbourg[*] has been taken, along with more landings on the coast of France.

Love to All.   Your loving son

Albert.

---

[*] The Allied invasion of northwest Europe began June 6, 1944. Cherbourgh was the first port that the Allies captured.

Amarillo, Texas

Al's Odyssey, from Catonsville to Japan
Edward Albert Aldridge II's World War II Letters

Sgt. E. A. Aldridge 33552323
3701 AAF Base Unit
Section A   Flight I
Amarillo, Texas

7 July 44

Dear Mom & Pop:

Received two letters yesterday when I returned from pass. I returned back to camp about two o'clock Thursday morning. We left camp at about four o'clock Saturday afternoon, that is two other fellows and myself. On the way down, we stopped at Vernon, Texas, where one of the fellows lives, and stayed until Sunday morning, then continued on to Dallas, Texas about four hundred miles from Amarillo. We went in one of the fellow's car that works in payroll with me.

We stopped at a Convention of the Walther League in Dallas. The league composed of the younger members of the Lutheran church. Representatives from all Lutheran churches of each town from the state of Texas were at the Convention.

I received the last money order that you sent, and also the application for insurance, that was made out at Fort Mead. I signed it and will send it back in my next letter, for it is in the barracks, and I can not get it now. You should have received a policy from the National Service Life Insurance Company. The application you sent was for that policy. If you do not have it, will you let me know, but be sure that isn't around the house somewhere. I have paid $6.50 every month since I have been in the Army, for the insurance so I want to make sure that it is effect. I was under the impression that the policy was sent to you, sometime last year.

I submitted my application for furlough today, and it was approved by the officers where I work, also by the furlough section, so therefore it should be approved without any further trouble. It

Amarillo, Texas

Al's Odyssey, from Catonsville to Japan
Edward Albert Aldridge II's World War II Letters

was for twenty days starting the 7th of August, so if I get it OK, I should be home the 8th or 9th.

      I will probably need about $20 bucks before the month is over, because the trip to Dallas cost most of my pay that I got on the 30th. You can also send me $30 dollars around the last of the month, for the railroad ticket, if I don't let you know different before then. Mail the first money order soon as you get a chance.

      I wonder of Pop could pick up a 16 – 600 tire sometime in the near future, because the spare on the Ford is not worth much. I suppose I also will have to get tags and a tax sticker too, when I come home, but don't bother the tags or sticker, until I am positive that I will make it.

      How was Elwin's birthday, did he have party, did he get many presents?

      Love to All

      Your loving son: Albert

Amarillo, Texas

Al's Odyssey, from Catonsville to Japan
Edward Albert Aldridge II's World War II Letters

Sgt. E. A. Aldridge 33552323
3701 AAF Base Unit
Section A   Flight 1
Amarillo, Texas

16 July 44

Dear Mom & Pop:

Received your package with the cookies, bread and cheese, and I really did enjoy it.

Everything here at the camp is about the same, as hot as ever. One of the fellows working here in payroll is getting a discharge today. He is thirty eight years old, and has several dependents at home. He is leaving tonight for Detroit, Michigan his home.

I won't be able to get a furlough until around the fifth of September now. I had my application OKed where I work, but the Section would not approve it until six months from my last furlough, which is the fifth of Sept. So you won't have to send me the money to come home on for some time yet.

I really was disappointed when they told me about it, for I was planning on leaving the first of next month. However, I hope the time will pass very fast between today and September.

We have a baseball team for the Unit Personnel Office, and we play several times a week. It helps pass the time between one week and the next.

Its time to leave the office for today, so I will close for the present.

     Love to All

         Your Loving Son
         Albert

     Amarillo, Texas

Al's Odyssey, from Catonsville to Japan
Edward Albert Aldridge II's World War II Letters

Sgt. E. A. Aldridge 33552323
3701 AAF Base Unit
Section A   Flight I
Amarillo, Texas

19 July 44

Dear Mom & Pop:

Received the money order you sent, several days ago.

Well it's the middle of July already, and it seems as if the summer has just started. The time seems to go so fast that I hardly realize what month it is. The weather here now is grand although it gets hot every afternoon, but at night is always nice and cool. The air is very dry all of the time, so when it gets hot, the perspiration is dried very fast. Just the opposite from Miami Beach Florida. We haven't had hardly any dust here this year compared with last. The rainy spells this spring helped the grass grow until there isn't very many spots of dry ground other than the drill field, and part of the air field, that is just dirt, where dust can blow.

We have had several thunder and lightening storms during the last two weeks, they are always violent, but you don't seem to mind them, for the rain never lasts too long. It usually rains in the night time, and is over by morning.

I went to the movies the other night and saw the *Ghost of Canterville.*, with Charles Laughton, Margaret O'Brien, and Robert Young. It was a very good picture, although it has the Army in it as most all pictures do now, but not very much action or fighting.

Amarillo, Texas

Al's Odyssey, from Catonsville to Japan
Edward Albert Aldridge II's World War II Letters

About the only thing that I do in camp now is to play baseball or go to the boxing matches, or take in a movie in the evenings. However, almost every night I manage to get some ice cream or a milk shake. We have a PX that is open until twelve o'clock at night, which makes it very easy to get almost anything to eat anytime day or night.

How is little Elwin enjoying his vacation. I bet he sure is sunburned now, playing in the sun every day. Does he still play with the boys? I have been thinking that Elwin must be big enough by now to ride a two wheel bicycle. If I remember correctly, I got my first one when I was nine years old, and Elwin must be taller than I was.

They have a B-17 school here now on the field, and every day you can see the airplanes flying around. Some so close the ground you wonder how they miss the buildings. The fellows learning how to fly the large planes sure must have a swell time. There are, also, a few B-26 and several P-38, as well as P-52's. The B-29, the new large bomber, is sure a smooth looking plane when it is flying. When you stand beside on the ground, it looks like a large building.[*]

How is Pop making out with the gas rationing now? It seems to me that it will be lifted, as well as tire rationing, this fall or in early November. Last Sunday Walter Winchell said that the war in Europe will be over by September the 15th or sooner, and I think he will be right if the Russians keep their present rate of conquest.[†]

---

[*] The B-29 was the most advanced and biggest bomber used during WWII. It still had severe reliability problems through the end of 1944 with its engines catching on fire.

[†] This was a very over optimistic assessment, but Al and most people tend to be optimistic. V-E Day was celebrated on May 8, 1945. V-E is victory in Europe.

Amarillo, Texas

Al's Odyssey, from Catonsville to Japan
Edward Albert Aldridge II's World War II Letters

However, then we will have to fight this war with Japan, but I don't think it will be too much after Germany falls.[*]

There seems to be a certain amount of faith that the army is going to discharge a lot of men that are over thirty eight years old. You would be surprised to know how many men that are in the army which this would affect.

Well as everything stands at present, I won't be home until the first of September, but it isn't too far away. If I can stay away from shipments, until then everything will be fine.

You mentioned in one of your letters about Oriole Park burning down[†], and that you would send me the newspaper. As yet I haven't received it. Where are the Orioles playing ball now? I understand that they are in first place, for once.

As I can't think of much more to say, I will close for the present.

Love to All

Your loving son

Albert

PS Don't mind the typewriting, for I don't do much practicing.

---

[*] V-J Day was August 15, 1945.
[†] Oriole Park burned down July 4, 1944. In spite of that, the Orioles won the Pennant in 1944. The team continued the season on 33rd Street at the old Baltimore Municipal Stadium which was never intended to be a baseball stadium. As Elwin recalls, it was an earthworks stadium with wooden bench type seats. No beer was sold there, and fans were very well behaved.

Amarillo, Texas

Al's Odyssey, from Catonsville to Japan
Edward Albert Aldridge II's World War II Letters

Sgt. E. A. Aldridge 33552323
3701 Base Unit
Flight 1 Section A, Bks 1822
Amarillo, Texas

27 July 1944

Dear Mom & Pop:

Received your letter of the 19th, and was surprised to hear the neighbors in the back are Philippine.*

It's just a little over a month, until I get my furlough. My first day of furlough is the 5th, so I should be home about the evening of the 6th. All I have to do now is to stay off shipments until then. But, if I go overseas I probably will get a delay in route. The overseas shipments from this field have slowed down for the present, however, how long this will last is the question. We are getting quite a few civilians in payroll for the last two weeks, the number about fifteen compared to the two a few weeks ago. So when a few new ones come in a few soldiers usually go out.

The war in Europe is going fine according to the latest reports over the radio. The Russians seem to be on fire, and in a week they should be in East Prussia. The reports from all sources indicate the war in Europe should be over sometime in September. I sure hope that it will, so the power can be concentrated in the East. Although, we are supposed to be winning the war with Japan, and taking the Islands in the Pacific, that Japan took from us, the main part of the battle will be on the land. In Indochina, Burma, and French Indo China, the Japanese are well fortified. Therefore, it will

---

* There was a diverse population in Baltimore County and Catonsville Manor, but I don't recall any other Polynesians or Orientals. I became good friends with their son. While the State schools were segregated for African-Americans at that time, he had no problem with acceptance in segregated schools or the neighborhood. We enjoyed playing baseball with African-American teams. If it was illegal, we did not know it.

Amarillo, Texas

Al's Odyssey, from Catonsville to Japan
Edward Albert Aldridge II's World War II Letters

take sometime to dig them out, as well as in China proper where the Japanese are making unusual progress every day. I just hope that China will be able to hold out, making it easier for the Allies. We have orientation classes once a week where we discuss the war from the different fronts as well as all of the latest news events, at home. It looks as if Roosevelt and Truman will head our next executive branch of the government. I don't think the Republicans will have too much of a chance, however, the election returns will indicate a turning to the more conservative view.

We lost first ballgame yesterday by the score of 4 to 1 it was a pretty close game. The trouble was that our team did very little hitting, I got on base twice, but wasn't able to get any hits. In fact for the last two games I haven't gotten a hit. We play again tomorrow night, so I probably will have better luck.

The bread that you sent was not stale, in fact it was quite fresh, but one of the fellows got some that was moldy, so I didn't think that you had better send any more until the weather gets a little cooler.

The weather here is still hot as ever. The days are always hot, with the nights very cool. In fact last night it was so cold that I woke up in the middle of the night, and had to get another blanket.

When I go to sleep, it is warm, so often, I just lie on top of the bed without blankets of anything, but before the night is over I always need some kind of cover.

I wonder if you could get an extra Sunday paper and send it to me once in a while, for it was good to see a Baltimore paper. I read the one that you send, about the fire in Oriole Park from one side to the other. I also would appreciate it if you could get a Monday Morning paper too, for it gives all of the scores and players of the sandlot games.

Amarillo, Texas

Al's Odyssey, from Catonsville to Japan
Edward Albert Aldridge II's World War II Letters

There isn't much more that I can think of to say at this time, so I will close for the present.

Love to All

Your loving Son:

Albert

PS: Add (Bks 1822) to my address
    As on envelope.

Al was shipped out before his furlough came. The war dragged on longer than he expected. The Allies had done such a good job of knocking out German supply lines in Europe that they had wrecked the infrastructure greatly slowing the advance of the Americans toward Germany.

Al's Odyssey, from Catonsville to Japan
Edward Albert Aldridge II's World War II Letters

Fort Myers, Florida

Buckingham Army Air Field Flexible Gunnery School[*] was located in the southwest region of Florida near the City of Fort Myers. It was a training site for gun operators who would fly in bombers to help defend them against enemy aircraft. The Gunnery School was started in 1942 on 7,000 acres of swamp that had been drained with canals. It must have been a humid, miserable place—some books describe the snake, blood-sucking bedbugs, and mosquito infestations. "Col. Delmar described the site as...the ugliest field in the nation."[†]

The Gunnery School initially had three 5,000 foot runways, and two oval tracks on the "Ground Moving Target Range", as well as skeet ranges and trap shooting ranges. Training was conducted in both air-to-air and air-to-surface gunnery. The air-to-air training employed a variety of aircraft, including T-6s, RP-63s, B-17s, and B-24s. For ground-based training, a number of facilities were used such as moving target ranges and gunnery simulators.

At the end of WWII, the base had a total of six concrete runways (the largest was 5,800' long), its target ranges were comprised of a 65,723 acres, and it had approximately 700 buildings, housing 16,000

---

[*] Osburne, R.E., <u>World War Sites in the United States</u>, Riebel-Roque Publishing Company, Indianapolis, IN, 2007
[†] <u>Florida's World War II Memorial, Buckingham Army Airfield</u>, www.flheritage.com/wwii/sites, July 19, 2008.

Al's Odyssey, from Catonsville to Japan
Edward Albert Aldridge II's World War II Letters

men. Buckingham closed in 1945, after graduating almost 48,000 aerial gunners.[*]

    Based on my memories and perceptions from these letters, Mom and Pop were convinced that Al wanted to get into combat. They were trying to encourage him to stay in office work, and Al was trying to assure them that he is OK and to explain the system.[†]

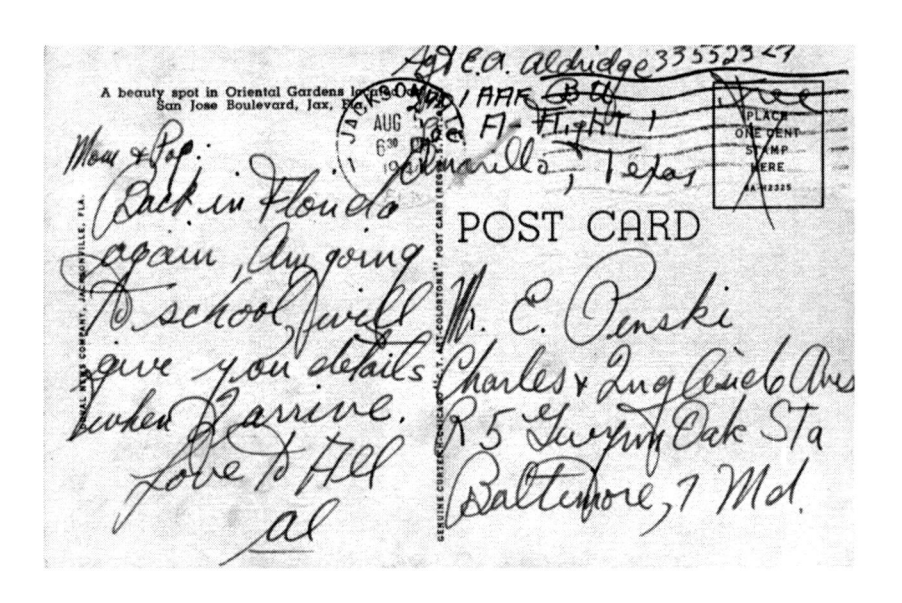

---

[*] Thole, L., Forgotten Fields of America, Volume III, Histories Publishing Co. Inc., 2003,
ISBN-13: 978-1575101026
[†] Legend has it that four leaf clovers are a sign of good luck

Fort Myers, Florida

Al's Odyssey, from Catonsville to Japan
Edward Albert Aldridge II's World War II Letters

U. S. Army Air Forces
Buckingham Army Air Field
Flexible Gunnery School
Ft. Myers, Florida Section Q

Sgt. E. A. Aldridge 33552323

Aug 6, 1944

Dear Mom & Pop:

    Arrived safe at Fort Myers, Florida at 10 AM o'clock 6 Aug 44. We left Amarillo Army Air Field 2:00 AM August 3, 1944, that is twelve other fellows besides myself. I was in charge of the shipment, and had to take are of all of the arrangements for the reservations and a dozen other things as well as keeping track of the fellows.

    The school I am supposed to go to, as you probably realize by the writing paper, is aerial gunnery school. I didn't volunteer for it; however I was not surprised when the order came out. They had to ship a certain number of permanent parties to this school. There were so few fellows qualified for combat crew in Unit Personnel that I didn't have much of a chance, to stay off of the shipment.

    I understand that the school here is only six weeks; however, there are so many fellows here at this camp that they don't have the equipment to take care of all of them. So it will take quite awhile longer.

    At the present time I don't know or have the faintest idea when I will get any kind of a furlough, so you won't be able to expect to see me for at least three more months.

Fort Myers, Florida

Al's Odyssey, from Catonsville to Japan
Edward Albert Aldridge II's World War II Letters

The camp here isn't anything like Amarillo; however there is a swimming pool here, as well as several large PX's, also two movies. The town which is about 13 miles from camp is very small, although I haven't seen much of it.

The trip down was swell we had several long layovers, the first at Dallas for about twelve hours, so we got to see most of the town. The next stop was New Orleans. It was a dirty city although there are a lot of very old buildings there as well as the water front with all of the levies, where the water is higher than the land. There are so many sailors in New Orleans, that you seldom see a soldier. The next layover was at Jacksonville, Florida. I saw a movie there as well as part of the town.

It is getting dark now, and we will have to get up in the morning at five o'clock, so I will say goodbye for the present.

    Love to All

           Your loving son

           Albert

My new address

    Sgt. E. A Aldridge 33552323
    AAF – BAAF
    Section Q
    Ft. Myers, Florida

        Fort Myers, Florida

Al's Odyssey, from Catonsville to Japan
Edward Albert Aldridge II's World War II Letters

U. S. Army Air Forces
Buckingham Army Air Field
Flexible Gunnery School
Ft. Myers, Florida

Section Q
Sgt. E. A. Aldridge 33552323

August 8, 1944

Dear Mom & Pop:

Well everything is OK with me at the present time, so don't worry about anything. The weather here is really sultry, all day and night, it is very hot. We are going to take a physical this afternoon, but I don't have any doubt about passing it.

The food here isn't as good as we got at Amarillo or the mess hall so clean. I guess we will be cleaning though as I understand that we will get KP very often before we start to school.

Yesterday morning we had to carry lumber out of a swamp and load it on a truck. For the afternoon we were supposed to go back, but we didn't show up, instead we went to the PX then got a haircut and went to the movies.

I miss the typewriter when writing letters. I just kind of got used to using it. Don't mind my handwriting for I am lying on the bed, while I am writing this letter.

I will need some more money before the month is over, as I spent a lot on the way down from Amarillo, and I also want to buy a swimming suit. You can send me $20^{00} around the 15th.

It is time to go to chow so I will close for the present. I think it would be better if you sent it registered instead of a money order

Al's Odyssey, from Catonsville to Japan
Edward Albert Aldridge II's World War II Letters

as I can't find a Post Office on the post and I don't know when I will be able to get a pass to go to town.

      Love to All

        Your loving Son

          Albert

Al's Odyssey, from Catonsville to Japan
Edward Albert Aldridge II's World War II Letters

U. S. Army Air Forces
Buckingham Army Air Field
Flexible Gunnery School
Ft. Myers, Florida

Sgt. E. A. Aldridge 33552323
Section Q

14 August, 1944

Dear Mom & Pop:

 Received your letter this afternoon that you sent directly to Ft. Myers. I have been here now for eight days and as yet not much has happened.

 We have had some kind of detail for the past seven day; however I spend more time getting out of work, than I spend actually working. Friday I had KP as well as the other fellows I came down with. We also get it again tomorrow. On KP you start at 2:30 AM and don't get off until 7:30 PM that night.

 I went up with two other fellows to the Post Headquarters to see if we could get a job, there while we were waiting to go to school. However, if they can't get us off of KP I don't think it would be worth while working there.

 I don't work hard when I get detail, only about four hours a day. For the last four days I have just been policing up the area. The sergeants usually get put in charge of a detail, but it is a lot better just being in a detail for you don't have to keep track of the men.

Fort Myers, Florida

Al's Odyssey, from Catonsville to Japan
Edward Albert Aldridge II's World War II Letters

I am getting a good sun-tan on my shoulders and arms, since I am out in the sun every day. We haven't been able to get a pass to go to town as yet. I understand that the town is small and clean with a large beach several miles down it.

I bought a swell pair of swimming trunks on the PX yesterday, it cost me $3.15.

It has rained here every day for the last four days. The rain has been making it cool in the evening and better sleeping.

I have to do my own washing now, and it sure is a lousy job.

There are quite a few airplanes on the field; you can always see B-24's and B-26s in the sky, all of the time, as well as several other types of airplanes.

It is getting late so I will close for the present.

      Love to All
             Your loving Son

          Al

Fort Myers, Florida

Al's Odyssey, from Catonsville to Japan
Edward Albert Aldridge II's World War II Letters

August 21, 1944

Dear Mom & Pop:

Well it is the 21st of August already; time really does pass fast, here. It has been over two weeks since I arrived.

I received the money that you sent and it comes in handy. As yet we haven't signed a payroll for this month, so I know we won't get paid before the 10th or next month, if even then.

This camp is so confused that I don't' see how they keep anything straight.

Talking about sunburn I have got quite a tan on my face, shoulders, and arms. I was out in the sun for every day for almost two weeks. I got my hair cut short, so I can keep as cool as possible.

It rains here consistently every evening at four o'clock, for about fifteen or twenty minutes then it stops, and the sun comes out again. The rain keeps it fairly cool in the evenings, although it gets very hot around one o'clock in the afternoon.

I have been working at the Post Headquarters here since Saturday. That way I get out of KP and get out of other details.

I don't work in payroll, but instead service records. I managed to acquire quite a bit of information about service records in Amarillo so the work isn't new to me. In fact if they would give me a chance I could give them a lot of short cuts, in their present system. However, I don't give them any ideas that I would like to stay here, for I wouldn't want to be assigned at this camp.

Fort Myers, Florida

Al's Odyssey, from Catonsville to Japan
Edward Albert Aldridge II's World War II Letters

I went swimming for my first time Sunday afternoon, and did enjoy it. The pool is very large and wasn't crowded.

I don't know how long it will be before I start to school, but I am anxious to get it over. There are about one thousand fellows before me, so it should be quite some time.

I caught a cold, a few days ago, but it is almost better now. I got my feet wet several times so I guess that was the cause of it.

Love to All

Your Loving Son

Albert

Fort Myers, Florida

Al's Odyssey, from Catonsville to Japan
Edward Albert Aldridge II's World War II Letters

U. S. Army Air Forces
Buckingham Army Air Field
Flexible Gunnery School
Ft. Myers, Florida

Sgt. E. A. Aldridge 33552323
BAAF Section Q

August 29, 1944

Dear Mom & Pop:

Received your two letters last night one you wrote on the 24th and the other on the 26th. I can't remember receiving a letter from little Elwin, did you send it with one of yours. I did receive the last letters that you sent to Amarillo, just after I arrived here. The letters are usually forwarded promptly as the Post Office keep a close check on all of the letters.

I certainly would like to get home next month but it will be impossible so the earliest I could get away from this field would be when I finished school. It takes six weeks to complete the course, and then I don't know when I would get shipped.

I started my basic week yesterday, which is more or less a processing week before you start school. So I hope to start the actual school next week.

There are four of the fellows that I came down here from Amarillo with, who are still with me.

Al's Odyssey, from Catonsville to Japan
Edward Albert Aldridge II's World War II Letters

Yesterday and today I went up to 38,000 feet in an altitude chamber. It was really quite an experience. I had to wear an oxygen mask after 10,000 feet, and at 30,000 I was breathing pure oxygen. But all of the time I stayed right on the ground, they just reduce the pressure which causes the same atmospheric conditions as at high altitude. Several of the fellows got the bends, and had to be removed from the chamber from the escape hatch.

I also heard several lectures about high altitude conditions and flying. I learned quite a few interesting things that a person very seldom thinks of but just takes for granted.

A B-29 airplane landed on the field this afternoon, while three others were circling the field. So almost everybody beat it for the runway to see what it looked like at close range. The number three motor was out so it was forced to land while the other planes continued on their way. It was the first B-29 that a lot of the fellows saw, however there were always several at Amarillo. Most of the fellows are going to be B-29 gunners so they were especially interested in the plane. It is just about the largest bomber the Army has at the present time. It is a pretty bomber, long and sleek, and almost looks like a huge fish in the sky. The most prominent feature is the huge tail, which can be spotted at a distance above all of the other airplanes.

I left my traveling bag and two sets of sun tan suits besides several other things, with a fellow at Amarillo to send home, so you can keep a look out for them and let me know when they arrive. You can send me the bag down here when you get a chance for I probably will need it. I was afraid to bring the extra clothing with me as you get clothing check when you leave a camp and again when you arrive at another. They take away all of the extra clothing away, so I thought it would be best to have it sent home.

Fort Myers, Florida

Al's Odyssey, from Catonsville to Japan
Edward Albert Aldridge II's World War II Letters

I haven't received the papers that you sent as yet, but I suppose they will come soon.

Don't worry about me changing my shoes and stockings when they get wet, for I always do it as soon as I can. It is raining now, and has rained off and on several times today. The rain is the only thing that keeps it cool at night, but I don't like the rain in the daytime, for the field when it starts, so you get soaking wet before you can get back to the barracks.

I want to take a shower before they put the lights out so I will say so long.

Love to All

Your Loving Son

Albert

Fort Myers, Florida

Al's Odyssey, from Catonsville to Japan
Edward Albert Aldridge II's World War II Letters

U. S. ARMY AIR FORCES
FLEXIBLE GUNNERY SCHOOL
BUCKINGHAM ARMY AIR FIELD
FT. MYERS, FLORIDA

September 3, 1944

Dear Mom & Pop:

    Received your letter today, just before I went to lunch. I also got paid for the month of August today. I don't know where all of the money goes, but every time I turn around I am buying something or having something cleaned.

    I haven't been to town since I arrived here, but I think I will have to see what it is like some time this week.

    I do my own washing now, and it always turns out that every Sunday I spend most of the morning scrubbing. I wash all of my cloths, even my sun tan uniforms, which I have found at the cleaners.

    I received the first newspapers, yesterday, and boy was it good to see a Baltimore paper again.

    Back to the old grind again of KP and detail for another week, however I feel sure that I will start school next week for sure.

    I went to the movies last night and saw an old picture *Kid from Spain*, with Eddie Cantor. It was very funny.

Fort Myers, Florida

Al's Odyssey, from Catonsville to Japan
Edward Albert Aldridge II's World War II Letters

It is very hot today; in fact you can't even stop perspiration, while just sitting in the barracks.
Love to All

Your Loving Son

<u>Al</u>

Fort Myers, Florida

Al's Odyssey, from Catonsville to Japan
Edward Albert Aldridge II's World War II Letters

U. S. Army Air Forces
Buckingham Army Air Field
Flexible Gunnery School
Ft. Myers, Florida

Sgt. E. A. Aldridge 33552323
Section P Flight A
Class 44-43
BAAF
Ft. Myers, Fla

September 10, 1944

Dear Mom & Pop:

Its Sunday again, the time does pass so fast. I moved yesterday to a new squadron, where I will be stationed until I leave this field.

I start to school Monday, however it looks as if I will also pull KP again Monday. However it will probably be the last time for this field. Only 13 men from the Headquarters get it each day and the NCOs will only have to keep track of the other men, so I won't have to do any work.

It should only be six weeks now until I get out of school. Then I hope to get a delay enroute to my next station. So if everything turns out OK, I should be home the later part of October.

I can't see how it always happens but I have been the first on the list on everything that happens since I have been on this field. There hasn't been a name alphabetically before my name in over 500 men. So any button that I have to wear has No 1 on it. Therefore you can see how I'm always first.

I am glad that Pop had Labor Day off, for I had KP for almost 18 hours. I didn't even realize what day it was until noon.

Al's Odyssey, from Catonsville to Japan
Edward Albert Aldridge II's World War II Letters

Elwin probably is in school again by now. He will be in the fourth grade already.

I guess that I got Grand Ma's letter, however I don't remember.

I got a letter from Emmy Ridgely the other day, and he also is overseas someplace. He doesn't say where, but the letter has an APO from New York and his letter was censored. It looks as if most of the fellows from Ellicott City are all overseas.

We haven't done anything today so far, but we are supposed to have a formation this afternoon. It is one o'clock now. As usual I finished my washing this morning. I am getting used to it now, although I don't get the clothes, as clean, as the laundry did as we have to use cold water, and don't get any chance to soak the clothes.

I have been watching the PX for a present for you for your birthday Mom; however they don't have much of anything at the PX on the field. So I would appreciate it if you would buy yourself something for me. I won't get a chance to get into town when the stores are open as I understand we don't get finished school until 6:45 in the evening. Get yourself something nice and don't worry about how much money you spend.

    Love to All

        Your Loving Son

        Albert

    Fort Myers, Florida

Al's Odyssey, from Catonsville to Japan
Edward Albert Aldridge II's World War II Letters

U. S. Army Air Forces
Buckingham Army Air Field
Flexible Gunnery School
Ft. Myers, Florida

Sgt. E. A. Aldridge 33552323
Section P Flight A
Class 44-43 BAAF
Ft. Myers, Fla

                    U. S. ARMY AIR FORCES
                    Buckingham Army Air Field
                    FT. MYERS, FLORIDA

                              September 25, 1944

Dear Mom & Pop:

      Received Pops letter the day before yesterday, and was certainly glad to hear from you.

      I would have really loved to get home this summer; however it was impossible for me to do so. But I expect to make it sometime around the end of October or the first of November -- just as soon as I can finish the school here.

      I am glad to hear that the apple tree has done so fine this year. I would like to have some of the apples. Also, if Mom could send a few cookies.

      I was very much surprised to hear last you have been sick and that you had lost so much weight. Don't work so hard all of the time and get a lot of sleep. I haven't gained any weight lately; however, I still average between 178 and 180 pounds.

Fort Myers, Florida

Al's Odyssey, from Catonsville to Japan
Edward Albert Aldridge II's World War II Letters

It also worries me about Elwin, for almost every letter I get he is either sick or has a cold. He doesn't seem to be able to stand the damp weather very good.* I think it would be a lot better for Elwin if he could live someplace in a warm dry climate. Myself I did never feel better or gain so much weight as I did in Amarillo.

Grandpa has been sick quite often the last six months hasn't he? If anything happened to him, I don't think I could get an emergency furlough, while I am in school, however, by the time you get this letter I will only have about 2½ weeks to go.

I really think it was better that I ended up in some kind of school as if I would have ended up overseas or in the infantry. Since I have left Amarillo several hundred of the permanent parties have been shipped out for overseas, and undoubtedly I would have been one of them. As my present situation stands, I wouldn't to be ready to go overseas for many months, and before I even left the country I would end up someplace as a clerk. For all of my records show my experience as a clerk in the Army. Most of the assigned personnel in the Sections on this field are graduates from the Gunnery School.

I received the papers that you sent several days ago. I haven't been off of the field since I have been here, so I haven't spent too much money this month. However, I will probably need some, when I get out of school to get home.

It is getting kind of late so I will close for the present.

                        Love To All

                        Albert

---

* In Fourth Grade, little Elwin was starting to get a lot healthier - he only missed 20 days of school.

Fort Myers, Florida

Al's Odyssey, from Catonsville to Japan
Edward Albert Aldridge II's World War II Letters

October 1, 1944

Dear Mom & Pop:

Well today is the first of October, and I have been in the Army for twenty months.

I received the papers you sent yesterday. It was good to see the Baltimore paper again. I read almost everything from the first page to the last page.

I am using the typewriter in the orderly of the room of the Section. It is the first time that I have typewritten for almost two months. I am getting a little rusty.

Three weeks of school are finished, and only three more to go, then I should be able to get out of this place for good. Everybody graduating from here has been getting delays in route. It usually amounts to about fifteen days plus traveling time to the next camp that we go. It will be probably either Lincoln, Nebraska, or Clovis, New Mexico. I just can't seem to get stationed anywhere near home.

Most of my shirts needed buttons, and several patches and stripes, so I spent the day sewing. It took me about two hours to sew about twelve buttons on my shirts. And about an hour to sew one patch on.

We have been very busy, for the last four weeks, and haven't had too much time to do much of anything. We are constantly kept busy from early in the morning until seven thirty in the evening. The last two Sundays we have had off, however, the rest of the Sundays we will be here we will probably fly.

Fort Myers, Florida

Al's Odyssey, from Catonsville to Japan
Edward Albert Aldridge II's World War II Letters

    Elwin must be busy with his school work now. As he has been going for almost a month now. I hope he doesn't get sick too often this year. For he gets so many colds each year, that cause him to miss so much in doing the work. I think he will find that most of the teachers are OK and they will treat his very nice. I always found out as long as you didn't give the teacher any trouble, they would always be all right.[*]

    Pop don't work to hard, for I would not like to see you become sick. And if you do ever get sick please let me know about it as soon as possible. For I am always thinking about you.
                   Love to All

                                       Your loving son

                                       Albert.

---

[*] Elwin's attendance was much improved in the fourth grade and thereafter.

                      Fort Myers, Florida

Al's Odyssey, from Catonsville to Japan
Edward Albert Aldridge II's World War II Letters

U. S. Army Air Forces
Buckingham Army Air Field
Flexible Gunnery School
Ft. Myers, Florida

Sgt. E. A. Aldridge 33552323
Section P BAAF
Class 44-43 Flight A
Ft. Myers, Fla

October 14, 1944

Dear Mom & Pop:

Received your letter this afternoon, and realized that I must also write to you.

Well! This is the last day of the fifth week of school, and only one week to go as I graduate next Saturday the 21st. Then if everything turns out all right I should get a delay enroute within a week or so after I graduate. So you had better send me about $35.00 as soon as possible, for I don't know how soon I will have after the 21st. I may get about $18.00 flying pay when I graduate, however if I leave before the 31st I will need the money.

I received the bag and clothes some time ago, as I must have neglected to tell you about getting it. I also received the package you sent with the apples and cookies, which I certainly enjoyed.

I have been flying three times this week in B-24's and have flown all over the southern part of Florida, as well as Havana. It gets very cold when you fly above 15,000 feet. So we have to wear clothes lined with sheep wool, as well as boots, and gloves.

Fort Myers, Florida

Al's Odyssey, from Catonsville to Japan
Edward Albert Aldridge II's World War II Letters

It has been cool here for the last several days especially at night time. I have had to wear a jacket every time that I leave the barracks. We have had a fire in the stove all day.

I have been receiving the papers that you have been sending. I always read them from front to the last page.

I have passed all of the tests and phase checks, with very good marks, as I want to finish this school, because if I wash out, I will have to go to radio school and would not have a chance to get home.

Love to All

Albert

Al's Odyssey, from Catonsville to Japan
Edward Albert Aldridge II's World War II Letters

October 22, 1944

Dear Mom & Pop

Yesterday, I should have graduated from this school, however, the Hurricane,[*] as you no doubt read about in the paper, set us back a week. Now I will graduate on Saturday the 28th.

Everyone on the field was evacuated, and taken into town. My flight and four others about 257 of us in all spent Wednesday night the 18th in one of the high schools in Fort Myers. We all had to sleep on the floor, with only a blanket and a raincoat. However, the only part of the Hurricane that came near Ft. Myers or the field was the tail end with comparatively small damage as far I have found out there were no injuries anywhere around here.

The wind was very strong as it blew down a number of trees, as well as several small houses. On the field the only damage was the loss of the tar paper on the roof of several buildings. The most damage was at the different shore sites.

Now that I will graduate on the 28th I should be home sometime, about the first week of November, or shortly after.

I sprained my ankle Friday evening, when I was coming out of the Day Room. After spending most of Saturday in bed and getting it taped up it feels O.K. now, although I still have a little limp.

How Elwin making out in school, he must be very busy now, with his homework.

---

[*] That was the Pinar del Rio Hurricane that killed 318 people. It struck land in nearby Sarasota, Florida on October 19, 1944.

Fort Myers, Florida

Al's Odyssey, from Catonsville to Japan
Edward Albert Aldridge II's World War II Letters

I received the money today, rather yesterday, and went to the Post Office today.

I can't say for sure as yet when I will be home, however I will let you know as soon as possible.

Your Loving Son.

Love to All

Albert

Al's Odyssey, from Catonsville to Japan
Edward Albert Aldridge II's World War II Letters

Naples, Florida

Naples Army Air Field was only a mile from Naples and near the Everglades. It was a sub-base to Buckingham Army Air Field activated in December 1943[*]. As many as several hundred men and 53 aircraft were assigned to the base. It is now Naples Municipal Airport.

FLEXIBLE GUNERY SCHOOL
U. S. ARMY AIR FORCES
BUCKINGHAM ARMY AIR FORCE
FT. MYERS, FLORIDA

October 31, 1944

Dear Mom & Pop

    Well, I have graduated from school at last; however, as yet I don't know when I will get home. I moved down to Naples, Florida Saturday after graduation, because they did not have any place to put us.

    Naples is about only 65 miles south of Fort Myers. We don't know when we will ship, it may even be a month, before we leave this place.

---

[*]Important Dates in Collier County History, Collier County Museum, www.colliermuseum,com, 2007.

Al's Odyssey, from Catonsville to Japan
Edward Albert Aldridge II's World War II Letters

I will let you know as soon as I can find out anything definite.

It is very nice here, for the camp is very small, and the barracks are clean. There are quite a few gunners that graduated before I did that haven't left yet, that is the reason for the delay.

I will write again tomorrow, for it is time to go to eat now.

    Love To All,
           Your Loving Son,

         Albert

Al's Odyssey, from Catonsville to Japan
Edward Albert Aldridge II's World War II Letters

U. S. ARMY AIR FORCES
BUCKINGHAM ARMY AIR FIELD
FLEXIBLE GUNNERY SCHOOL
FT. MYERS, FLORIDA

Sgt E. A. Aldridge 33552323
Section P. Flight A
Class 44-43 BAAF
Ft. Myers, Florida

November 5, 1944

Dear Mom & Pop:

    Another Sunday has come and almost passed at Naples, Florida. Two fellows that I went through school with came down from Ft. Myers (Aerial Gunnery School) Saturday and left this afternoon. We spent this morning and afternoon walking around the town and down along the beach. Naples is on the Western shore of Florida right on the Gulf of Mexico. It is more or less a summer resort, or should I say a winter resort.

    I don't do very much of anything here, for I am supposed to be in charge of details that do odd jobs around the field. However, starting tomorrow night I am going to be in charge of painting the mess hall, although I will work only every other night, just three nights a week.

    Two hundred fellows that graduated from school Saturday came down here Saturday night. All this field is used for is to provide a base for the P-39s that are used to simulate attacks from the air. The gunnery students shoot at the P-39 s from B-24's. They don't shoot bullets but take pictures of where they would be shooting.

Naples, Florida

Al's Odyssey, from Catonsville to Japan
Edward Albert Aldridge II's World War II Letters

I understand that was of the B-29 gunnery graduates here will leave before the 23rd of this month. Therefore, I should be home, before then, if everything goes all right.

It seems that every letter I write it is always a little later, when I will be able to get home. However, I am sure that I will be home this month, probably the later part. I hope I will be home for Thanksgiving, as I haven't been home for any holidays, as yet.

I have two army manuals on Army and Naval identification, with lots of pictures of Airplanes and Boats that I got for Elwin.

       Love to All

                Your Loving Son

            Albert

Al's Odyssey, from Catonsville to Japan
Edward Albert Aldridge II's World War II Letters

Sgt. E. A. Aldridge 38552323
Section P Flight A
Class 44-43 BAAF
Ft. Myers, Fla

November 8, 1944

Dear Mom & Pop:

    Received your letter today, and thought I would answer it at once. I am impatient, to get out of this state and get home. All I am doing now is just wanting to be shipped out. You see, that when I am shipped, I will get a delay enroute, for any where from about nine to fifteen days. During this time I will be able to come home while enroute to my next station.

    I don't know exactly when I will leave here, however, I am sure it will be this month. And I hope it will be before the 23rd. I will let you know as soon as I get any definite information.

    Don't send me anything here as far as Christmas presents or cookies, apples, etc, as I am not sure when I will leave, and I certainly hope I will be home before Christmas.

    At this moment I am in the mess hall, and it is about 9:30 PM. I am in charge of a painting detail, and I work every other night, as the Mess Hall is being used during the day. I only work about five hours a night so you can see that I don't have much to do. So during the daytime all I do is wander around the Western side of Florida and spend money. In fact, I am down to the thirty five dollars that you sent me plus about five more of my pay. I bought a pair of shoes while I was at Fort Myers, however I want to get another pair, as I have another certificate. G.I. shoes are so heavy and clumsy that I get tired of wearing them so I switch to civilian, once in a while.

Naples, Florida

Al's Odyssey, from Catonsville to Japan
Edward Albert Aldridge II's World War II Letters

    I suppose that I could use about $20^{00} more, as I have several other things to buy. Just drop me a money order, and if I don't get it before I ship it will be OK.

    I was surprised to hear the Joseph[*] was shipped overseas, as I still thought he was in Missouri. I suppose I am quite lucky to be able to stay on this side so long.

    Love to all

                          Your son

                           Albert

---

[*] Joseph Shear, Al's cousin from Pittsburgh.

Al's Odyssey, from Catonsville to Japan
Edward Albert Aldridge II's World War II Letters

Sgt. E. A. Aldridge 38552323
Section P Flight A
Class 44-43 BAAF
Ft. Myers, Fla

November 10, 1944

Dear Mom & Pop:

    Everything is just about the same as usual; nothing seems to happen here, so there's not much to write about.

    Having nothing better to do, I though I would write some letters. I am working tonight again, but the work doesn't amount to very much.

    My ankle seems to be better now, although it was sore quite awhile, as I wasn't able to keep off of it very much. I had it taped several times, but every time the tape wore blisters on my foot. So I had to always take it off.

    We are trying to get up a ball team now, to play the other three teams that they have here. I tried to get one before but didn't have too much luck. The fellows all promise to come out in the evenings, but don't seem to make it.

    After seeing the other teams play, a lot of the fellows claim now that we could beat them. So we are going to try it again. Tomorrow night we are supposed to practice. I don't know if I will be able to play yet because of my ankle, but I will be able to coach the fellows.

Naples, Florida

Al's Odyssey, from Catonsville to Japan
Edward Albert Aldridge II's World War II Letters

I just got finished doing a little painting and I have more paint on me then I put on the Mess Hall ceiling. Its kind of rough painting the ceiling that is about one hundred feet long and about thirty-five feet wide. It is really not the ceiling, but the underside of the roof. There are rafters about every two and one half feet apart, and a million and on a different boards supporting the roof. It's better then doing nothing.

Will write again if I get any news about coming home in near future.

Love to All

Your Loving Son

Albert

Al's Odyssey, from Catonsville to Japan
Edward Albert Aldridge II's World War II Letters

Sgt. E. A. Aldridge 38552323
Section P Flight A
Class 44-43 BAAF
Ft. Myers, Fla

November 16, 1944

Dear Mom & Pop:

It's the 16th of November already, and at one time I had expected to be home by now. However, everything does not always turn out the way we would like them to, but I still expect to make it sometime in the near future.

I got a letter from Mrs. Ridgely yesterday. Emery has been overseas for some time now. He is in France now. She also said that Roger Mellor is back from overseas, and has been married. His mother certainly must be happy about him coming back to this country.

Jessie Phelps, another one of the fellows from Ellicott City is in Germany now. His mother died while he was overseas.

There have been quite a few shipments to CIS, that is instructor's school in the last few weeks. I don't know yet as how I will make out, about going to this school. If I do, it will be another 3 months before I get home.

I just got two letters, one that you sent on the 13th and the other you sent by air mail, with the money order.

Also about Roger Mellor, well that's how things happen.

Naples, Florida

Al's Odyssey, from Catonsville to Japan
Edward Albert Aldridge II's World War II Letters

  There is not much to do around here, but sleep and play ball, several of us play 500[*] sometimes in the afternoon. I go to the show several times a week. Last night I saw *Conspirator*. It was a very good picture.

    Love To All

        Your Loving Son

        Albert

---

[*] A card game

Al's Odyssey, from Catonsville to Japan
Edward Albert Aldridge II's World War II Letters

Sgt. E. A. Aldridge 38552323
Section P Flight A
Class 44-43 BAAF
Ft. Myers, Fla

November 28, 1944

Dear Mom & Pop:

I am still in Naples, waiting for something to happen. I don't know anymore now about my leaving this place than I did a month ago.

The time passes very fast here. I go to the show about three times each week. The movies are very good, the last one I saw was Danny Kaye, in *Up in Arms*.

I am still playing ball, since the weather here is very nice, in fact today it is hot. We seldom have any rain, and every day is sunny.

I was very disappointed when I was not able to be home for Thanksgiving. But, that is the way things always happen.

I really hope to be home before Christmas however I can't find out anything definite. I could use a new wallet, as I wore out the one you sent me, and I am using the one that I had when I came into the Army. I could use some cookies and cake, but don't send me any presents, until I let you know. In case I stay here until after Christmas, I will try to let you know as soon as possible.

I will not need my muffler or gloves, as long as I stay here so you won't have to bother sending them to me. I should be able to get them when I get home.

Naples, Florida

Al's Odyssey, from Catonsville to Japan
Edward Albert Aldridge II's World War II Letters

I have been going to church since I have been down here, almost every Sunday, and also on Thanksgiving eve.

Elwin must be getting big now, what does he want for Christmas this year.

Love to All

Your loving Son

Albert

ENLISTED MAN'S TEMPORARY PASS

Aldridge, Edward A.   Sgt.   33552323
(Name)   (Grade)   (Army serial No.)

Section N
(Organization)   (Station)

is authorized to be absent—

From 13:30 2 Dec, 44 To 02:00 3 Dec, 44
To visit Naples, Florida

Signed Howard C Evans
Commanding Officer.

HOWARD C. EVANS, 2nd. Lt., AC. (OVER)

*This form supersedes W. D., A. G. O. Form No. 7, 8 September 1942, which may be used until existing stocks are exhausted.

Naples, Florida

Al's Odyssey, from Catonsville to Japan
Edward Albert Aldridge II's World War II Letters

Sgt. E. A. Aldridge 38552323
Section P Flight A
Class 44-43 BAAF
Ft. Myers, Fla

Dec. 3, 1944

Dear Mom & Pop:

Receive your letter of the 28th yesterday evening. Yes, I am still here, and everything is all right.

I received the package that you sent a few days ago, and I was very glad to get it. The apples were very good, and tasted fine. While I was eating one of them, I thought about the apple pies you make. And hoped that I would be home soon, to eat one.

There was a shipment that went this week, however, I was not lucky enough to be on it. One of the fellows that was on it, told me that there probably be another leaving next week. As several of the fellows that were in my class left this week, I should be on the next shipment that goes out. It certainly would be wonderful if I could be home for Christmas this year.

The reason that I did not write for a week was that the rumors for shipment where so many that I put off writing, hoping that I might let you know that I was coming home.

Naples, Florida

Al's Odyssey, from Catonsville to Japan
Edward Albert Aldridge II's World War II Letters

My address is still the one to Ft. Myers, although, I am at Naples. This field is the base of Ft. Myers, so the address is the same. As far as giving anyone my address, I suppose Ft. Myers is the best for anything sent there will follow me wherever I go.

I had hoped to be home in time to buy some Christmas presents, however I would appreciate it if you would go ahead, and buy presents for Elwin and Pop; and yourself for me.

As for sending me any presents here I would rather that you wouldn't, as I hope to be home sometime this month. I feel almost positive that I will be on the next shipment.

Love To All

Your loving son

Albert

Naples, Florida

Al's Odyssey, from Catonsville to Japan
Edward Albert Aldridge II's World War II Letters

Sgt. E. A. Aldridge 38552323
Flight A   BAAF
Section P
Ft. Myers, Fla

Dec. 12, 1944

Dear Mom & Pop:

Well, I am still in Naples, Florida, and there is still, no news of my coming home. However, there is still a good chance that I may leave here Friday and ship from Fort Myers about Wednesday of next week.

If I do not leave here this week, I am certain that I will be here until after the first of January. As the Army usually does not let the men travel over the holidays.

I received the cookies and apples that you sent as I think I said, in my last letter.

I was pleased to get a letter from Elwin, and tell him I will get him a boat as soon as I can get a chance to leave Naples. As there are not any stores that I can buy toys at in Naples. I am not sure, when I will be able to get it, however the first chance I get I will buy him one. We can not get any passes at the present time to go anyplace besides Naples.

My ankle is completely better now, and I have been playing ball on it for the last several weeks. Ball is about the only recreation we have around here. However, there is not anything I would rather do than play ball. This is about the only place that I could be playing this time of year.

Naples, Florida

Al's Odyssey, from Catonsville to Japan
Edward Albert Aldridge II's World War II Letters

What makes you think that I would not go to a Christian church? You don't think that I would have any reasons to go to any other kind.

If I get any news I will let you know as soon as possible.

Love to All

Your loving son

Albert

Al's Odyssey, from Catonsville to Japan
Edward Albert Aldridge II's World War II Letters

Sgt. E. A. Aldridge 33552323
Section P BAAF
Flight A
Ft. Myers, Fla

Dec. 20, 1944

Dear Mom & Pop:

Its only five more days until Christmas, and this will be another Christmas, that I will be away from home. They promised us shipments for the last week, but put it off from one day until the next.

I don't know when I will be home now, but I am sure, that it won't be until sometime next month.

Everything is about the same here as usual, with nothing to do. This place is certainly getting terrible as there is nothing to do. Everybody here is getting disgusted around here. Just laying around, and doing details.

About the check, keep it until I get home, as I probably couldn't even get it cashed here.

I hope this letter gets home before Christmas, so you won't be looking for me to come home.

At the present time I don't know what I will be doing on Christmas or New Years.

I am in good health and feel fine, as my ankle is better now.

Merry Christmas to Mom, Pop, and Elwin.

       Your Loving Son

          Albert

       Naples, Florida

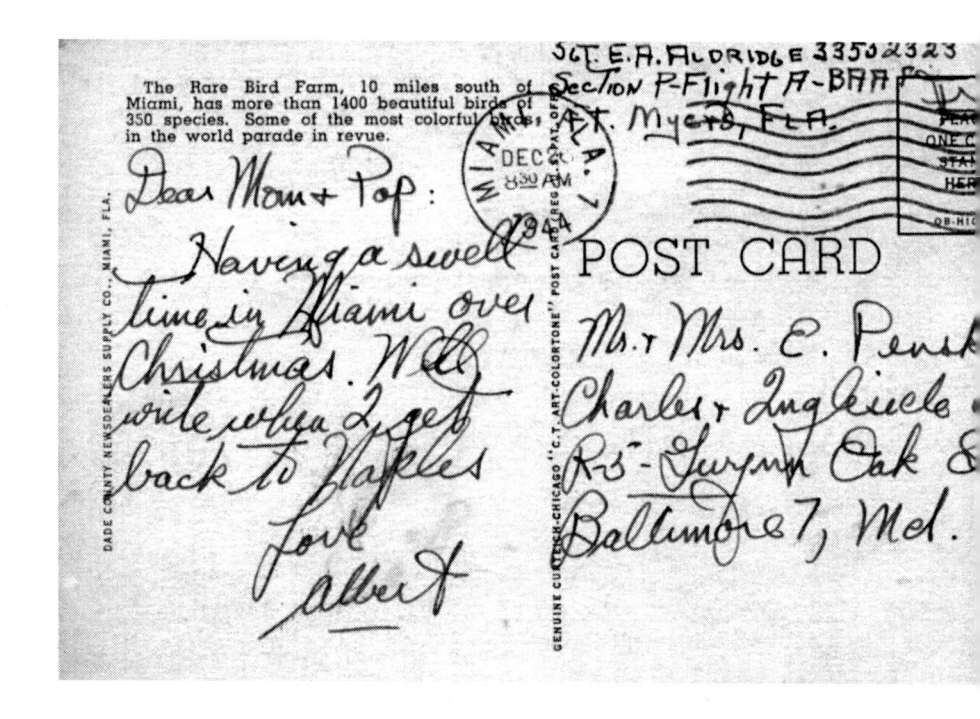

Al's Odyssey, from Catonsville to Japan
Edward Albert Aldridge II's World War II Letters

Sgt. E. A. Aldridge 38552323
Flight A   BAAF
Section P
Ft. Myers, Fla

Jan 2, 1945

Dear Mom & Pop:

    It has been a week since I have written last. I can hardly keep track of the time it seems to pass so fast.

    I spent a nice Christmas in Miami; however it couldn't come anywhere near as fine as a Christmas at home would have been. Four of the fellows and myself went down there together. It was a

192

Naples, Florida

Al's Odyssey, from Catonsville to Japan
Edward Albert Aldridge II's World War II Letters

lot better than spending Christmas in camp. Miami was very crowded and we had to spend an extra night there or we could not get a bus back to Naples. We came back about seven hours after our pass was over, but quite a few of the fellows had the same trouble, it was overlooked.

Did Elwin, Pop, and yourself have a nice Christmas. I bet Elwin had a lot of fun running the trains. He is just the right age to enjoy them the most. He is probably sorry that the holidays are over, as he starts school again, today. I wanted so much to get him a boat, I tried to get one in Miami, but they didn't have one that I thought he would like.

Your fruit cake arrived today, and I enjoyed it very much. One of the fellows said it was the best he has ever eaten.

I receive a lot of candy from Aunt Rolly, and a toilet set and some cookies from Aunt Sophie, for Christmas. The present from Aunt Sophie came in handy for it was what I needed most. I am going to write and thank them for the presents, but you will have to send me Aunt Sophie's address as I lost it someplace. I kept the address off of the package, but I must of lost it as I was looking for it tonight. I am sure Aunt Rolly's address is 2510 Plainview Ave.

Everything is just about the same with me now. I am in good health, but am getting tired of staying around this camp doing nothing. The weather is still nice here, although sometimes it gets chilly in the evenings. I am still playing ball as my ankle is better now. I suppose I will have to write for money again, when I get my orders to leave. So don't be surprised if you get a telegram, from me for money sometime in the near future. I didn't get too much money this month as they took out all of my laundry charges for the last five months out of this month pay, rather last months pay. However, I still have around forty dollars at the present time.

Naples, Florida

Al's Odyssey, from Catonsville to Japan
Edward Albert Aldridge II's World War II Letters

The question of coming home is just about the same as usual. I can just wait, for the orders to come out. As I said before it should be soon, but how soon I don't know.

It is almost two years now that I have been in the Army. That is quite a long time, but looking back now, as yet it hasn't been too bad. The time surely has passed very fast.

I spent New Years Eve in the barracks, and just wasted time talking to the other fellows.

Love To All,

Your loving son,

Albert

Al's Odyssey, from Catonsville to Japan
Edward Albert Aldridge II's World War II Letters

Sgt. E A. Aldridge 33552323
Flight A Section P-BAAF
Ft. Myers, Fla.

Jan 15, 1945

Dear Mom & Pop:

As the days and weeks pass I am still waiting to leave this camp. Shipments now are few and far between. We don't get any news as to what is going to happen to us. Rumors that we might have to go back to school have been floating around. But I hope they aren't true.

Elwin must have had a nice Christmas, for he certainly received a lot of presents. Did he run the trains under the Christmas tree?

I am working in the Orderly Room now, the job helps pass the time. In fact the last two weeks sped by so fast that I cannot recall one day from another.

I was going to call over New Years, however there were so many calls placed that the operators said it would be about eight hours before I could get the call through.

There isn't much to write about so I will close for the present.

Love to All

Your Loving Son

Albert

Naples, Florida

Al's Odyssey, from Catonsville to Japan
Edward Albert Aldridge II's World War II Letters

Lincoln, Nebraska

Lincoln, the State Capital, is in the south east corner of Nebraska. The local airport, five miles northwest of town, became a staging area for combat troops during WWII. It was also a combat crew processing and distribution center. In 1946, the Army declared it surplus, and it became Lincoln Municipal Airport.[*]

Sgt. E. A. Aldridge 38552323
LAAB – Squadron H
Lincoln, Nebraska

February 8, 1945

Dear Mom & Pop:

    Well, everything is all right, I arrived in Lincoln, Nebraska about eleven o'clock yesterday, morning. I went out to the camp from Lincoln about six o'clock in the evening.

    I am in the Receiving Section now, probably until tomorrow or the next day. I haven't as yet received an address here, so don't send me anything or write to the address on the envelope. I will let you know as soon as I get into another Section and I get an address.

    The weather here is all right during the day but it gets very cold at night. There isn't any snow at all here at the present time.

---

[*] Osburne, R.E., <u>World War Sites in the United States</u>, Riebel-Roque Publishing Company, Indianapolis, IN, 2007

Al's Odyssey, from Catonsville to Japan
Edward Albert Aldridge II's World War II Letters

The fellows here say that so far this winter that when it would snow one day, it would melt the next day.

    I had a very nice time in Pittsburgh, and am glad now that I stopped there. I did feel very bad when Aunt Florence told me about Edward. But they still have hopes that he may be OK. The telegram only said that he was missing in action, not killed. So most anything could of happened. Aunt Florence is certainly worried about him.

    Aunt Rolly, Uncle Joe, and Ruth[*] came over to Aunt Florence's Tuesday, for dinner. Then they took me to the station to get the eleven o'clock train.

    Grandma is still going along as ever, she is just as active as ever, and she looks very well.

    Joe is in the Marianas; he left Hawaiian Islands, a few weeks ago. He still is in the signal corp. These islands contain Saipan.

    It is getting late and I have to get up at four o'clock in the morning, so I will close for the present.

    Love To All

                      Your Loving Son

                      Albert

---

[*] Ruth was Joseph Shearer's wife.

Lincoln, Nebraska

Al's Odyssey, from Catonsville to Japan
Edward Albert Aldridge II's World War II Letters

1 LT Edward J. Kampel,

MISSING IN ACTION*

ID: **O-757492**

Entered the Service From: **Pennsylvania**
Rank: **First Lieutenant**
Service: **U.S. Army Air Forces, 545th Bomber Squadron, 384th Bomber Group, Heavy**
Died: **Wednesday, January 10, 1945**
Memorialized at: **Cambridge American Cemetery**
Location: **Cambridge, England**

Awards: **Distinguished Flying Cross**
Air Medal with 4 Oak Leaf Clusters
Purple Heart

---

* Registry, National WWII Memorial, Washington, D.C., 2007

Al's Odyssey, from Catonsville to Japan
Edward Albert Aldridge II's World War II Letters

Edward Joseph Kampel, October 1943, Pittsburgh

Lincoln, Nebraska

Al's Odyssey, from Catonsville to Japan
Edward Albert Aldridge II's World War II Letters

Edward Joseph, a navigator, died on his 32nd and last B-17 mission over Germany.

A B-17, Boeing "Flying Fortress" Heavy Bomber[*]

Sgt. E. A. Aldridge 33552323
Provisional Squadron F
LAAB 2nd Air Force
Lincoln, Nebr.

                                                                       Feb. 12, 1945

Dearest Mom & Pop:

    I received the letter that you wrote to Fort Myers this morning. It was the first mail that I have received since I have been

---

[*] <u>Recognition Pictorial Manual</u>, War Department, Washington, D.C., FM 30-30, June 1943.

200
                        Lincoln, Nebraska

Al's Odyssey, from Catonsville to Japan
Edward Albert Aldridge II's World War II Letters

here. Finally got an address that I will have as long as I will be here. It is, Provisional Squadron F, LAAB, 2nd AF Lincoln, Nebr.

As yet I don't know exactly how long I will be here. However, from prospects it will probably be from one to two months. I will then go to some training center, perhaps Kansas, Texas, or New Mexico.

I have started processing today, and will continue to for about four days, after that I will just wait for shipment. I had another physical and passed it OK. However, they seem to think that my eyes have gotten weaker since I took my last one. However, I haven't noticed any change myself. I think it was just the glare, where I took the test.

The weather here has been very good here although it getting too cold at night. It gets warm every afternoon, around 2 o'clock, and stays warm until about 12 at night. There are three stoves in each barrack, and they keep it warm enough at night. The only trouble is that we have to keep getting coal for them.

The Post Exchange here does not have identification bracelets. It is not as complete as the once at Fort Myers.

I met a fellow here that I went to school with who lives in Lansdowne. He is just across the street, in a barracks just opposite mine. I am going to try and move into his barracks tomorrow.

The food here is very good, a lot better then it was in any camp I have been in before. However, the Mess Hall is quite a distance from the Squadron that I am in.

Love to All

Albert

Lincoln, Nebraska

Al's Odyssey, from Catonsville to Japan
Edward Albert Aldridge II's World War II Letters

Clovis, New Mexico

Clovis is on the central east edge of New Mexico. Clovis Municipal Airport was taken over by the Army in 1942 to train glider pilots which were used in the invasion of Europe. In the later months of the war, Clovis Army Air Field (CAAF) became a training field for B-29 crews. In 1957, it was renamed Cannon Air Force Base and remained in operation throughout the Cold War. It is now the home of the 27th Special Operations Wing.*

Sgt. E. A. Aldridge 33552323
Combat Crew Section
CAAF
Clovis, New Mexico

    February 18, 1945
Dearest Mom & Pop:

    I suppose you will be surprised when you see the address on this letter. I left Lincoln Friday night and arrived here this morning.

    The shipment certainly was a surprise to me as well as most of the other fellows on it. I was only at Lincoln for one week. During which time I was kept very busy processing.

---

* Osburne, R.E., <u>World War Sites in the United States</u>, Riebel-Roque Publishing Company, Indianapolis, IN, 2007

Al's Odyssey, from Catonsville to Japan
Edward Albert Aldridge II's World War II Letters

I am here for almost three or four months further training. We have been formed into crews, and our training will be based around the crew itself. Working together as well as cooperation among the crew members will be very much stressed.

Clovis is about one hundred miles from Amarillo, Texas. I probably will get a chance to go to Amarillo several times, and visit some of the fellows that are left there.

The field here seems to be OK, however, I haven't seen too much of it as yet. My barracks is next door to the Mess Hall, and the food so far is fine. So now I guess I will do most of my eating there.

I collected fifty one dollars and a few cents travel pay for the trip from Fort Myers to Lincoln. It cost me fifty-two dollars from Fort Myers to Baltimore to Lincoln. So it worked out fairly well. I also collected my rations for the delay in route.

I am going to send a money order home for about one hundred dollars, so you can keep an eye out for it. I won't be able to send it with this letter because the Post Office isn't open today.

The weather here isn't much better then at Lincoln; however, I don't think it will be quite as cold.

Love to All

Your loving son

Albert

Clovis, New Mexico

Al's Odyssey, from Catonsville to Japan
Edward Albert Aldridge II's World War II Letters

The attack on Iwo Jima, the most costly battle in the history of the Marine Corp, started at dawn February 19, 1945. There were 26,504 U.S. casualties, and of the 21,000 Japanese on the Island, only 216 survived to become prisoners of war. One reason given that Iwo Jima was captured by the Marines was because it was on the path of the B-29s flying from the Marianas to bomb Japan. The B-29s, when laden down with a full load of bombs and fuel, were very vulnerable to Japanese fighter planes based on Iwo Jima. After its capture, Iwo Jima proved useful for emergency landings and refueling of the B-29s. Over two thousand B-29 landings on Iwo Jima were made during the war. It was also used for rescuing crews that went down in the Pacific.

Some academic historians have argued that Iwo Jima was not worth the high price, but it seems that the decision makers at the time were doing the best they could with poor intelligence. They did not anticipate the large number of Japanese on the Island, their well planned strategy, or their degree of preparedness.

Clovis, New Mexico

Al's Odyssey, from Catonsville to Japan
Edward Albert Aldridge II's World War II Letters

Army Air Base Feb 22, 1945

Sgt. E. A. Aldridge 33552323
C. C. 8 CAAF
Clovis, New Mexico

Dearest Mom & Pop:

 Just a few lines, before I have to go to my afternoon classes.

 I am enclosing a money order in this letter for one hundred dollars.

 This morning I had to take another physical, it was just the same as all of the others that I have taken. I passed everything OK.

 I received the two letters that you sent to Lincoln this morning. Thanks, for the valentine. I didn't get a chance to see Felix in Chicago, as it was snowing very hard when I was there. So I didn't get very far from the station.

 I have been very busy since I have been here, except for the first two days.

 The instructors say that we will be kept very busy for the next two months.

Clovis, New Mexico

Al's Odyssey, from Catonsville to Japan
Edward Albert Aldridge II's World War II Letters

I have met all of my crew except the Bombardier. The fellows seem to be OK. We have a Captain as Commander, and he seems to be quite a swell fellow.

I also got a letter from Mrs. Ridgely this morning. She said that Roger Mellor was home just after I left.

It's time to go to class again, so I will close for the present.

    Love to All

                    Your Loving Son

                        Albert

Clovis, New Mexico

Al's Odyssey, from Catonsville to Japan
Edward Albert Aldridge II's World War II Letters

Sgt. E. A. Aldridge 33552323
C. C. 8 CAAF
Clovis, New Mexico

March 3, 1945

Dear Mom & Pop:

    Today being Saturday, it has been my day off for the last two weeks. I am supposed to fly again tomorrow. So far my crew has only flown once. That was Thursday evening and night for about four and one half hours. We have to fly over one hundred hours before we can graduate, about one hundred and twenty five hours. So you can see that I have quite a long ways to go. The day set for graduation of my class is May 17.

    I received your package, with the handkerchiefs, yesterday. It took quite a while to get here. I can use them now as most of mine are in the laundry. At present, I have week's laundry in the laundry over fifty pieces. The bad part is they only allow twenty five pieces at one time. I still have about a dozen pair of dirty socks plus some handkerchiefs and some under clothes. As well as dirty sun-tan uniforms, at the barracks.

    I am getting paid for February in a few days, so you can expect another money order for about twenty-five dollars in the near future. I don't like to keep too much money with me here. I am on the go so much now that I am liable to lose it or something. I should be receiving my flying pay also around the end of this month. It will be about eighty dollars, if I get paid flying pay for February.

    The weather should be changing this month, but it can't get warm too soon for me. This has been a pretty bad winter everyplace. Elwin, too, must be looking forward to the warmer weather.

Clovis, New Mexico

Al's Odyssey, from Catonsville to Japan
Edward Albert Aldridge II's World War II Letters

I guess that you might as well renew the insurance policy on the car. It might come in handy sometime.

I think I will put some of my flying pay into a couple of war bonds, when I get it.

No, I don't have Joe's address, so you had better send it to me.

Love to All

Albert

Clovis, New Mexico

Al's Odyssey, from Catonsville to Japan
Edward Albert Aldridge II's World War II Letters

Sgt. E. A. Aldridge 33552323
C. C. 8 CAAF
Clovis, New Mexico

March 7, 1945

Dear Mom & Pop:

Today it is a month since I reported to Lincoln. However, it seems much longer then that. The time here goes so fast, that I have a hard time keeping track of the days.

With the present schedule, I don't get much time off. I don't know when I will even get a day off. Sometimes, I only get about four hours sleep a night. We fly here both day and nights, one day in the day time and the next at night.

I bought myself an identification bracelet in town the other day. It wasn't too expensive, about like the ones they wanted twelve dollars for. But I haven't had a chance to have my name put on it yet.

I received the watch too several days ago; it arrived in good condition.

I also receive Little Elwin's valentine. I like it very much. I wouldn't know what to tell you about the bus situation. But I don't think it would be a good idea for you to ride on the bus once in awhile. In the long run, it would probably cause more trouble. As you wouldn't be able to do it every day. I don't see why the bus driver should put him off, unless he starts the fights.[*]

---

[*] Little Elwin does not remember exactly what this was about. Mom was probably over reacting as usual. There was a lot of bullying, harassing, and fighting on the buses and at school. Usually the older boys goaded the younger boys into fights. The bus drivers and teachers mostly ignored it unless parents complained. When Elwin became one of the bigger boys, all fighting around him stopped.

Al's Odyssey, from Catonsville to Japan
Edward Albert Aldridge II's World War II Letters

Don't worry about me, especially about me going overseas. If I do go I will be able to let you know about it. If everything here goes along OK, I should be able to get home, when I finish school here.

I am glad to hear that Pop's father is a lot better, because he certainly did look bad when I saw him.

I don't get paid my flying pay until about the 10th, so don't look for a money order before then.

      Love To All,

           Your loving son

              Albert

Clovis, New Mexico

Al's Odyssey, from Catonsville to Japan
Edward Albert Aldridge II's World War II Letters

Sgt. E. A. Aldridge 33552323
C. C. 8 CAAF
Clovis, New Mexico   March 11, 1945

Dear Mom & Pop:

    Well today is Sunday, however, I went to school all day.

    Yesterday I was supposed to fly; however, we had trouble with No. 3 engine, on the ship and could not get off of the ground. I will not get a day off now for at least three weeks. We are supposed to fly two days, and go to school the third for the next three weeks.

    You asked me about flying. Well, there isn't much to tell you about it. When the ship is in the air, it seems as if it is standing still, if you don't look at the ground.
    When the weather gets bad, the air gets rougher. Then the ship bounces around a little. This makes some people sick, but it doesn't bother me. When the plane is landing or taking off, while it is on the ground, it feels like riding in a train. The B-29 has two cots like beds in the radar room. On long missions the crew gets a chance to rest. The plane also has a pressurization system whereby, after it goes higher than 8,000 feet, the pressure remains the same, as it is at 8000 feet. For that reason oxygen and oxygen masks are not needed. Also, the heat remains the same, although it is much colder outside. 10,000 feet is about the freezing level this time of year.

    I received Pop's letter yesterday, and I was certainly glad to hear from him. You can use my car anytime you want to.

    A lot of the fellows that I worked with at Amarillo, who were transferred to the infantry, just left Fort Meade for overseas. I probably would have been with them, if I would have been able to stay in Amarillo.
                      Love to all, Your loving son, Albert

Clovis, New Mexico

Al's Odyssey, from Catonsville to Japan
Edward Albert Aldridge II's World War II Letters

Sgt. E. A. Aldridge 33552323
C. C. 8 CAAF
Clovis, New Mexico

March 14, 1945

Dear Mom & Pop:

    Time is passing fast now, the days run together and a week passes, before I can turn around.

    I got my second filling in one of my teeth, that is the second in my mouth. There was just a very small cavity one of my teeth. Three Dentists looked at it before they decided to fill it.

    I was called for a dental check up the day before yesterday. But, I guess it is better that it is filled now, for it may have bothered me later.

    When I receive a letter from Grandma, I will answer it as soon as I can. I have been keeping up on my correspondence fairly well lately.

    The weather here is pretty good now although it gets windy once in awhile and the dust gets quite thick, almost as bad as it was in Amarillo two years ago.

    I understand there is some sort of curfew in Baltimore now. I haven't heard much about it though.

Al's Odyssey, from Catonsville to Japan
Edward Albert Aldridge II's World War II Letters

Several of the fellows and myself, have been trying to build a radio. However, we have had some trouble getting a transformer. I wonder if Pop might be able to help us out. All of the radio stores in town do not have the type we need. It has to be one with forty-five and ninety volts output. Maybe some of the radio stores in Baltimore have them. I would appreciate it if Pop would try to get one for me.

There isn't much to write about at the present so I will close for the present.

Love to all,

Your Loving Son

Albert

Clovis, New Mexico

Al's Odyssey, from Catonsville to Japan
Edward Albert Aldridge II's World War II Letters

Sgt. E. A. Aldridge 33552323
C. C. 8 CAAF
Clovis, New Mexico

March 19, 1945

Dear Mom & Pop:

    Today is an exceptional one as I got all of the morning off. They seem to be rushing us through school here. My crew finished our first phase last week. All of us except the pilot have been checked out, that is we can now fly without an instructor going with us.

    I received the letters that you sent me sometime ago in your letter. I forgot all about them. I have been keeping them in my wallet, so that I will not lose them.

    It is about time that Elwin is growing out of the colds he used to get. I always felt sorry for him, when he was sick so much for he is too young to be sick so often.

    Flying isn't all fun, there is quite a bit of work connected with it. Also, it gets very cold at high altitudes. Yesterday at 28,000 ft, it was 27° below zero -- that is on the centigrade scale, where zero is freezing.

    I haven't as yet received the packages that you sent; however, it usually takes them much longer than it does letters. I guess that I will receive them in a few days.

Clovis, New Mexico

Al's Odyssey, from Catonsville to Japan
Edward Albert Aldridge II's World War II Letters

    I don't know whether Mrs. Mellor has told you, but <u>Emery Ridgely died of wounds the middle of last month, in Germany.</u>[*]

    Have you heard anything else from Aunt Florence about Edward? I wrote to Larry[†] in Las Vegas Nevada, sometime ago, however he hasn't answered me as yet.

    Love to All

Your loving son

Albert

---

[*] Emerson M. Ridgely, "Emery" of Ellicott City, died in combat in 1945. He served in Company B, 747th Tank Battalion, U.S. Army. (<u>National WWII War Memorial, Registry</u>, Washington, DC, 2008.)

[†] Larry Kampel, Al's cousin and Edward Joseph's younger brother.

Al's Odyssey, from Catonsville to Japan
Edward Albert Aldridge II's World War II Letters

Sgt Edward A. Aldridge 335?2323
CCS CAAF
Clovis, New Mexico

March 28, 1945

Dear Dad,

Received your letter the day before yesterday, however, I haven't had a chance to answer until this morning. Yesterday morning my crew my crew had to get up at 3:00 AM, and we didn't get back until 6 PM. After flying over Clovis for a while, we made 1000 mile trip to Galveston, Texas. Then we flew over the Gulf of Mexico for a short time and back to Clovis.

The whole trip took about 9 hours, and we used 4,500 gallons of gasoline. That's quite a bit for one day. Our average speed was about two hundred miles per hour. The ships here are not flown as fast as they could be, because of their condition. The B-29 will go over four hundred miles per hour.

As to the radio that we are trying to build, it's just about like the one that you built and we used in the kitchen. It has 30 tubes. I don't know much about it as you know, but our radio man another gunner got most of the parts. We have everything for the set itself, as well as a rectifier tube and condensers for the power part or whatever it is. They say that all that is needed is just the transformer. We tried every radio store in Clovis, but couldn't get one.

We are going to try to make a transformer since it's so hard to get one. The way that we planned the set won't take up much room, but if we make up a whole power pack, it will be larger than the whole set itself. I will let you know how we made out.

The weather here is very nice now; it is warm in the daytime, but cool at night. There is a quite a bit of dust here now. There are very few trees and hardly enough grass to mention, so every little gust of wind blows dust all over the field.

Clovis, New Mexico

Al's Odyssey, from Catonsville to Japan
Edward Albert Aldridge II's World War II Letters

I have to fly again this afternoon, but I like flying in the afternoon better than I do in the morning. It will be around twelve or 1 o'clock before we will land though and I won't get to bed before two or two-thirty tomorrow. It's quite a long day, considering that school starts again at 6 o'clock tomorrow morning.

If I finish school here before the 17th of May, I might be able to come home again. But the way things go on this Field you can't count on it too much.

It's almost time to go to lunch so I will close for the present.

                Love to all. Your loving son: - Albert

Clovis, New Mexico

Al's Odyssey, from Catonsville to Japan
Edward Albert Aldridge II's World War II Letters

Sgt. E. A. Aldridge 33552323
C. C. 8 CAAF
Clovis, New Mexico

April 3, 1945

Dear Mom & Pop:

    Received a card from Grandma, yesterday afternoon.

    There isn't much to write about at the present time. Everything here is about the same as usual. Just flying and going to school.

    It's very cold here today, the wind is very bad. This morning, there were snow flakes blowing around, but I don't think it will snow very hard this time of year. At least I hope it doesn't, for I like the warm weather too much.

    I am getting quite a few days off now. Two last week, and most of today. I am getting plenty of time to sleep now. In fact, most of the time, I am getting too much.

    I tried to call Sunday; however, there was a delay from six to eight hours. And I was unable to get the call through. Did everybody have a nice Easter? It was just like another day here although we had the day off. Late dinner, at one of the fellow's homes, that has his wife here in Clovis. It was a nice change.

    Love to All

                   Your Loving Son

                   Albert

Clovis, New Mexico

Al's Odyssey, from Catonsville to Japan
Edward Albert Aldridge II's World War II Letters

COMBAT CREW SECTION
CLOVIS ARMY AIR FIELD
CLOVIS, NEW MEXICO

April 7, 1945

Dear Mom & Pop:

I received the Ellicott City paper this morning. I was glad to get it. I also noticed the article about Delawders; was that the same family that used to bring wood?

Emmys sister wrote me about his death, also a couple of other people in Ellicott City. He was a very well liked fellow with everyone who knew him.

Yes, I received the cookies that you sent for Easter. I must have forgotten to mention them in my letters.

I guess that you can expect Elwin to a little more running around the place now, for he is getting older. I suppose when I was his age I did quite a bit of running all over the Manor.

I was surprised to here that Charley Hershmann was around, for it has been sometime since I have seen him myself. It's good to hear that Roger Mellor is well again, for he has been sick quite a few times since he has been in the army.

Al's Odyssey, from Catonsville to Japan
Edward Albert Aldridge II's World War II Letters

I haven't written Larry again since you sent me his address. But I want to do it sometime today, as I haven't anything to do all day. I expect to get quite a few letters written today.

Everything here at camp is about the same as usual.

Love To All

Your Loving Son

Albert

Clovis, New Mexico

Al's Odyssey, from Catonsville to Japan
Edward Albert Aldridge II's World War II Letters

Sgt. E. A. Aldridge 33552323
C. C. 8 CAAF
Clovis, New Mexico

April 26, 1945

Dear Mom & Pop:

It has been quite some time since I have written, but I have been waiting to find out if I could give you any definite news as to my coming home. I am not positive as yet, when and if I will be able to make it.

However, I feel certain that we will finish here before the fifth of next month. I hope to spend a few days at home between the fifth and fourteenth of May. My crew is finishing our last missions the first of next month. We leave here as a crew, so none of the crew can get a leave until everyone in the crew is finished.

We are going on another long range mission tonight. I don't know where as yet. It will be in the direct that the weather is the best. One of the missions is over Pittsburgh, I hope the weather is good in that direction, we might be able to go there. Although during these missions we don't land. We have to fly 3,000 miles non stop.

The mission that I wrote you about in my last letter to California was made OK. We landed in Tucson, Arizona on the way back, because the weather was bad over Clovis. However, we left Tucson the next morning and came back to Clovis.

When I come home, I won't have to write for money as I have been saving enough. That is the reason I haven't been sending any of my flying pay home.

Clovis, New Mexico

Did you write Mrs. Ridgely a letter? I think she mentioned something about getting a letter from you in her last letter.

How is Elwin making out with his school work? I bet he is looking forward to this summer. He is getting to be a big boy now.

I will write soon again.

    Love To All

                        Your loving son

                        Albert

Clovis, New Mexico

Al's Odyssey, from Catonsville to Japan
Edward Albert Aldridge II's World War II Letters

April 27, 1945

Dear Mom & Pop:

I haven't written for a few days now, as I have been quite busy. I am flying six days this week. Tomorrow my crew is taking a long range mission. We leave Clovis around seven in the morning and will return around 12:00 PM the same day. We go to El Paso Texas, then to Tucson, Arizona and then on to Los Angeles California and San Francisco California and back to Clovis, the whole mission is supposed to be over 3,000 miles, without stopping or refueling.

To date here at Clovis my crew has around 82 hours in the air. The training here consists of about 120 hours in the air plus about the same amount of hours of ground school. Two of the fellows on my crew that were privates, were promoted to Corporal. Both of them have been in the army longer then I have. However, they spent quite a bit of time in Cadet training, but didn't finish it. Now there is 3 Corporals, 2 sergeants and 1 staff sergeant, besides the officers.

I received several papers that you sent to me. I do enjoy reading them, although they are a little old.

The weather here is nice again; however, it was snowing the day before yesterday. I hope the warm weather is here to stay this time. Elwin must be outside quite a bit now. I know how he likes to play outside, for there is so much more to do. He hasn't quite two months of school left. I'll be he is waiting for the vacation to start. I know I did every year, when I was in school.

Clovis, New Mexico

Al's Odyssey, from Catonsville to Japan
Edward Albert Aldridge II's World War II Letters

    I am sorry to hear that Grand Dad is very sick again. He was always so nice to everyone, but he is quite old.

    I haven't sent any money home, as I have been saving some, for I would just have to send home for some if I get enough time off, when I finish here. My class is scheduled to ship out of here around the 17th of next month. So if I get a furlough, it will be before the 17th.

    Everyone was certainly surprised to hear of President Roosevelt's death.[*] It certainly came very unexpectedly. Pop always did say that he looked very bad when he saw him in the movies, or other pictures. I don't think they will find a man very easy to take his place. Truman will move up to President, now.

    It's almost time to go to bed so I will close for the present.

    Love To All,

        Your loving Son

        Albert

---

[*] Beloved President Franklin Delano Roosevelt (January 30, 1882 – April 12, 1945) was expected to die during his fourth term, thus Democratic Party leaders replaced pro-Communist Vice President Henry Wallace with a little known Senator, Harry S. Truman. After a few weeks as Vice-President, all the tough problems of ending the war, transition, economy redirection, occupation of Korea and Japan and dealing with the impending Cold War fell on to his unprepared shoulders.

Clovis, New Mexico

Al's Odyssey, from Catonsville to Japan
Edward Albert Aldridge II's World War II Letters

V-E Day[*] was celebrated May 8, 1945, but the Germans surrendered on May 7, 1945.

Sgt. E. A. Aldridge 23552323

May 15, 1945

Dear Mom & Pop:

Arrived Clovis 4:00 PM Monday afternoon. The trip was fine, but riding the train got very tiring. I made fine connections in Pittsburgh and Chicago.

As soon as the train left the station, I realized that I had forgotten my shoes.

I am leaving Clovis and am going to Topeka Kansas, so don't mail them here. I would like you to mail them to <u>Topeka Army Air Base, Topeka, Kans.</u> I think they will reach me at that address. If you send them as soon as possible, I think I will be able to get them if I don't stay their very long. Make sure that you wrap them securely and put a return address on the package, as they may have to follow me around.

When I had to catch the train at Baltimore, I had to get on a certain car. You have to get on the car that is going to the furthest distance. So I had to find the car that was going to Chicago. Pop told me just as I was entering the train that I wasn't on the car to Harrisburg, but that wasn't the right car.

I didn't have a chance to stop to see anyone at Pittsburgh, as the connection there was very close.

---

[*] V-E Day was Victory in Europe Day.

Clovis, New Mexico

Al's Odyssey, from Catonsville to Japan
Edward Albert Aldridge II's World War II Letters

I haven't anything to do today so I will be able to take it easy, and get some sleep.

I do want Mom to get herself something for Mother's day although it is a little late.

Also let Pop get himself a birthday present. I will be traveling so I probably won't be able to get a present for Pop.

I will write again tomorrow.

      Love To All

                              Your Loving Son

                              Albert

Clovis, New Mexico

Topeka, Kansas

Topeka Army Air Field was 7.5 miles south of Topeka which was 50 miles west of Kansas City. The Air Field was built in 1942 with the first troops arriving in August, 1942. A total of 2,766 B-29s bombers were built by Boeing in Wichita Kansas at the plant of the old Stearman Aircraft Company.[*] They were tested at the Topeka Army Air Field starting in 1944. The crews for the B-29s were assembled there. The Field is now a civilian commercial field named Forbes Field.[†]

---

[*] B-29 Superfortress, www.boeing.com/history, 2008
[†] Osburne, R.E., World War Sites in the United States, Riebel-Roque Publishing Company, Indianapolis, IN, 2007 and Forbes Field (ANG) Topeka Airport, www.globalsecurity.org, 2008.

Al's Odyssey, from Catonsville to Japan
Edward Albert Aldridge II's World War II Letters

Sgt. E. A. Aldridge 23552323
CL-5-17
% General Delivery
Prov Sq. 349-36
TAAB
Topeka, Kans.

KAY HOTEL
200 Rooms - 200 Baths
9TH AND MAIN STREETS
Kansas City 6, Mo.

May 21, 1945

Dear Mom & Pop:

We arrived in Topeka, Kansas on Saturday the 19th. As soon as I got there they gave us a pass, so several of us went to Kansas City.

We have to be back to camp tomorrow at noon. I received the letters that you wrote when I got back to Clovis. I hope that I will get the tennis shoes before I leave Topeka.

At the present time I don't know exactly how long I will stay at Topeka. But I don't think it will be much longer then two weeks.

I will write again as soon as I get back to camp.

Your loving son

Albert

Topeka, Kansas

Al's Odyssey, from Catonsville to Japan
Edward Albert Aldridge II's World War II Letters

Sgt. E. A. Aldridge 33552323
Class 5 – 17 - % Gen Del
Prov Sq. 349 – 36 – TAAB
Topeka, Kansas

SERVICE CLUB
TOPEKA ARMY AIR FIELD
Topeka, Kansas   May 24, 1945

Dear Mom & Pop:

    Received your letter yesterday that was forwarded from Clovis, New Mexico. I left Clovis on the 18th of May, so I didn't have much chance to write while I was there.

    You didn't mention my shoes in your letter so I suppose that you hadn't noticed that I forgot them.

    I still have the other four leaf clover that you mailed to me sometime ago. I am keeping both of them now in my wallet. When we were coming back from Kansas City, I found another along the

Topeka, Kansas

Al's Odyssey, from Catonsville to Japan
Edward Albert Aldridge II's World War II Letters

road. I think it was the first one that I have ever found myself. I am putting it in this letter.

I received a short letter from Aunt Sophie yesterday also. She sent me the pictures that we took while in New Cumberland. I am sending them to you, all except two of them, which I am going to keep.

I sent my black bag home, with a few things in it. The supply office here is going to mail it for me. There is a carton of cigarettes in it. You can send them to Uncle Jack if you find time. There are also a few pictures that I collected, some from Amarillo and some from Clovis. I guess the only way you will be able to tell which are from Amarillo and which are from Clovis, is that the ones from Clovis, some of the fellows are wearing wings.

We have just about completed our processing here, although our Airplane Commander is in the hospital now. He has a slight case of the flu.

The weather here in Kansas is quite nice, although it is raining today. This is about the best field that I ever have been on. The barracks are two storey and they are clean. There is a good PX here as well as a Movies, Gym, and Library where I am writing this letter.

I mailed Pop a birthday card from Kansas City. I suppose he has received it by now.

Elwin must be happy about his vacation, which isn't very far off now. I bet he spends most of his time outside with the boys now. He probably will do quite a bit of running around this summer.

        Love to All   `Your loving Son
                                           Albert

Topeka, Kansas

Al's Odyssey, from Catonsville to Japan
Edward Albert Aldridge II's World War II Letters

HEADQUARTERS
TOPEKA ARMY AIR FIELD

SPECIAL ORDERS)   Topeka, Kansas
                  E-X-T-R-A-C-T   24 May 1945
NUMBER   144)

1. Under the provisions of AR 605-115 and AR 615-275 the following Officers and EM, of the combat crew indicated, attached unasgd, Sq "K", 272nd AAF Base Unit (SS), this station, are granted leave and/or furlough for a period eight (8) days beginning 25 May 1945. Personnel will report to CO Sq "K", 272nd AAF Base Unit (SS) on or before 2400 1 June 1945. EM listed hereon were last rationed to include supper 24 May 1945.

CREW NO. 349-36

1ST LT	LONNIE V DUNCKELMAN	02067676	Box 165, Montgomery, La
F/O	JOHN P JERO	T139324	229 S Lombard Ave, Oak Park, Ill
F/O	WALLACE J HUTCHENS	T-9447	7414 Jaboneria Rd, Bell, Calif
1ST LT	ROBERT M MORY	0676996	176 Rowland Rd, Fairfield, Conn
S/Sgt	A J Whitlock	18040777	Box 942, Cisco, Texas
Sgt	Edward A Aldrich	33552323	Rt 5, Gywnn Oak Sta, Baltimore, Md
Sgt	Edward B Dalkiewicz	33466430	775 Bennett St, Luzerne, Pa
Sgt	Claudie S Gonzales	33619035	Box 21, Pompeys Pillar, Montana
Sgt	Alvin E Pettit	14102721	Box 383, Greer, South Carolina
Cpl	John R King	34345140	Amory, Miss

*   *   *   *   *

BY ORDER OF LIEUTENANT COLONEL HORGAN:

NEIL C SMITH
Capt., Air Corps,
Asst Adjutant

OFFICIAL:

NEIL C SMITH
Capt., Air Corps,
Asst Adjutant

232

Topeka, Kansas

Al's Odyssey, from Catonsville to Japan
Edward Albert Aldridge II's World War II Letters

Sgt. E. A. Aldridge 33552323
Prov Sq. 349 – 36
General Delivery
% Base Post Office
TAAB - Topeka, Kans,

SERVICE CLUB
TOPEKA ARMY AIR FIELD
Topeka, Kansas

June 2, 1945

Dearest Mom & Pop:

Arrived in Topeka 8:00 PM on the 1st. The trip was OK, about the same as the rest of my train rides.

I hope that this letter finds you a lot better, as I hated to leave home while you were sick. But I know it won't be too bad for you as long as Grandma is there.

My pilot is out of the hospital now. We had to fly this morning at six thirty, so I didn't get too much sleep last night. However, I expect to make up for it tonight.

They are keeping us very busy now, so I suppose we won't be here very long. The plane we have now seems to be a pretty good ship. The pilot and engineer said it flys very well.

It's getting a little late so I am going to close for tonight

Love To All

Your Loving Son
Albert

I sent my tickets in for refund, and told them to send the refund home. However, it should take quite some time.

Topeka, Kansas

Al's Odyssey, from Catonsville to Japan
Edward Albert Aldridge II's World War II Letters

> **NOTICE OF CHANGE OF ADDRESS**
> (Sufficient cards will be distributed to each soldier when his mail address is changed to permit him to send one to each of his regular correspondents and publishers.)
>
> Date *JUN 7*, 194*5*
>
> This is to advise you that my correct address now is—
> *SGT* *Edward A. Aldridge* *33552323*
> (Grade) (Name) (Army Serial No.)
> *349-36* *A C* *UNSGD*
> (Company or comparable unit) (Regiment or comparable unit)
> APO No. *19390-AM-37* % Postmaster *SAN FRANCISCO, CALIF*
> (Strike out if not applicable) (Name of post office)
> Signature *E A Aldridge*
>
> NOTE.—Newspapers and magazines may need your old address for correct processing.
>
> My old address was ....
>
> W. D., A. G. O. Form No. 204* (1 November 1943)
> *This form supersedes W. D., A. G. O. Form No. 204, 8 April 1943, which may be used until existing stocks are exhausted.

Sgt. E. A. Aldridge 33552323
Prov. Sq. 349 – 36
General Delivery
% Base Post Office
TAAB - Topeka, Kans,

June 8, 1945

Dear Mom & Pop:

    Received two of your letters this afternoon. One mailed on the fourth and the other on the sixth. I am very sorry that you do not feel any better. You didn't mention anything about yourself in the last letter you wrote so I do hope you will be well soon.

    My writing is very poor as I am writing in the airplane. We have it all loaded with our equipment and clothes, etc. So we have to keep it closely guarded all of the time. The ship has been loaded for the last three days, but we haven't as yet left. However, it probably will be our last night here.

Topeka, Kansas

Al's Odyssey, from Catonsville to Japan
Edward Albert Aldridge II's World War II Letters

I have been thinking of Elwin's birthday ever since I have been back. But I wasn't able to find him a decent present in town. We are restricted to the field now so I won't possibly get another chance to get him anything. I suppose he could pick out something himself that he likes better than I could anyway. Tell him to buy anything he wants and I will pay for it.

I and several other fellows played several rounds of golf in our spare time. We wanted to play again yesterday, and today, but it has been raining here off and on for the last four days.

My cold is just about better now. I took the rest of the bottle of Family Physician. I usually don't keep a cold very long.

I mailed a card with an emergency address; however, don't send me any packages or anything like that at that address, as I will send another as soon as I get one.

I am sending two pictures of a B-29 in this letter. I wish you would keep them for me.

      Love To All

                         Your Loving Son

Topeka, Kansas

Al's Odyssey, from Catonsville to Japan
Edward Albert Aldridge II's World War II Letters

The B-29 had a top speed of 365 mph, a range of 5830 miles, and a ceiling of 31,850 feet. The crew areas were pressurized, but the tail gunner had a separate pressurized area from the rest of the crew. He could not be helped in an emergency by the rest of the crew.[*]

Notice in his crew picture that follows that Al had not designated his crew position. All the crew positions are filled except the tail gunner. Elwin recalls asking Al if he was the tail gunner and he replied that he was blister gunner and engineer. They called the Plexiglas bubbles in the turrets blisters, and the side gunners were called blister gunners. They probably were trained to fill more than one position.

---

[*] B-29 Superfortress, www.boeing.com/history, 2008

Topeka, Kansas

Al's Odyssey, from Catonsville to Japan
Edward Albert Aldridge II's World War II Letters

The hand writing on the picture is Al's

Topeka, Kansas

Al's Odyssey, from Catonsville to Japan
Edward Albert Aldridge II's World War II Letters

TRUE CERTIFIED CONSOLIDATION
HOLLIS J EVANS, 1st Lt. A.C.
Hollis Evans

WAR DEPARTMENT
A.A.F. Form 121
Revised 1 October 1944

INDIVIDUAL A. A. F. ISSUE RECORD   A

NAME	GRADE
EDWARD A. ALDRIDGE	CPL.
RATING: Gunner TG	ASN: 33552323

ARTICLES (Nomenclature, Type or Stock No.)	Qty Issued	Qty Turned In
Bag, flyers clothing, B-4	1	1
Bag, flyers kit, type A-3	1	
Cylinder, oxygen bailout, H-2	1	1
Flashlight, complete, TL-122	1	
Gloves, winter, A-11, w/insert	1	
Gloves, summer flying, B-3	1	
Gloves, insert, rayon	2	
Goggles, flying, B-8	1	
Headset, HS-38	1	1
Helmet, summer flying, AN-H-15	1	1
Helmet, flying, inter, A-11	1	1
Jacket, flying, inter, B-10	1	1
Mask, oxygen, w/ adaptor Type A-14	1	1
Microphone, ANB-M-C1	1	
Parachute A-4 42226388	1	
Packet, first aid, parachute	1	1
Kit, emergency, type C-1 Sustenance	1	1
Shoes, flying, winter, A-6	1	
Suit, summer flying, B/C	1	1
Trousers, flying, inter, A-9 //	1	
Vest, life preserver, B-4	1	
GLASSES, SUN FLYING	1	

Individual's initials
Issuing officer's initials

238

Topeka, Kansas

Al's Odyssey, from Catonsville to Japan
Edward Albert Aldridge II's World War II Letters

Mather Field, California

Mather Field was twelve miles east of Sacramento, the capital of California. It was built during World War I, and in 1944-45, it was used as a port of aerial embarkation to the Pacific in preparation for the final bombardment and invasion of Japan. In 1990s, Mather Air Force base was closed.[*]

Sgt. E. A. Aldridge 33552323
APO – 19390 – AM – 37
% Post Master
San Francisco, Calif.

June 14, 1945

Dear Mom & Pop:

I am at Mather Field in California at the present time. I suppose that you have received my watch by this time, as I sent it as soon as I got here. It seems I broke it playing basketball in Topeka, Kans. You can get it fixed, however do not send it to me. I don't think I will need it, at least for the present.

My crew is still all together, and I hope we will all be able to stay together from now on out.

I do pray by now that you are better Mom, as I hate to leave as long as you are sick, as I haven't received mail for almost a week.

---

[*] Osburne, R.E., World War Sites in the United States, Riebel-Roque Publishing Company, Indianapolis, IN, 2007

Al's Odyssey, from Catonsville to Japan
Edward Albert Aldridge II's World War II Letters

I sent Elwin a birthday card yesterday; I hope he got it before his birthday.

The weather here is very warm, but it is nice with the sun shining all of the time. There is a swimming pool and bowling alleys on the post, but I don't think I will get too much chance to enjoy them.

The APO number on this letter is a temporary one. We are told that we will get another later on.

I am fine, and my cold is just about better now, so don't worry about me too much.

I just got your letter mailed to Topeka, Kansas. One of the fellows just came back from the Post Office.

I received the shoes when I got back to Topeka. I bought a pair of light moccasins here so I have plenty of shoes now. They are very comfortable and I wear them all over the camp.

There are flowers here, all around the post. Just about every barracks have bright red and pink flowers around them. The grass is so nice and green also. It helps make everything look so cool and nice.

I don't imagine we will be here very long, I can't tell you when we are going to leave.

I will write again as soon as I can.

       Love to All

          Your loving Son

          Albert

            Mather Field, California

Al's Odyssey, from Catonsville to Japan
Edward Albert Aldridge II's World War II Letters

In 1943, the United States started planning for the invasion of Japan[*] with the assumption that whole population of Japan would oppose the invasion. The coast of Japan had few suitable beaches and the island Kyushu (the southern most island of Japan) was chosen as the most suitable target. The largest naval armada in history was to be assembled for the invasion, and the assault was set at November 1, 1945. The Japanese expected to use 10,000 kamikaze aircraft and hundreds of suicide boats. They estimated that they could sink over 400 American ships. Some Americans estimated that there would be as many as a million Allied casualties. About 500,000 Purple Hearts medals were manufactured for the attack. As the time of the invasion approached, the prospects for Allied success without unacceptable losses seemed more and more doubtful.

The "total" war had totally disrupted or shattered everybody's lives, had turned businesses upside down, and had frustrated politicians' plans. As a result, everyone was very impatient to get the war over no matter how or what the cost. The B-29s would prove to be the answer.

---

[*] Allen, T.B., and Polmar, N., Code-Name Downfall, Simon and Schuster, New York, !995.
Frank, R.B., Downfall: The End of the Imperial Japanese Empire, Random House, New York, 1999.
Skates, J.R., The Invasion of Japan: Alternate to the Bomb, University of South Carolina Press, Columbia, S.C., 1994.

Mather Field, California

Al's Odyssey, from Catonsville to Japan
Edward Albert Aldridge II's World War II Letters

Tinian in the Pacific

Tinian[*] is best known for being the air base from which the atomic bomb attacks on Japan were launched, but it was the B-29s dropping conventional bombs that reduced Japan's fuel supplies to zero and really convinced the Japanese to surrender. Tinian is in the Mariana Islands, which are an archipelago made up by the summits of fifteen volcanic mountains in the north-western Pacific Ocean that extend 1,565 miles from Guam to near Japan. The Northern Mariana Islands include the islands of Saipan,[†] Tinian and Rota. Tinian is about the size of Manhattan, NY, about 1500 miles south of Japan, and Guam is about 200 miles south of Tinian.

Japan took the Mariana Islands in 1914, during WWI, from Germany. The Germans and Japanese changed the natural history of the island forever by the removing the native vegetation and planting sugar cane. The Marianas were officially turned over to Japan by the League of Nations in about 1922. This was one of the reasons that the United States refused to join the League. When Japan began preparing for its control of the Pacific, Tinian was turned into a major military base with the Japanese 1st Naval Air Fleet commander stationed at Ushi Airdrome on the flat northern end of the island. The Japanese installed defensive cannons, bunkers, and anti-aircraft guns.

---

[*] Farrell, Don A., Tinian, Micronesian Productions, 1999
[†] Farrell, Don A., Saipan: A Brief History and Tour Guide, Moore's Marauders, Scottsdale, Arizona, 1990.

Al's Odyssey, from Catonsville to Japan
Edward Albert Aldridge II's World War II Letters

The Marianas Campaign was the most important victory of World War II in the Pacific.[*] From there shipping and communication lines of the Japanese were cut and the long range B-29s could bomb Japan. Tinian was captured by the United States in July 1944 in a surprise, near perfect, military operation. At Suicide Cliff, hundreds of Japanese soldiers and civilians jumped to their deaths in full view of offshore Americans.[†]

"When the jig was up they lined the cliffs like spectators at a yacht race. We did our best to talk them out of it, using loud speakers. Why should helpless old men and women and their kids bash themselves on the rocks?

"'Give Up' we told them. 'Surrender to our troops and you won't be harmed.' That went for Japanese soldiers too, for we wanted prisoners.

"But it seldom worked. The dazed scared civilians thought surrender meant torture. The Japanese soldiers had drummed into their heads that we were American devils.

"So the women threw their kids off the cliffs and then jumped after them. They dressed in their best cloths for the occasion. Sometimes a husband would hug his wife before they leaped together. The sea was littered with their bodies. They piled up on the rocks

---

[*] Saipan, GlobalSecurity.org, 2005.
[†] Your Victory, Mid Pacific Command and Pacific Ocean Areas (MIDPAC), about 1946.

Al's Odyssey, from Catonsville to Japan
Edward Albert Aldridge II's World War II Letters

with bright garments flapping in the breeze.

"When these civilians changed their minds about taking the leap, there were always Japanese soldiers to give them a push. The weird crazy show went on for days."[*]

The Japanese lost nearly all of the 9,162 soldiers who defended the island.

The U.S. Navy Seabees quickly transformed the entire island, excepting its three highland areas, into the largest military airbase in the world, housing 50,000 personnel. Also, it was the busiest airbase of the war, with two B-29 airfields (West and North) having six 8,500 foot runways. Meanwhile, several hundred Japanese troops held out in the jungles for months.

The Japanese garrison on Aguigaun Island off the southwest cape of Tinian, held out until the end of the war. The last Japanese holdout on Tinian was not captured until 1953, eight years after the war. More than 13,000 civilians, mostly Japanese, were detained on Tinian until the end of the war.

Al left the United States on June 15, 1945 bound for Tinian. On the same day, President Truman received a memo from the War Department that just taking Kyushu, Japan by invasion would result in an estimated 131,500 Americans casualties. The invasion of Okinawa resulted in over 85,000 American

---

[*] Your Victory, Mid Pacific Command and Pacific Ocean Areas (MIDPAC), about 1946.

casualties, and fighting lasted from late March 1945 until June 15, 1945. The Navy sustained more casualties in that operation than in any other battle of the war due to kamikaze attacks. Kamikaze in English usually refers to Japanese suicide attacks by flying explosive filled airplanes into ships. It was a destructive desperation effort in the closing months of World War II. The Japanese even used men in bombs and torpedoes to guide them to their targets.

While the nation prepared for an invasion of Japan, everyone hoped it would not be necessary. Meanwhile, the Japanese leaders were trying to form an alliance with the Russia against America and were intending to fight until all the Japanese were dead.

Tinian in the Pacific

Al's Odyssey, from Catonsville to Japan
Edward Albert Aldridge II's World War II Letters

June 15, 1945

Dearest Mom & Pop:

Well, everything is fine, and my cold is completely better now.

I'm somewhere in the Pacific, but I can't tell where, as all of my letters will be censored from now on.

The crew is still together, and I hope it will remain that way, as all of the fellows are swell.

I sincerely hope that Mom is much better by now and that Grandma is still there to help her out.

Elwin must be ready to celebrate his birthday now. I hope he received my card before the 18th.

Tell Aunt Lilley that I was sorry; I wasn't able to see her on my furlough, and send me Vernon's address.

Tinian in the Pacific

Al's Odyssey, from Catonsville to Japan
Edward Albert Aldridge II's World War II Letters

There's not much more to say so I will close for the present.

    Love to All

                                Your Loving Son
                                Albert

Tinian in the Pacific

Al's Odyssey, from Catonsville to Japan
Edward Albert Aldridge II's World War II Letters

Sgt. E. A. Aldridge 33552323
APO – 19390 – AM – 37
c/o Post Master
San Francisco, Calif.

AIR MAIL

June 23, 1945

Dearest Mom & Pop:

It's been about a week since I have written last. But at last I have reached the destination. We are stationed on the Island of Tinian. It is one of the Marianas, about three miles from Saipan.[*]

I am OK and really feeling fine. It is quite warm here, and it rains very often. But you don't mind the rain so much as it helps a little to keep it cool.

We live in huts here, with about twenty fellows in each hut[†]. It isn't bad at all. We stopped in Hawaii overnight on the way over. But I didn't have enough time to find Vernon.[‡] The Coast Artillery Camps are spread all over the islands. Since I didn't have his address, it would have been quite a job locating him.

---

[*] The 20th US Army Air Force, 313th Bomb Wing located on Tinian at North Field included the 6th, 9th, 504th, 505th, and the 509th Bomb Groups. Al was in the 9th Bomb Group, 99th Bomb Squadron. His planes tail ID was a circle X. There were several squadrons in each bomb group.
[†] Instant barracks and Quonset huts had no air conditioning, no insulation, and primitive heating. The barracks were cold, hot, and drafty. Housing around military bases was so scarce that people lived in tents, converted chicken coops, barns, and one room shacks. On returning home, Al talked of very large spiders that joined him in bed at night.
[‡] Vernon Rice was Al's cousin. He was the son of Lillian Rice, Pop's sister.

Tinian in the Pacific

Al's Odyssey, from Catonsville to Japan
Edward Albert Aldridge II's World War II Letters

We stopped at several other islands on the way here. But the best one was a small one. It was one mile long and one half mile wide. We went swimming there in the Pacific. It was about the best water I have ever been swimming in. I also got a little sun burn there.

Several fellows that I left Amarillo with are here too. But I haven't had a chance to look them up yet.

There is a show here, in fact one in each group that is free. There is a different show each night. That is about the only way to spend the nights here. Just about everybody goes to the show, whether they have seen it before or not.

The fellows say that stationery is hard to get here. So I would appreciate it if you would send me some from time to time.

Mom I pray that you are better by now. I hated to leave home, while you were sick. But it makes me feel better to know that Grandma is there to help you.

As yet we haven't done much since we have been here, but I suppose we will get a lot of lectures and such before we start flying.

I will write again tomorrow.

    Love to All

                Your Loving Son

                Albert

Tinian in the Pacific

Al's Odyssey, from Catonsville to Japan
Edward Albert Aldridge II's World War II Letters

Sgt. E. A. Aldridge 33552323
9th B.G. – 99th Sq.
APO – 247 c/o PM
San Francisco, Calif.

June 25, 1945

Dearest Mom & Pop:

    Everything is just about the same. The weather is still pretty good and hot, although it rains several times each day. But the rain helps a little to keep it cooler. It always seems to rain during the shows in the evening. It seems quite strange to see all of the fellows going to the show with raincoats on their arms while the sun is shining. But they sure do come in handy.

    They have our crew separated some for the present with two of us in each hut. However, we hope to get in the same hut sometime.

    The enlisted men here have a nice club with ping pong, pool tables and a large writing room. Also, it is a place to gets drinks, such as Coca Cola and Beer, when they have it. About all you can get is one bottle a day. The buildings are in the center of a clump of trees. The trees are young pines, just about thirty feet high.

    We haven't much to do at present, although we are still getting more schooling. Yesterday we had the morning off and today the afternoon. Eight of us went to church yesterday morning. The services here at church include all Protestant services at one time. So all of us, except three on the crew, go to church together.

Tinian in the Pacific

Al's Odyssey, from Catonsville to Japan
Edward Albert Aldridge II's World War II Letters

The food here isn't too bad, although we are using mess kits again. The heat and the mess kits remind me of when I was at Miami Beach. But that's about all.

I am getting a little sun tan, although I suppose I will get a good one, before I get out of here.

I am constantly going to the mailroom; however, mail hasn't reached us yet here. I keep wondering how Mom is getting, but I can just pray for the best. I am sure by the time you get this letter Mom will be entirely well.

I read that the gasoline rations have been increased. So I guess Pop won't be so short from now on.

    Love To All

                      Your Loving Son

                      Albert

Tinian in the Pacific

Al's Odyssey, from Catonsville to Japan
Edward Albert Aldridge II's World War II Letters

Sgt. E. A. Aldridge 33552323
9th B.G. – 99th Sq.
APO – 247 c/o PM
San Francisco, Calif.

June 27, 1945

Dear Pop:

    Received your letter yesterday evening that you sent on the 8th. It took quite a while to catch up with me. As I left Topeka, the day after you mailed it, it has been the only letter I have received since I left the states.

    I was surprised to hear about Mother's operation,[*] and I pray it wasn't too hard on her. By the time I received the letter, Mom must be back home again. I hated very much it leave home, when she was sick. But I know the good Lord will take care of her.

    I am fine so don't worry about me. Everything here is about the same. I am still going to school here.

    The weather here is still very warm, although it cools a little in the evenings.

    Japan seems to be taking quite a beating so let us pray the war will be over very soon. I will write again tomorrow.

    Love To All

        Your Loving Son

        Albert

---

[*] Appendicitis

Tinian in the Pacific

Al's Odyssey, from Catonsville to Japan
Edward Albert Aldridge II's World War II Letters

Sgt. E. A Aldridge 33552323
9th B6 99th Sq
APO – 247 - c/o AM
San Francisco, California

June 28, 1945

Dear Mom & Pop

I didn't write yesterday, so I am taking advantage of this morning. It rained all night and very hard this morning. I went to school all day yesterday, it was mostly review. But since it has been two months since we finished at Clovis, it helps.

Well, it is raining again now. I guess this must be the rainy season.

I have only received the one letter that Pop wrote since I have been here. However, I should get more any day now. It takes quite awhile for the mail to catch up.

Mom must be a lot better by now as it has been about three weeks since the operation.

In the V-Mail letter I sent with my address is also a cable address. In case of an emergency just add the rest of my address it. And you could cable me.

I am still in the best of condition and really feel swell. Don't worry about me.

Tinian in the Pacific

Al's Odyssey, from Catonsville to Japan
Edward Albert Aldridge II's World War II Letters

Did Elwin have a nice birthday? He is getting to be a big boy. Tell him I will write to him. The rest of the fellows and playing outside must be taking up most of his time since his vacation.

I wrote a letter to Grandma several days ago. I suppose you must have received it before this letter.

I will write again tomorrow.

Love To All

Albert

Tinian in the Pacific

Al's Odyssey, from Catonsville to Japan
Edward Albert Aldridge II's World War II Letters

Sgt. E. A Aldridge 33552323
9th B.G. 99th Sq
APO – 247
San Francisco, California

July 4, 1945

Dear Mom & Pop

    Everything is about the same as usual here on Tinian. Not much to write about, as all we are doing here is going to school.

    I got paid for June. I am enclosing a money order for Sixty Dollars. There isn't many places to spend money here.

    The only letter that I have received since I have been here is the one Pop wrote on the 8th of last month.

    I have been worrying about Mom. As I haven't heard how she was making out since the operation.

    There isn't much to write about so I will close until tomorrow.

        Love to All

            Albert

Tinian in the Pacific

Al's Odyssey, from Catonsville to Japan
Edward Albert Aldridge II's World War II Letters

July 7, 1945

Dear Mom & Pop

I just got back from swimming. The water here is really nice, but a little salty.

To date, my crew hasn't done anything here as yet. We have been going to school for the last two weeks.

I sent a money order for sixty dollars in my last letter. Let me know, when you receive it. I have only received the one letter that Pop wrote to Topeka on the 8th of last month, so far. But I guess it must take quite awhile for the mail to catch up.

It is still very hot in the daytime here. And it rains quite often. Usually several times each day.

Well, Mom I pray that you are better by now. Since it has been one month since your operation I have been looking everyday for a letter as I really don't know much of the operation.

I could use a few more T shirts. The kind I wore at home, with the printing on the front. I would appreciate it if you would send me some.

Gene Autry[*] is here tonight in person. Everyone is leaving to go. So I will close for today.

       Love To All

                Your Loving Son
                Albert

---

[*] Gene Autry (1907-1998) was a very popular singing cowboy on stage, radio, TV, and in the movies. He owned the Los Angeles Angels from 1961 until his death in 1998. As a young man, he was an outstanding baseball player.

Tinian in the Pacific

Al's Odyssey, from Catonsville to Japan
Edward Albert Aldridge II's World War II Letters

July 9, 1945

Dearest Mom & Pop:

Yesterday evening I received four letters from you and two more this afternoon. These letters were the first I received here, except for the one Pop wrote on the 8th of last month.

I feel a lot better now that I know you are a lot better now Mom. It was kind of hard, when I received Pop's letter about the operation, and then not hearing again, for about two weeks. But now I hope the letters will come regular.

I haven't as yet received the letter that Grandma wrote; I hope she received the one from me before she left for Harrisburg.

The last letter I received that was mailed on the 30th of last month. It was addressed to my old or temporary APO. So you must not have received any letters that I wrote from here, on or before the 30th. I haven't been writing much in my last few letters as there isn't too much to write about from here. Also, it's kind of hard to write a lot when I hadn't received any letters in quite some time.

I think it would be better to write letters air mail. For the fellows here say that Air Mail is about the fastest, and V-Mail takes the longest.

Tinian in the Pacific

Al's Odyssey, from Catonsville to Japan
Edward Albert Aldridge II's World War II Letters

I was very much surprised to hear about Dolores[*] joining the Spars. I wish she hadn't as I don't think that she will like it very much. Its not that I mean the Spars especially, but any of Women's forces connected with the Army, Navy, etc. I haven't met very many Wac's or Waves that liked it very much. Most of them would like very much to get out.[†] But I suppose she will have to find out for herself. And I wish her the best of luck.

I am glad that Elwin helped you with some of the work. He certainly is a good boy. I knew he would pass OK in school, for his marks always have been good. I would certainly have liked to have had some of that candy that he made. But I don't think it would be advisable to send any all the way here. I'll bet Elwin and all of the other fellows do have a lot of fun on the diamond Pop made for them in the field[‡].

I have another small check from a bus company in New Mexico, which I am enclosing in this letter. I have endorsed it on the back, so I suppose you can get it cashed. The refunds from the train tickets were more than I expected.

The letters that are written to me are not censored. Just ones that leave here are.

---

[*] Dolores Smith, Al's cousin from Harrisburg, PA.
[†] About 400,000 women volunteered to serve their country in World War II.
[‡] The field was near the intersection of Charles Street and Ingleside Avenue in Judic's field. Pop wanted to get the boys where we would not break windows so he used his scythe like the grim reaper to cut a small space in the field. Unfortunately, it was so overgrown that balls were lost constantly. Thus, it was used only one or two times.

Tinian in the Pacific

Al's Odyssey, from Catonsville to Japan
Edward Albert Aldridge II's World War II Letters

As far as the Crew pictures are concerned, I don't care if you give them away as long as you keep a large one for yourself and one for me. But I do want the pictures of the airplane as I had quite a time getting them. I hadn't realized that I had so many pictures lying around, until I got them together and sent them home.

Larry is certainly lucky to be stationed in Richmond, Va. It isn't very far from home. He must be at Camp Lee.

You were right about that letter that I asked for Vernon's address. I was in Hawaii. But I stayed there only a short time.

I am going to write Aunt Rolly for Joes address. He is on the next island Guam. I want to write him a letter, before I try to contact him.

I will write again tomorrow.

    Love To All

                      Your Loving Son

                      Albert

Tinian in the Pacific

Al's Odyssey, from Catonsville to Japan
Edward Albert Aldridge II's World War II Letters

July 12, 1945

Dear Mom & Pop:

The time here passes very fast. As usual, the different days of the week have no individual meaning except perhaps Sunday, when we go to church.

Everything is fine and I am feeling wonderful although I spent most of today washing. Today is the first one for over a week my crew hasn't had anything to do.

The weather here is still very warm. But the rain still comes on time everyday. I saw a pretty good show here the other day *Music for Millions.*

I have stopped smoking cigarettes.[*] But I could use some tobacco for my pipe. It comes in handy to help pass away the time, when there isn't too much to do. It comes in pound cans or boxes. I would appreciate it very much if you could get me some if you get a chance.

Mom, don't work too hard, for you may get sick again. I am glad to hear that you are getting better fast.

As yet our crew hasn't flown on a mission from here however, the fellows here tell us not to be in any hurry.

---

[*] During World War II, soldiers overseas were given free cigarettes daily. In 1944 service men received about 75% of all cigarettes produced. The war was a bonanza for the tobacco industry in that it increased the number of people that were smoking enormously. Many of the movies of the time glamorized smoking and drinking.
http://healthliteracy.worlded.org/docs/tobacco/Unit1/2history_of.html, World Education, Boston, MA, 2006.

Tinian in the Pacific

Al's Odyssey, from Catonsville to Japan
Edward Albert Aldridge II's World War II Letters

How is Pop making out with Elwin's bicycle?[*] I don't think he will have much trouble though as there is plenty of parts lying around in the cellar. Just about everything but petals.

It is just about time to go to the show.

    Love To All

                                        Your Loving Son
                                        Albert

---

[*] Elwin's bike was put together from old parts, some from about 1910. During the war you could not buy new things made of metal, except maybe lead. Pop managed to assembly an ancient bicycle, and it was greatly appreciated and well used by Little Elwin.

Tinian in the Pacific

Al's Odyssey, from Catonsville to Japan
Edward Albert Aldridge II's World War II Letters

On July 16, 1945, Al flew a combat mission to Kuwana, Japan taking 14 hours and 25 minutes.[*] Mission 273: 94 B-29s attacked the Kuwana urban area destroying 77% of the city.[†] On July 16, 1945, General Curtis LeMay took control of the 20th Air Force.[‡]

Sgt. E. A Aldridge 33552323
9th BG 99th B. Sq
APO – 247 - c/o PM
San Francisco, California

July 19, 1945

Dear Mom & Pop

    I have been receiving your letters regularly now. It takes about eight or nine days for them to get here. That isn't too bad. I think that Air Mail is a little faster then regular mail or V mail.

    I received a letter from Mrs. Ridgely several days ago. She always writes and gives me the news of all of the other fellows from Ellicott City. Her son Russell joined the Air Corp several months ago. But I don't think he will have to go overseas though. He is in Denver, Colorado at present. She asked me to ask you to stop in to see her if you would. She said she would like to meet you. I think I told you that she moved to Ingleside Ave, next to Ruffs near Edmondson Avenue. Her address is 410 Ingleside Avenue.

---

[*] Al's flight records
[†] The USAAF in WWII, http://paul.rutgers.edu/~mcgrew/wwii/usaf/html/,
[‡] US Army Air Force in World War II: Combat Chronology, Air Force History Studies Office, Washington, D.C., January 3, 2006.

Tinian in the Pacific

Al's Odyssey, from Catonsville to Japan
Edward Albert Aldridge II's World War II Letters

I hardly realized that it was so late in the month. As Pop usually takes his vacation around the last of July, I would like to go swimming with you. It would be a lot nicer then here. As we usually swim off of the rocks along the edge of the island. There isn't much sand, and a lot of coral.[*]

Grandma wrote me a letter from Harrisburg. She said that it was very warm in Baltimore. And that she could not stand the heat. She is getting old and I imagine it is hard for her.

We made our first mission here. It was just like a training flight back in the states. We couldn't see a thing as it was night time, when we were over the target. We didn't encounter any enemy action of any kind. Except for the long flight the missions from here are very easy.

It is getting late so I will have to close.

    Love To All

               Your Loving Son

               Albert

---

[*] Coral often is very sharp.

Tinian in the Pacific

Al's Odyssey, from Catonsville to Japan
Edward Albert Aldridge II's World War II Letters

July 21, 1945

Dear Mom & Pop:

Received your letter today, which was mailed on the 11th. I have been getting a letter from you about once a day. I mailed a letter this morning that I wrote yesterday. I suppose you will get that one the same time as the one I am writing now.

I would like to go with you to Bay Shore and Tolchester[*]. But I guess we have to postpone it for a little while.

We have a ball team here now. So I get some exercise playing. We play the Officers of our Squadron this afternoon. I would like very much to beat them as my Copilot is the manager of their team.

Joe[†] wrote me a letter from Guam, and said that he would try to get over here to see me. I hope he can make it. As yet, I don't know how good my chances are of going to see him myself, but I hope one of us can make it.

The weather here is still OK. It is kind of hot, but I don't mind that too much. The rain is still plentiful too.

---

[*] Bay Shore Park (1906-1947) was located at Sparrows Point on the Patapsco River in Baltimore County, MD. It had a vast shallow beach and an amusement park. It closed when it was taken over by Bethlehem Steel Corporation. (Dundalk Patapsco Historical Society, Dundalk, MD) Tolchester Beach (1877-1962) was located on the eastern shore of the Chesapeake Bay north of Rock Hall. It was 155 acres and the destination of numerous steamers and ferrys. It was an amusement park with a small steep beach. (Maryland Online Encyclopedia , mdoe.org, 2008.)
[†] Joseph Shearer was Al's first cousin.

Tinian in the Pacific

Al's Odyssey, from Catonsville to Japan
Edward Albert Aldridge II's World War II Letters

The Navy and the Air Forces are certainly dealing out a great deal of punishment to Japan. I don't think it will be too long before Japan will have to quit.

You haven't mentioned receiving the money order that I sent from here on the 1st of this month. Will you let me know if you received it yet? The money order was for sixty dollars.

As I mentioned in my letter yesterday we still have only one mission so far.

        Love to All

                Your Loving Son

                Albert

Tinian in the Pacific

Al's Odyssey, from Catonsville to Japan
Edward Albert Aldridge II's World War II Letters

On July 24, 1945, Al flew a combat mission to Tsu[*], Japan taking 14 hours and 10 minutes. Missions 288 and 289: 113 B-29s hit the urban area of the city of Tsu.[†]

A total of three hundred and sixty B-29s were lost bombing Japan. They were hit by anti-aircraft fire, rammed by Japanese kamikaze pilots, shot down by Japanese interceptors, and stricken by mechanical failures.[‡]

July 25, 1945

Dear Mom & Pop:

I have been receiving your mail very regular at present. I have been getting about a letter a day.

It is very hot today. In fact it is one of those days where one doesn't want to do much of anything, but sleep. However, it is even too hot to sleep.

You mentioned putting a money order of mine in the bank. I have been wondering if it was the one for sixty dollars that I sent from here, around the first of the month. Have you received a bond, for the month of June yet? One should come every month starting with June.

---

[*] Al's flight records
[†] The USAAF in WWII, http://paul.rutgers.edu/~mcgrew/wwii/usaf/html/
[‡] Takaki, T. and Sakaida, H., B-29 Hunters of the JAAF, Osprey Publishing, 2001.

Tinian in the Pacific

Al's Odyssey, from Catonsville to Japan
Edward Albert Aldridge II's World War II Letters

We made our second raid yesterday. It was a day time raid, and I got to see a little of Japan. I understand that Japan took quite a beating yesterday from both the Army and the Navy.

Perspiration is getting all over this paper, so I am going to close this letter. I will write again tomorrow.

Love To All

Your Loving
Son

Albert

On July 16, 1945 the Heavy Cruiser Indianapolis left San Francisco for Tinian with a top secret cargo – parts for the atomic bombs.[*] It crossed the Pacific at record speed.[†] It arrived in Tinian on July 26th, discharged its cargo, and headed for Guam. On July 28th the Indianapolis left Guam and steamed toward Asia. It was sunk by a Japanese I-58 submarine. This sinking was the most tragic loss in American Naval history. Also, it was the last major ship lost by the US Navy in World War II. No one knew of its sinking for five days, decreasing the number of survivors.

On July 24th the following orders were received on Tinian, "*The 20th Air Force will deliver its first special bomb as soon as weather permits visual bombing*

---

[*] Statement of Dr. William S. Dudley, Director of Navel History, before the Senate Armed Services Committee on the USS Indianapolis.
[†] The Indianapolis crossed 5000 mile of Pacific in ten days.

Tinian in the Pacific

Al's Odyssey, from Catonsville to Japan
Edward Albert Aldridge II's World War II Letters

after 3 August, 1945 on one of the following targets, Kokura, Hiroshima, Nigata or Nagasaki."

On July 26, 1945, Al flew a combat mission with the target being Tokuyama, Japan taking 1 hours and 30 minutes.[*] Since the time was so short, the mission was probably aborted due to engine problems. After the war, Al told us about a mission where an engine caught on fire and they had to land on Iwo Jima which is between Tinian and Japan. Iwo Jima was probably about 1 hours and 30 minutes from Tinian.

During the night of 26/27 July 1945 the Twentieth Air Force had 350 B-29s fly 3 incendiary missions against secondary cities; 1 B-29 was lost. Mission 294: 97 B-29s hit the Tokuyama urban area destroying 37% of the city area.[†]

Meanwhile, at the Potsdam Conference, Japan was warned to surrender without conditions or face "devastation of the Japanese homeland." Since the Potsdam Conference included Joseph Stalin, they were warned that the Soviet Union would not help them.

On July 28, The Japanese Prime Minister rejected the Potsdam peace ultimatum.

---

[*] Al's flight records
[†] The USAAF in WWII, http://paul.rutgers.edu/~mcgrew/wwii/usaf/html/

Tinian in the Pacific

Al's Odyssey, from Catonsville to Japan
Edward Albert Aldridge II's World War II Letters

July 28, 1945

Dear Mom & Pop:

Received your letter yesterday mailed on July 18th. I also received the one you sent regular mail the day before. It took about five days longer then the Air Mail letter. It took a little time to get your first letters, but now they take around nine days, seldom longer.

Elwin is getting to be a big boy now. He must enjoy going to the movies every Saturday with the other fellows.[*]

I am fine so don't worry about me. The weather here is OK, except sometimes the heat gets you down a little. But I think that I like hot weather better than cold any time.

I received a letter from Grandma, as I think I said before. Also one from Joe, I think we will be able to see each other sometime before long. At least I hope we do.

Japan is still taking quite a beating. Since they haven't accepted the terms offered them, I suppose they will even get it more. Let us all pray that the war will be over soon.

        Love To All

                Your Loving Son

                Albert

---

[*] Elwin walked through Judic's Field to the Westway Theater every Saturday. The theater was located on Edmondson Avenue near North Bend. Mom gave Elwin 25 cents with which he bought a ticket, a coke, a candy bar, and some penny pretzels. They usually had cartoons, a serial, war news, and a feature action movie, which to young boys was great.

Tinian in the Pacific

Al's Odyssey, from Catonsville to Japan
Edward Albert Aldridge II's World War II Letters

On July 28, 1945, Al flew a combat mission to Uji-Yamada, Japan taking 13 hours and 20 minutes.[*] During the night of 28/29 July 1945, the Twentieth Air Force had 554 B-29s fly 6 incendiary raids on secondary cities. Mission 300: 93 B-29s hit the Uji-Yamada urban area destroying 0.36 square mile or 39% of the city area.[†]

TOPEKA ARMY AIR FIELD[‡]

August 1, 1945

Dear Mom & Pop:

Received a letter yesterday from you, and there is another in my mail box, but I can't get it yet. Well everything here is just about the same. I am feeling fine, so don't worry about me.

As yet, I haven't received the stationery that you sent. But I hope it will come any day now. The fellows here say that packages take about a month to get here.

The pictures of the crew that I sent home are for you. Just as long as you keep one for me, you can give some of the rest away if you want. The only ones I meant for you to save for me, were the smaller ones of the B-29. I had quite a bit a trouble getting them.

I have just received one letter that you sent regular mail. It took about four or five days longer then air mail. If you have written any more, I haven't received them as yet.

---

[*] Al's flight records
[†] The USAAF in WWII, http://paul.rutgers.edu/~mcgrew/wwii/usaf/html/
[‡] Paper was in short supply; Al was still using paper from Topeka.

Tinian in the Pacific

Al's Odyssey, from Catonsville to Japan
Edward Albert Aldridge II's World War II Letters

Yes, I hope that Larry gets a discharge.[*] I don't see why Aunt Florence hasn't received further word about Edward -- unless he was killed in the crash.[†]

I have met several of the fellows that left Amarillo with me here on Tinian. But none of them are in the same Group, with me.

I was looking through my belongings yesterday and I came across this paper I got from the Service Club in Topeka. I still have other writing paper left.

One of the fellows on my crew handed me the letter I mentioned being in my box. Yes, I have been receiving your letters, just about every day.

I suppose Dad must be very busy around the house now. There is always a lot of things to do, especially with a garden too.

I have to go to chow now. I will write again, tomorrow.

Love To All

Your Loving Son

Albert

---

[*] As Little Elwin recalls, Larry got a medical discharge.
[†] The rest of her life, Aunt Florence lived in hope of her son Edward Joseph walking through the door.

Tinian in the Pacific

Al's Odyssey, from Catonsville to Japan
Edward Albert Aldridge II's World War II Letters

On August 1, 1945, Al flew a combat mission to Nagaoka, Japan taking 16 hours and 20 minutes.[*] Twentieth Air Force Mission 308: 125 B-29s attacked the Nagaoka urban area destroying 1.33 square mile, 65.5% of the city.[†]

On August 5, 1945, Al flew a combat mission to Maebashi, Japan taking 12 hours and 20 minutes.[‡] Mission 313: 92 B-29s hit the Maebashi urban area destroying 1 square mile, 42.5% of the city.

The first atomic bomb was dropped on Japan on August 6, 1945. The B-29 bomber that dropped the nuclear bomb was flown from Tinian. The pilot was Paul Tibbets, who helped develop the B-29. The B-29 that he used was stripped of armor except for the tail gunner position, and the plane was souped-up to fly higher and faster.

The following translation of the leaflet is an example of the warnings the United States issued to Japan about August 6, 1945.[§]

---

[*] Al's flight records
[†] The USAAF in WWII, http://paul.rutgers.edu/~mcgrew/wwii/usaf/html/
[‡] Al's flight records
[§] Harry S. Truman Library & Museum, Miscellaneous historical document file, no. 258, Independence, MO, www.trumanlibrary.org, 2007

TO THE JAPANESE PEOPLE:

America asks that you take immediate heed of what we say on this leaflet.

We are in possession of the most destructive explosive ever devised by man. A single one of our newly developed atomic bombs is actually the equivalent in explosive power to what 2000 of our giant B-29s can carry on a single mission. This awful fact is one for you to ponder and we solemnly assure you it is grimly accurate.

We have just begun to use this weapon against your homeland. If you still have any doubt, make inquiry as to what happened to Hiroshima when just one atomic bomb fell on that city.

Before using this bomb to destroy every resource of the military by which they are prolonging this useless war, we ask that you now petition the Emperor to end the war. Our

president has outlined for you the thirteen consequences of an honorable surrender. We urge that you accept these consequences and begin the work of building a new, better and peace-loving Japan.

You should take steps now to cease military resistance. Otherwise, we shall resolutely employ this bomb and all our other superior weapons to promptly and forcefully end the war.

EVACUATE YOUR CITIES.

The second atomic bomb was dropped on Japan on August 9, 1945. The B-29 bomber that dropped the nuclear bomb was flown from Tinian.

On the August 10, 1945, soldiers throughout the Pacific prematurely and inappropriately celebrated the end of the war with their weapons. Several soldiers were killed in the celebrations.

The Emperor wanted to surrender, but the Japanese all powerful military leaders felt they had to fight to their deaths.

Tinian in the Pacific

Al's Odyssey, from Catonsville to Japan
Edward Albert Aldridge II's World War II Letters

August 10, 1945

Dear Mom & Pop:

I received another of your letters this afternoon. In the last three days I have received about six letters you. During the last few days, I have been very busy.

By now I think that all of the checks from the bus & railroads {should have gotten home}. You mentioned two before and the one I sent in my letter. I was a little worried about the money order I sent from here.

Everything here on Tinian is about the same as usual. The weather here is still very warm. The rain here only usually lasts for about 20 minutes at one time. Once in awhile through it rains longer. It doesn't usually bother anyone very much except for the mud.

I was surprised to hear that Grandma came to Baltimore again so soon.

I am glad that you gave Uncle Carl one of the pictures. What kind of a job did he have in Baltimore? It is too bad that the weather was too hot for him.

You certainly did have a lot of company this summer so far. I certainly will have to visit the Aldridge's the next time I go to Pittsburgh. Did Emily[*] stay very long with you? I have always neglected going to see them. As I never did see the Aldridge's very often, I suppose I hardly realized that they were really so closely related to me.

---

[*] Emily was Al's aunt, his father's, Ed's, much younger sister.

Tinian in the Pacific

Al's Odyssey, from Catonsville to Japan
Edward Albert Aldridge II's World War II Letters

I will write Elwin s letter tomorrow. As soon as I saw V mail letter in my box, I told one of the fellows that it probably from my brother. I did enjoy getting a letter from him. I will write to him V mail, so he can see what they look like when you receive one.

According to all present indications, the war should be over very soon. With Russian declaring war on Japan, and the United States attacking from China and us on the other side it shouldn't last very long. The destruction caused by this new bomb should hasten their surrender.

We have to go to some sort of a meeting now so I will close for now. If several days pass and you don't hear from me, don't worry, as often I can't write every day.

Love To All

Your Loving Son

Albert

Tinian in the Pacific

Al's Odyssey, from Catonsville to Japan
Edward Albert Aldridge II's World War II Letters

On August 14-15, 1945, Al flew a night combat mission to Kumagava, Japan taking 14 hours and 50 minutes:[*] Mission 329: eighty one B-29s dropped incendiaries on the Kumagaya urban area destroying 0.27 square mile, 45% of the city area. These night missions were the last B-29 missions against Japan in WWII.[†] **The prime minister of Japan admitted that night raids of B-29s caused him to end the war.**

The following mission was flown during the night of August 14-15 1945: Mission 328, the longest nonstop, unstaged B-29 mission from the Mariana Islands, 3,650 miles (5,874 km), One hundred and thirty two B-29s bombed the Nippon Oil Company at Tsuchizakiminato. Some historians claim it was the night missions against Japan's oil supply that really ended the war. "There wasn't enough oil left to drive a jeep through Tokyo."[‡]

---

[*] Al's flight records
[†] The USAAF in WWII, http://paul.rutgers.edu/~mcgrew/wwii/usaf/html/
[‡] Tourtillott, M., A Secret of WWII Revealled,. www.markettrends.net/WWIIsecret , 2007

Tinian in the Pacific

Al's Odyssey, from Catonsville to Japan
Edward Albert Aldridge II's World War II Letters

The evening of August 14, 1945, Japanese Army elements tried to seize the palace and launch a coup to prevent surrender. The next day, the Emperor of Japan announced to his people on radio that the war was over. By the end of August, American troops were moving into Japan.[*] Their objective was demilitarization of Japan, changing the form of government to a Democracy, and eliminating Japanese patriotism from the schools.

August 15, 1945

Dear Mom & Pop:

    We just received the news of the war being over. However, since the previous announcements there hasn't been much celebrating.

    We made our sixth raid of Japan yesterday, and I am thankful that it was the last. I don't think that none of us wanted in the least to make it, but it was the easiest one we made. Our Engineer did not fly as he had some trouble with one of his eyes.

    I suppose we will be over here for sometime. But I don't care so much as there shouldn't be any more fighting.

    I have been receiving your letters very regular for the last month. But as yet I haven't received any of the packages that you sent. I suppose they will get here some time soon.

---

[*] <u>Initial Occupation of Japan</u>, Naval Historical Center, Washington Naval Yard, Washington, D.C., 1999.

Tinian in the Pacific

Al's Odyssey, from Catonsville to Japan
Edward Albert Aldridge II's World War II Letters

    I certainly would have liked to see Aunt Emily and her family. But I probably will get plenty of chances sometime in the future.

    Sometimes when I haven't much to do, I often wonder just what I will do, when I get out of the Army. I am not too eager to go back to the Doughnut Corporation of America. Once in a while I think about going back to school and taking up mechanical or architectural drawing. If I can get the government to pay for the school and the fifty dollars a month that they will pay, I could make out fairly well.

    Time here certainly passes very fast. Most of the time, I can hardly remember what day it is.

    I have wanted to write to Elwin for the last few days. I will write him this evening.

    I am going with several of the fellows to see a baseball game, so I will close for the time being.

        Love To All
            Your Loving Son

        Albert

Tinian in the Pacific

Al's Odyssey, from Catonsville to Japan
Edward Albert Aldridge II's World War II Letters

August 19, 1945

Dear Mom & Pop:

Haven't been doing too much for the last few days. The signing of the terms by the Japanese is still hanging in the fire. I don't know what we are going to do here at the present time. There is a rumor that some of the planes and crews are going to be used for hauling cargo.

Yesterday I wrote Elwin a few lines, which no doubt he has received already. I also received the packages of writing paper that you sent. I forgot to check the date stamped when you mailed the package, but it takes quite sometime for them to get here.

Yesterday afternoon four of us were sailing off the island. Our navigator made a small boat out of two gas tanks. It works fine.

It is still very hot here, but I have gotten used to the heat now. There is almost always a breeze; as if you can stay out of the sun it isn't too bad.

We heard over several days ago that gas rationing was discontinued. Now Pop won't have to worry so much about that situation.

    Love To All

        Your Loving Son

          Albert

Tinian in the Pacific

Al's Odyssey, from Catonsville to Japan
Edward Albert Aldridge II's World War II Letters

August 23, 1945

Dear Mom & Pop:

I received two letters from you this morning. It seems that I get your mail about every other day. Usually I get two of them at the same time.

Several days ago, I receive a letter from Aunty Emily. I was glad to hear from her. The next time I go through Pittsburgh, I will have to stop and visit them.

At the present time, I am doing very little of anything. Some of the planes here are going to be used for carrying supplies; however, I don't think the gunners will go along on these trips. So I don't suppose I will be doing too much flying for awhile.

There hasn't been any word as to when we will be able to leave Tinian. But I am sure that it will not be much chance of leaving for several months.

I have been wanting to write Grandma a letter, but I don't know where to write it.

I received Dad's letter a few days ago. I remember the Davis that he mentioned in his letter. I am glad to hear that Wennett[*] got his student's pilots license, but I think I have had enough of flying myself. When I get home I will be satisfied to stay on the ground for awhile.

I am using the writing paper that you sent Mom, but I haven't received the T-shirts that you sent yet. Packages don't arrive here too often, but I hope they will come soon.

---

[*] Pop's nephew, his sister Freda's son.

Tinian in the Pacific

Al's Odyssey, from Catonsville to Japan
Edward Albert Aldridge II's World War II Letters

Don't worry about me, as I am fine. I am getting quite a sun-tan, from playing ball and sailing the boat. The food here isn't too bad, but it took a little while for me to get used to it. About the only thing we don't get here is milk.

I spent yesterday morning and all of this morning washing. I seem to get all of my clothes dirty at once.

Several of the fellows want me to go sailing with them, so I will close for today.

Love to All

Albert

Tinian in the Pacific

Al's Odyssey, from Catonsville to Japan
Edward Albert Aldridge II's World War II Letters

August 27, 1945

Dear Mom & Pop:

Received one of your letters yesterday afternoon. They are coming very regular at the present time.

Saturday we had a parade of the 313th wing on the Air Field. It was for the Commanding General, who is leaving the wing. This morning I have to go on a training flight. It will probably be just formation flying around the islands here.

My pen doesn't write very well, I suppose it needs a cleaning.

There isn't much for us to do here now. I spend quite a bit of my time sailing around the island. We try fishing once in awhile, but seldom catch anything.

As yet I haven't received the second package that you sent, but packages are kind of slow getting here.

I will finish this letter when I get back from flying this afternoon. ___ We landed just awhile ago. The weather was kind of bad, so we had to down early.

A lot of packages just came in, I will let you know if I got one in my next letter.

> Love to All –
>
> Albert

Tinian in the Pacific

Al's Odyssey, from Catonsville to Japan
Edward Albert Aldridge II's World War II Letters

Sgt. E. A. Aldridge 33552323
9th B.G. 99th B. Sq.
APO – 336 - c/o P.M.
San Francisco, California

August 31, 1945

Dear Mom & Pop:

Received a letter from you today dated August 21. In which you said you had not received any of my letter since August 11. During that time I recall writing several letters, which you have no doubt received by this time.

I suppose I am not writing as often as I should. But I will try to write you as often as possible. There isn't much to write about now and sometimes the days pass faster then I realize.

I spent all morning washing again. My clothes seem to always get dirty so fast.

Yes I have a new APO No which you said was blotted out on the V mail letter. It is APO 336, however the rest of my address is the same.

The rest of my crew flew over to Saipan this morning, since I did not have to go, I decided to stay here and wash.

There hasn't been any news as yet as to when we will be able to leave Tinian for the states. I don't think we will have to stay here too long though.

Once I get back to the states I think I may have a good chance to get a discharge. However, if anyone finds out about my previous personnel work, I may get caught in some separating center.

Tinian in the Pacific

Al's Odyssey, from Catonsville to Japan
Edward Albert Aldridge II's World War II Letters

Elwin must be ready to start school again. I guess by the time you receive this letter it will be almost your birthday.

I wish you Mom the happiest and best wishes in the world. And would give anything to be at home on your birthday and give you the nicest present I could buy.

Today is pay day again so you can keep your eye out for a money order that I will send for forty-five dollars.

Did you receive two checks from the government this month for forty dollars? I don't remember you mentioning anything about them in your letters.

I have to close now as I have to go down on the line and do some work.

                Love To All

                Albert

Tinian in the Pacific

Al's Odyssey, from Catonsville to Japan
Edward Albert Aldridge II's World War II Letters

On September 2, 1945, V-J Day, Al flew a mission to Yawata, Japan taking 15 hours and 30 minutes as Japanese officials signed the provisos of surrender aboard the battleship *USS Missouri* in Tokyo Bay. The B-29 fly over was a "show of force" to convince all units of the Japanese military that surrendering was the best course of action.

Sept. 2, 1945

Dear Mom & Pop:

Well! Today the peace terms were signed with Japan. I suppose we all should thank God that these last five or six years of destruction are over.

We flew over Japan today for several hours in formation. About nine o'clock this morning, Japan time the terms were signed, about the same time we flew over Tokyo[*] From what we saw, Japan certainly did take a terrible beating from the air.

The country of Japan certainly looks beautiful from the air. The mountain slopes with green trees all over them seems very peaceful. Small villages, with almost all of the houses and buildings alike just dot the country side. With small patches of land surrounding the villages, that must be farms or rice patties. There are quite a lot of small streams or rivers all through the land. It seems as if every person must own a small boat, for every place you can see water; there are flocks of small boats.

---

[*] The formal surrender ceremonies took place in Tokyo Bay on board the battleship USS Missouri. (Formal Surrender of Japan, Naval Historical Center, Washington Naval Yard, Washington, D.C., 1999.)

Tinian in the Pacific

Al's Odyssey, from Catonsville to Japan
Edward Albert Aldridge II's World War II Letters

It has been over two and one half months since I left Mather Field in California, but it seems as if I just arrived here last week.

I received the package that you sent with the T-shirts and tobacco yesterday.

We just go back about two hours ago and I am a little tired, so I will close for now.

Love to All

Albert

Tinian in the Pacific

Al's Odyssey, from Catonsville to Japan
Edward Albert Aldridge II's World War II Letters

Down sizing was a complex and difficult task for the Air Force after World War II. Bombs and other ordnance had to be safely stored. At the high levels, it was realized the Communists were a serious threat and that a significantly strong defense was still necessary. At the same time, there was a considerable effort to be fair to the personnel while maintaining a reduced but competent military capability. In evenhandedness, it was necessary to release the most experienced personnel first, which made for considerable confusion.

Al told me once that tons of new equipment was just bulldozed into the Pacific Ocean. It took until May 1947 to reduce the Air Force to its minimum size. Hundreds of bases had to be closed and equipment had to be relocated, maintained, and inventoried.[*] Prisoners had to be located and returned to their homes. Some isolated Japanese soldiers still had to be convinced that the war was over and that it was safe and not dishonorable to surrender.

---

[*] Clancey, P., Hyper War: World War II, Hyper War Foundation, www.ibiblio.org/hyperwar/AAF/, 2007.

Al's Odyssey, from Catonsville to Japan
Edward Albert Aldridge II's World War II Letters

September 3, 1945

Dear Mom & Pop:

Today being a group holiday, there isn't too much to do. Several fellows and I played a little baseball this morning.

I received your letter this morning. Usually I receive two of your letters at the same time. I received another letter from Grandma from Pittsburgh. Did she come to Berwyn[*] with Aunt Florence and Uncle Larry?

It is pretty nice for Larry to be stationed so near to relatives. He is the only one in the family that was ever stationed close to home.

We aren't doing too much now around here. But when we will be able to leave is still unknown.

If the Army sticks to the point system it will be quite some time before I will be able to get out. To date I have about 44 points, and it takes around 80 some to get a discharge.

I want to go to the show tonight to see a picture with Fred Allen & Jack Benny. So I will close until tomorrow.

Love To All

Albert

---

[*] Uncle Ben's and Aunt Kate's home

Tinian in the Pacific

Al's Odyssey, from Catonsville to Japan
Edward Albert Aldridge II's World War II Letters

Sept. 6, 1945

Dear Mom & Pop:

Received two letters from you today. Also one from Aunt Rolly. She said they had gotten back from a vacation in Canada.[*]

It was almost a family reunion at Aunt Kate's, when everyone was there. It has been sometime since you have seen Aunt Florence and Uncle Larry. I and glad that Larry did not have to leave the States, as Aunt Florence hasn't received any word of Edward.

I am enclosing a money order for sixty dollars with this letter. Since the war is over, our mail isn't censored any more.

Yesterday, I made a crystal set[†] but as yet I haven't been able to pick up anything but the range station here on Tinian. I am using two razor blades for a crystal. I have tried several other things including pennies, nickels and dimes, but the blades seem to work the best.

I am going to get some parachute cloth, it is nylon; maybe you will be able to make something out of it.[‡]

---

[*] Uncle Joe was covered with red sores which he said were from fly bites.
[†] The first radios were made with metallic crystals of galena (lead sulfide) around 1900.
[‡] Nylon, a synthetic fiber, became popular right before World War II for women's' stockings. During the war, the military used all the nylon and silk for parachutes and tires. Thus nylon was a valuable commodity until after the war. Ultimately, such synthetics liberated people and especially women from ironing cloths.

Tinian in the Pacific

Al's Odyssey, from Catonsville to Japan
Edward Albert Aldridge II's World War II Letters

Aunt Rolly said that Joe wasn't able to get a pass, since I am not a close enough relative. But I think that I will be able to get a pass though since I may get a little time off.

Love to All

Albert

Tinian in the Pacific

Al's Odyssey, from Catonsville to Japan
Edward Albert Aldridge II's World War II Letters

Sept. 8, 1945

Dear Mom & Pop:

Everything here on Tinian is just about the same. I am not doing anything at the present time. I haven't flown since the day peace was signed. Some of the crews are hauling supplies to the prison camps that haven't been reached yet. I suppose in a day or so we will have to make a trip or so carrying them also.

I want to go over to Guam and see Joseph; however I don't want to miss any flights, as the number made may determine when we can go home.

Rumors of all kinds float around as to when the group will leave and etc. But I don't think many people do know just when we will be able to leave.

About the only ones that are leaving have enough points to get out of the army. I do hope to get home in time for Christmas, but I really can't do anything but hope for the best.

Yesterday I made a belt out of the shroud lines of a parachute. I think it looks real nice. But you will have to finish it, as I haven't anything to make a buckle out of. It's also a little too long, but you can shorten it easily.

There isn't much that happens around here to write about, so I will close for the time being.

Love to All

Albert

Tinian in the Pacific

Al's Odyssey, from Catonsville to Japan
Edward Albert Aldridge II's World War II Letters

Sept. 10, 1945

Dear Mom & Pop:

It is raining outside this morning, as for the last few days we have had a lot of rain. I say outside, because often when it rains hard, it rains inside of the Quonset* too.

Yesterday being Sunday I went to church in the morning and spent most of the afternoon, watching a baseball game.

Elwin must be having a swell time riding his bicycle now that Pop as fixed it for him. Tell him to be careful and to watch out for automobiles, especially if he ever goes on Ingleside Avenue. As I know, when I was his age, I used to be reckless.†

I am sending a few pictures of some of my crew with this letter. They aren't too good, but the light here is so intense it is hard to take good pictures. Also with the equipment for developing I think they are fairly good.

Dad's father certainly is having a bad time, he has been confined to bed for a long time now.

I too hope that I will be home before December but we will have to just wait and hope. After all of the prisoners of war are released there won't be too much for us to do here. So I can't see why the Army should keep all of the B-29s here. As they will be more trouble then they are worth. I just hope we will be able to fly

---
* Quonset is a trade mark for a prefabricated building used by the military, usually referred to as "Quonset hut."
† Elwin was forbidden to ride on Ingleside Avenue, but the rest of the roads were dirt and traffic was light, so Elwin could still go everywhere.

Tinian in the Pacific

Al's Odyssey, from Catonsville to Japan
Edward Albert Aldridge II's World War II Letters

one back to the states. The transportation problem here is very critical and flying back would save about a month of travel.

Since gas rationing has been stopped, you will be able to do a little more traveling. I guess they will release tires soon, as most of the factories will be converting over to civilian goods very soon.

The rain doesn't seem to want to stop. It is raining hard now. This certainly is the rainy season.

Love To All

Albert

Tinian in the Pacific

Al's Odyssey, from Catonsville to Japan
Edward Albert Aldridge II's World War II Letters

Sept. 11, 1945

Dear Mom & Pop:

Today I received the can of tobacco that you sent. It sure will come in handy.

I spent all afternoon down at the Photo Lab helping another fellow work on some pictures. It was something I haven't done before and was very interesting. I expect to spend quite a bit of time at the Lab.

Since the war is over, we have to do quite a few details and do KP. But it helps in passing the time.

This will have to be a short letter as we are flying formation tomorrow and have to get up at 3:00 AM. There is going to be some sort parade or something over on Guam. So we are going to have to fly over during the show.

It's almost eleven so I will have to close for the present.

Love To All

Albert

Tinian in the Pacific

Al's Odyssey, from Catonsville to Japan
Edward Albert Aldridge II's World War II Letters

```
                    NINETY NINTH BOMBARDMENT SQUADRON
                         NINTH BOMBARDMENT GROUP
                       Office of the Squadron Commander

ORDERS )                                          APO 336, c/o Postmaster,
       :                                          San Francisco, California,
NO. 21 )                                          12  September      1945.

    1. The following named Officers and Enlisted Men are assigned to
duties within Flights and Crews as indicated. All previous orders issued
in conflict with the following are hereby rescinded:


                              CREW 9-4A
AC        1st Lt       Waddell, Charles R.       0746487      1093
P         2nd Lt       Dunckelman, Lonnie V.     02067676     1092
NDR       F/O          Jero, John P.             T-139324     1034
B         F/O          Hutchens, Wallace J.      T-9447       1035
V         1st Lt       Mory, Robert M.           0676096      0142
FE        T/Sgt        Whitlock, A. J.           18040777     737
ROM       S/Sgt        Gonzales, Claudio S.      39619035     2756
CFC       S/Sgt        Pettit, Alvin E.          14102721     580
RG        Sgt          King, John R.             34345140     611
LG        S/Sgt        Dalkiewicz, Edward B.     33466430     1685
TG        Sgt          Aldridge, Edward A.       33552323     611
```

Tinian in the Pacific

Al's Odyssey, from Catonsville to Japan
Edward Albert Aldridge II's World War II Letters

Sept. 15, 1945

Dear Mom & Pop:

Time here is passing very fast as I hardly can keep track of the days.

This morning the 9th Group had a parade. Most of the combat crews were given metals. I receive of the Air Metal along with the rest of my crew. I am going to send it home so you can keep an eye out for it.

Yesterday we had to fly formation and tomorrow I think we will have to fly some supplies to prisoner of war camps. Some how or other we are kept busy most of the time now.

I don't know whether or not you should send me Christmas presents here. As I haven't the slightest idea, when we will leave, if you do send some, I think it would be better to send them as soon as possible. Don't send me anything that is valuable as all of the package sent from the states don't get here, and if I left before they got here, they might get lost.

Tonight, we are having some sort of a squadron party at the mess hall. I suppose just about everyone in the squadron will be there.

It seems that it takes longer for my letters to get to you, than letters coming from the states to here. The transportation from here to the states is very bad now, since they have been trying to get all of the soldiers out of some of the areas.

Love to All

Albert

Tinian in the Pacific

HEADQUARTERS TWENTIETH AIR FORCE
APO 234, c/o Postmaster
San Francisco, California

25 August 1945

General Orders No. 44

Section IV

AWARD OF THE AIR MEDAL – By direction of the President . . . by Headquarters United States Army Strategic Air Forces . . . announcement is made of the award of the Air Medal to the following . . .

For meritorious achievement while participating in aerial flights as crew members in successful combat missions against the Japanese Empire. All missions were flown under rapidly changing and often-times adverse weather conditions. The flights were subject to enemy anti-aircraft fire and fighter opposition. There were constantly present difficult navigational problems, danger of engine failure, and consequence of ditching many miles at sea. Under long periods of physical and mental strain, and undaunted by the many hazards faced regularly and continuously, each crew member displayed such courage and skill in the performance of his duty as to reflect great credit on himself and the Army Air Forces.

Al's Odyssey, from Catonsville to Japan
Edward Albert Aldridge II's World War II Letters

99th Bombardment Squadron, 9th Bombardment Group

Sergeant EDWARD A. ALDRIDGE, 33552323, Air Corps, United States Army, from 16 July 1945 to 7 August 1945.

Tinian in the Pacific

Al's Odyssey, from Catonsville to Japan
Edward Albert Aldridge II's World War II Letters

Sgt. E. A. Aldridge, 33552323
9th B.G. 99 B. Sq
APO – 336 - c/o P.M.
San Francisco, California

Sept. 17, 1945

Dear Mom & Pop:

I believe that I mentioned before that the T-shirts and the tobacco arrived here safely. It seems to me that you must not be receiving all of my letters.

We lost the boat several days ago. Several fellows borrowed it from our navigator, and the motor stopped. They didn't know how to sail it back to shore so they caught a patrol boat and tied the boat on back. It got turned over by the patrol, boats wake and they cut it lose.

Now I am spending most of my off time in the Photo Lab. We are doing a lot of work for the fellows in the Group.

I will write Elwin a letter on V-Mail stationary. As I still have a few V-Mail letters left.

The picture with Judy Garland and Robert Walker was here at our show some time ago. In fact, I saw the picture twice here.

We are still waiting to fly the supply mission that I mentioned in my last letter. I think that we may have to leave on it sometime tonight.

There is a rumor going around that the 9th Group may be transferred to Hickum Field in Hawaii, but that is just rumor.

Tinian in the Pacific

Al's Odyssey, from Catonsville to Japan
Edward Albert Aldridge II's World War II Letters

Today being Monday, Elwin is already starting his second week of school. He must be in the fifth grade now. Just two more years and he will be in High School[*].

                Love to All

                Albert

---

[*] Al must have moved to the High School building in the 7th grade. Little Elwin did not move until 8th grade.

Tinian in the Pacific

Al's Odyssey, from Catonsville to Japan
Edward Albert Aldridge II's World War II Letters

Sept. 22, 1945

Dear Mom & Pop:

Everything here on Tinian is just about the same. We have a new Commanding Officer of the 9th Bomb Group. Most of the Combat Crew members don't care much for him as he keeps us very busy. According to his schedule we have to fly twice each week, ground school two days each week and details two days each week. So now the only day we get off is Sunday.

The latest announcement on discharges states that the point system will be lowered to 70 points in October, 60 points in November, and by late winter men with two years service will be able to get discharges. By December 15th I will only have 50 points so I guess that I will fall into the class that will get out on over two years service. However, by that time I will have over three years service, so I should be among the first to get out. As things are going here I still have hopes of getting back to the states before Christmas. But we haven't any definite news, when we will leave here.

In our spare time several of us have been building a front porch on our Quonset. If we can find time we expect to finish the job this afternoon. All we need is a little more screen so we can finish screening it.

The tobacco you sent to me certainly comes in handy as it is hard to get it here at the present time.

I suppose a lot of the things that I write about seem to be different each time that I write. But that's the way things are around here. One week we are very busy and have all kinds of details, and the next we don't do anything.

Tinian in the Pacific

Al's Odyssey, from Catonsville to Japan
Edward Albert Aldridge II's World War II Letters

I never did say anything about the natives on this island. There are several hundred here I imagine. They look somewhat like Japanese people, but I suppose a lot of them are part Japanese. They are classified as Korean type of race. They are small and most of them look kind of young. They are not black but brown and the men are not very bad looking. They do odd jobs around the island. Their village is in the center of the island and is restricted to all service men. They live in small huts made of scrap lumber with grass roofs.

Well, today is another wash day for me. It rained very hard last night and most of this morning. The sun seems to be coming out now.

It has been several days since I wrote last, but I will follow this letter with another tomorrow.

                    Love to All

                    Albert

Tinian in the Pacific

Al's Odyssey, from Catonsville to Japan
Edward Albert Aldridge II's World War II Letters

Sept. 27, 1945

Dear Mom & Pop:

Today the right gunner and bombardier of my crew processed to leave for the states. Both of them have over eighty points. Quite a few are leaving from our squadron. So perhaps it won't be too long before the rest of us will be able to leave.

I spent most of today working on the porch. We got some blue paint down on the line, and painted part of it.

The pictures that I sent to you were not taken in front of my Quonset, however the one I live in is just about the same as the one in the picture. There aren't any trees in front of it, but we have some nice rock gardens, with flowers in them.

With a little luck, I may be home before Christmas, but for we can't get any definite news on when we will leave.

I am enclosing a few pictures in this letter; Elwin may want the one of a B-29.

We were going to fly tomorrow, but the flight had been postponed for twenty-four hours. Someone said that we were going to fly to someplace in Northern China, but that would be a long trip to make. We wouldn't be able to land there as the airfields are not large enough to handle B-29's. Therefore, we would have to make a round trip flight without stopping.

Tinian in the Pacific

Al's Odyssey, from Catonsville to Japan
Edward Albert Aldridge II's World War II Letters

The weather here isn't changing very much now that winter is approaching. The days are getting a little shorter. Perhaps it doesn't get so hot now as it did, but there isn't too much change.

It is about six o'clock in the evening now. Most of the breeze has stopped, but it is very comfortable here sitting on the front porch.

We have been getting ice cream here every other day for the last two weeks. And I want to get mine for tonight, so I will close for the present.

       Love to All

            Albert

Tinian in the Pacific

Al's Odyssey, from Catonsville to Japan
Edward Albert Aldridge II's World War II Letters

Sept. 30, 1945

Dear Mom & Pop

Received your letter this morning. I have been receiving your letters very regular. Usually I get two of them in one day, as usually mail does not come here every day.

I did not fly to Korea, as I said in my last letter. My Airplane commander was taken sick and was sent to the hospital. The rest of the crews just returned this evening.

Several other crews flew to Iwo Jima to bring back soldiers to Saipan, so they could return to the states. Some of them have as many as forty-two months of overseas service.

I did not write yesterday as I spent the day on KP. It wasn't very hard, as there isn't too much to hear.

I received a letter from Granma several days ago. She said that Dolores[*] was stationed in Washington D.C. That shouldn't be bad at all for she will be close to home and, also, to quite a few relatives.

It has been raining here very often for the last few days. This evening several of us went to the show to see *Woman in Green*. It rained during the whole show, so they left out one reel to make it shorter.

There isn't much to write about today so I will close for the present.

                        Love to All

                            Albert

---

[*] Al's cousin, Dolores Smith from Harrisburg, PA.

Tinian in the Pacific

Al's Odyssey, from Catonsville to Japan
Edward Albert Aldridge II's World War II Letters

Oct. 4, 1945

Dear Mom & Pop:

It is still raining here off and on. When it stops raining the sun comes out for awhile and starts to dry up the ground, then it starts raining again. Everything here is damp and we have plenty of mud.

Quite a few of the fellows here are getting ready to leave tomorrow morning, for Saipan, and then to the States. Two of my crew are among these. John King the right gunner from Mississippi and Hutchens the bombardier. They have more points then the rest of us, as John has two children, and the bombardier has been in the army for about six years.

I wrote Elwin a letter V-mail last night which will just about arrive the same time as this one will.

We may have to fly some sort of a training flight tomorrow. But unless the weather clears, I don't think they will be able to take the planes off the ground.

There has been another battle star given to this Group, which will make my total points 55. If another comes out soon I will have enough points to clear Tinian some time in November However, it is still rumored that we will leave here for Hawaii as a group; sometime the last of this month or the first of next. I would rather have the group go to Hawaii as it takes just about one month to get to the states from here by boat while it takes only five days from Hawaii. From Hawaii I would probably fly home.

Tinian in the Pacific

Al's Odyssey, from Catonsville to Japan
Edward Albert Aldridge II's World War II Letters

At the present time I can not say definitely when I will get to come home. I hope it won't be too long before I see you again. I still have a little hope of being home before Christmas, but it doesn't seem to be too probable.

I have my washing on the line now. With the wind blowing as hard as it is now, it will be all over the place in the morning.

It is getting late and I am kind of tired tonight, I will say goodbye until tomorrow.

Love To All

Albert

Tinian in the Pacific

Al's Odyssey, from Catonsville to Japan
Edward Albert Aldridge II's World War II Letters

WAR & NAVY
DEPARTMENTS
V-MAIL SERVICE

OFFICIAL BUSINESS

Oct. 5, 1945

Dear Mom & Pop:

I haven't any Air Mail stamps, so I will have to write this letter on V-Mail stationary. I did not write for two days as there was a Typhoon here. It rained for two days straight today was the first day in a week that it didn't rain. The wind here was very strong as several tents were blown away, and all of the fellows got caught in the rain. We didn't get too wet in our Quonset; however, it was crowded as all of the fellows in the tents moved in too, and some building that was more stationary. We had about two inches of water on the floor of our Quonset.

The last letter I wrote was on the night of the Typhoon. Also I sent the pictures the same night.

I will write again tomorrow when I get some air mail stamps.

Love To All

Albert

Tinian in the Pacific

Al's Odyssey, from Catonsville to Japan
Edward Albert Aldridge II's World War II Letters

October 10, 1945

Dear Mom & Pop:

I haven't written in several days, however, I have been on several search missions. Two B-29s ditched and we have been looking for survivors. The first plane left Okinawa for Guam and had to ditch. Another Navy ship cracked its hull trying to land on the ocean, when it tried to pick some of the men up. This afternoon another plane from Iwo Jima ditched about 3 1/2 hrs north of here. We have to get up at 3:15 AM again to go out and search again.

We haven't been getting too much sleep for the past few days.

I received two of your letters today. We still have quite a few B-29s here on Tinian.

Some B-29's from the 58th Wing left here for the states. However, there still are several hundred B-29's here, as well as about 100 from Okinawa.

I am fine so don't worry about me Mom.

Love To All

Albert

Tinian in the Pacific

Al's Odyssey, from Catonsville to Japan
Edward Albert Aldridge II's World War II Letters

October 12, 1945

Dear Mom & Pop:

It seems as if the weather here is going to clear up for a while. Although, it rained often, the sun comes out enough to dry the ground before it rains again.

Yesterday, we searched the ocean for about six hours but we didn't find much of anything. There were quite a number of objects floating around, but still three members of the ships crew are missing. One of the three is a General; I guess that is why the searching continues.

I agree with you that since the war is over there shouldn't be too much to do here on Tinian. But I think someone else looks at the situation just the opposite. As during the war the combat crew members were not subject to details, but now we are getting everything that comes along.

The other evening I saw the picture *Back to Bataan*. It was very good. Tonight there is going to be a USO show here. I think it is going to consist of mostly Hill Billy songs. But that shouldn't be too bad here.

Yesterday we hear the last game of the World Series while we were flying. I think it was a very interesting series as both teams where evenly matched. I picked Detroit to win myself, but most of the other fellows on my crew were for Chicago.

Three of the members of our original crew are leaving the island. One leaves this morning another is going to leave probably tomorrow and the third in a week or so. We have three replacements from other crews that were broken up, when the Airplane Commander was eligible to leave for the states.

Tinian in the Pacific

Al's Odyssey, from Catonsville to Japan
Edward Albert Aldridge II's World War II Letters

    It looks as if I will be here on Tinian for sometime, but we never know what the Army will do next. It is still rumored that we might move to Hawaii; but when I don't know. I think that there may be a good chance of us moving soon as out of about twenty crews that were in the 99th Squadron about a month ago there is only six complete crews here now. I guess that is the reason we are flying so often now. As the Airplane Commanders have usually been in the Army for sometime most of them have a lot of points. Each time a Commander leaves, the crew has to be broken up. So if we don't leave here soon there won't be hardly enough pilots to fly the ships anywhere.

    When I read what I have just written it looks as if I am writing in circles.

    Colder weather must be on its way in Maryland now. I haven't seen too much cold weather for the last two years, so I dread a little going back to it. But for a chance of going back to the States I wouldn't mind seeing a lot of it.

    I keep wondering how everything will be when I get out of the Army. It seems such a long time since I was able to call myself a civilian. All that I am actually doing now is trying to pass the time in the easiest way I possibly can until I get out. Most of the fellows here haven't much ambition to do anything at all here, since the war ended. When we were flying missions over the Empire, everyone hated to miss just one chance to fly so they could get home. Now everyone tries in every possible way to keep from flying more then four hours each month. Just enough time to get paid for flying.

    It is almost time to go to chow, so I will close until tomorrow.

                                      Love To All
                                            Albert

                      Tinian in the Pacific

Al's Odyssey, from Catonsville to Japan
Edward Albert Aldridge II's World War II Letters

October 14, 1945

Dear Mom & Pop:

Today is Sunday here on Tinian. I got up a little early as John King, our left gunner, left for Saipan this morning. I am glad that he got a chance to go home, as he has two children.

We had a meeting for all of the Ninth Group yesterday afternoon. The Commanding Officer mentioned three more battle stars may be given to the group. Each battle state means five points to our total discharge score. Capt. Waddell my AC[*] who is also Operations Officer said that one star is already out. That will give me 50 points so now I am hoping that another will come out before Nov 1. As with 60 points I will be able to leave here sometime in November.

The mail here is a little slow now, as we didn't get any yesterday. I have only ten minutes to get this letter up the Post Office, so that it will leave today. Therefore I won't be able to write a very long letter.

---

[*] Aircraft Commander

Tinian in the Pacific

Al's Odyssey, from Catonsville to Japan
Edward Albert Aldridge II's World War II Letters

Since our AC is Operations Officer I don't think we will have to fly very often. However, I imagine we will have to fly supplies to Okinawa. The Typhoon destroyed almost everything there and the food is very low.[*] I understand that Sam Turnbull[†] is at Okinawa.

I am fine, and the weather now is very nice at present.

Love to All

Albert

---

[*] "On 9 October 1945, when the storm passed over the island, winds of 92 miles per hour and 30-35 foot waves battered the ships and craft in the bay and tore into the Quonset huts and buildings ashore. A total of 12 ships and craft were sunk, 222 grounded, and 32 severely damaged. Personnel casualties were 36 killed, 47 missing, and 100 seriously injured. Almost all the food, medical supplies and other stores were destroyed, over 80% of all housing and buildings knocked down, and all the military installations on the island were temporarily out of action. Over 60 planes were damaged." <u>Typhoons and Hurricanes: Pacific Typhoon at Okinawa</u>, October 1945 Department of the Navy, Naval Historical Center, Washington Navy Yard, Washington, D.C.

[†] A relative of his natural father, Edward Albert Aldridge I

Al's Odyssey, from Catonsville to Japan
Edward Albert Aldridge II's World War II Letters

October 15, 1945

Dear Mom & Pop:

I receive two letters from you this morning dated the fifth and sixth.

The bus running into town will be very convenient for everyone.[*] It is about time that someone finally got the idea to run it. In the future it will probably run oftener, if enough people use it. So is the bus run by the Baltimore Transit Co?

I think it would be better if you didn't send any more packages at the present time. Although I don't know when I will leave Tinian, according to the Commanding Officer of the Ninth Group, we should be in Hawaii sometime around Christmas. So if I don't get enough points to leave next month, I won't be here for Christmas. Packages will take sometime to get here now.

I sort of hate the "War Time" to be stopped as I thought it would be a good idea all of the time.[†]

We are flying again tomorrow morning on another search mission. We are still looking of a General that was lost almost two weeks ago. I can't see how they could expect us to find him after such a long time.

---

[*] He is talking about an independent bus line that ran from Woodlawn up Ingleside Avenue to Catonsville and on to Southern Baltimore County. It connected to all the street car lines.

[†] President Roosevelt instituted year-round daylight savings time, called "War Time" from February 9, 1942 until September 30, 1945.

Tinian in the Pacific

Al's Odyssey, from Catonsville to Japan
Edward Albert Aldridge II's World War II Letters

Our engineer began to clear today to go home. Slowly but surely they are getting around to almost everyone, that have enough points to leave.

It is getting late and I want to get to sleep as we have to get up early again.

Love To All

Albert

Tinian in the Pacific

Al's Odyssey, from Catonsville to Japan
Edward Albert Aldridge II's World War II Letters

October 18, 1945

Dear Mom & Pop:

Just a few lines this evening to let you know that everything is all right. I spent most of the day moving from my Quonset to another. We just got our Quonset all fixed up to make it a comfortable as possible, then we were told to move to another.

At the show tonight it was announced that the point system will be lowered again in December. Therefore, I should for almost certain be able to leave here for the states before the end of the year. But I hope it will be a lot sooner than the first of the year.

I certainly will be glad to get back to see everyone -- most of all to be able to stay with my own folks.

The weather here is nice again, although it has been very hot today. The rain has seemed to be ended for awhile. Today is the first day that it hasn't rained in quite some time.

It is getting late so I will have to close until tomorrow.

Love To All

Albert

Tinian in the Pacific

Al's Odyssey, from Catonsville to Japan
Edward Albert Aldridge II's World War II Letters

October 19, 1945

Dear Mom & Pop:

I received one of your letters this afternoon as there wasn't mail yesterday.

Everything on Tinian is just about the same as usual. The main topic of all conversation is either points or when we are going home. Rumors are changes are coming out every day. But the situation stands as I said in my letter yesterday.

Tomorrow we are having a meeting at the Group Theatre and some of the fellows are getting the Distinguished Flying Cross. Several fellows said that also the Group was getting the Presidential Citation tomorrow. The Ninth Group has done very much in the Air War against Japan according to the higher Headquarters.

Last night I mentioned that it hadn't rained yesterday, well just as I got back to the Quonset the rain poured down. However, it hasn't rained today as yet.

I just got back from the show, I saw Gary Cooper and Loretta Young but I don't remember the name of the picture. It was a very funny picture about the west.

There isn't too much news today, but I will write again tomorrow.

Love To All

Albert

Tinian in the Pacific

Al's Odyssey, from Catonsville to Japan
Edward Albert Aldridge II's World War II Letters

October 21, 1945

Dear Mom & Pop:

Today I received two letters from you mailed on the 9th and the 11th. It seems that the mail is taking a littler longer to get here now then it did before.

I spent all afternoon today down at the 504th group. One of the fellows that left Amarillo with me is going home tomorrow. We went through gunnery school together, and have been together ever since we left Amarillo.

This morning I received a letter from a fellow that I knew in Amarillo. His is stationed in Hawaii now. It seems as if most the fellows that I was with at Amarillo were overseas now. One is in Germany two are in Egypt and another is in the Pacific somewhere.

The movies we have here is open air. All of the movies on the island are just about the same as ours. The show in the Ninth Group is one of the largest on the island.

I can get about all of the candy I want here at the PX. They let you have anywhere from one to four bars each day. That is more than I usually want to eat.

I am going to try to start a baseball team here in our group. This is the first place I have been able to play baseball although I have been playing a lot of soft ball ever since I have been in the army.

There isn't anymore news about my leaving here at present.

Love To All

Albert

Tinian in the Pacific

Al's Odyssey, from Catonsville to Japan
Edward Albert Aldridge II's World War II Letters

October 24, 1945

Dear Mom & Pop:

There isn't much too write about at the present time. The weather here is getting a little better then it has been for sometime.

Lately, I haven't been doing very much of anything. Tomorrow we are going to have to fly some sort of a training flight.

It has been over a week since I have flown last. Since Capt Waddell has been Operations officer our crew we haven't done too much flying.

There hasn't been anymore news about leaving for the states. But all I can do is hope for the best.

It is getting late and I will have to get up early to fly so I will close for the present.

Love to All

Albert

Tinian in the Pacific

Al's Odyssey, from Catonsville to Japan
Edward Albert Aldridge II's World War II Letters

October 28, 1945

Dear Mom & Pop:

I haven't written for two days as I have been processing here. At first I thought that I would get a chance to come home soon. However, the processing was for in the future. As the Headquarters figured if the points were lowered again on the first of December we would be ready to go home.

But now I haven't any more news as to when we will leave Tinian. All of the airplane pilots have to check out for all regulations as it is again rumored that we will move as a group to Hawaii.

The weather here is very nice now. It isn't raining too often. During the daytime it is very hot, but it usually gets cool in the evening. I haven't used any blankets here, for about two months.

I received a letter from Grandma yesterday. She said that Joe was stuck over here too and wouldn't be able to get home for awhile. I guess he has about the same number of points as I have.

There isn't any more news, so I will close until tomorrow.

Love To All

Albert

Tinian in the Pacific

Al's Odyssey, from Catonsville to Japan
Edward Albert Aldridge II's World War II Letters

October 30, 1945

Dear Mom & Pop:

I received two letters this morning one from you and the other from Grandma. She mailed me a few newspaper clippings that she forgot to put in her last letter.

This evening while I was at the show it rained hard as it has here in two weeks. Everyone got kind of wet, although we always take our raincoats with us to the show. When it doesn't rain, the raincoat swerves a cushion for the seat.

It seems as if nothing happens around here lately. We don't have much to do now except fly several times each week.

Yes, if the points are lowered to 50 in December, I may get a chance to get home before Christmas. But at the present time I can't say what will happen.

The show tonight was *Her Highness and the Bell Boy*. It was very good picture as every one enjoyed it.

It is getting late so I will close for now.

Love To All

Albert

Tinian in the Pacific

Al's Odyssey, from Catonsville to Japan
Edward Albert Aldridge II's World War II Letters

November 1, 1945

Dear Mom & Pop:

Time is certainly passing fast since I came overseas. It is hard to believe that I have been here on Tinian since June 20, and I do hope that it won't be too much longer before I leave.

Taking everything into view I feel sure that I will leave here sometime this month. As I am still processing to leave, I don't know just when they will release fifty point men. It is possible though that I might be able to leave here other than on points, as several ships are going to fly back to the states. But I will need a little luck to do it.

Tomorrow we are flying again; the crews are still completing Air Transport Regulations. It still is possible that the 9th Group will leave here together.

I don't write as often as I should, but there isn't much to write about. It seems as if every day here is the same, for I do just about the same things every day.

It seems that I usually write all my letters just before going to bed. I have most of the day to write, but I put it off until the last minute.

Love To All

Albert

Tinian in the Pacific

Al's Odyssey, from Catonsville to Japan
Edward Albert Aldridge II's World War II Letters

November 2, 1945

Dear Mom & Pop:

Received your two letters mailed on the 23rd and 25th of last month and also Pop's letter.

I am very sorry to hear that Dad's father died. He was very old, and we can be thankful to the Lord that he lived such a long life. As you said in your letter he has been suffering very much. But I know he meant very much to all of his children, as he worked very hard to raise all of them. I wish very much that I had been able to see him before he died.

You said in your letters that it did not look too encouraging for me to be home soon. I guess I been writing a little too much of the different rumors the float around here. As what I write about what is going to happen, or what I think will happen, everything seems to change from the time I write it until I write again.

It looks as if the Group is going to move, but I don't think I will go with it. As I should leave here around the first of December on the point system. But as I said in my last letter, it is possible to leave a little sooner.

The General that was lost, was never found along with several other members of the ships crew. I think only two out the whole ship were found alive. Although several other were found dead.

Tinian in the Pacific

Al's Odyssey, from Catonsville to Japan
Edward Albert Aldridge II's World War II Letters

We did not fly tonight as I said we would yesterday. Our ship was not ready for flight as the ground crew has been working on it for several days. Something wasn't working proper in No 1 engine. So our flight was called off. My crew has had the same airplane since July, and I think the ground crew who make all repairs and keep it in condition are very good. I suppose Capt. Waddell our airplane commander thinks so too, as he is operations officer and can have any ship in the squadron that he wants.

I originally wanted to write this letter to Pop, but before I knew it I had addressed it to both of you. I appreciated it very much receiving Pop's letter today, as I know that you always are busy Pop and don't get around to writing very often.

Love To All

Albert

PS. You probably noticed I had already addressed the envelope before I wrote the letter.

Tinian in the Pacific

Al's Odyssey, from Catonsville to Japan
Edward Albert Aldridge II's World War II Letters

November 5, 1945

Dear Mom & Pop:

I didn't do any writing yesterday as I was feeling pretty bad. I had to take a typhoid shot and they make me sick for a day or so. I didn't mind taking the shot as much as I usually do, as it was part of the processing to clear. The 50 pointers are still getting ready to leave here, if the points are lowered on Dec 1. So if you hear about Congress lowering the points to 50 you will know that I will be able to leave here.

There still isn't much for us to do here now. We fly twice each week and have a little ground school each week. Twice each week we are supposed to have details, but we spend most of time getting out of them.

It is very warm here now, and it rains very seldom in the daytime.

It is getting late so I will close for the present.

Love To All

Albert

Tinian in the Pacific

Al's Odyssey, from Catonsville to Japan
Edward Albert Aldridge II's World War II Letters

November 5, 1945

Dear Mom & Pop:

Just a few lines tonight to let you know that everything is fine. I feel much better today, the effects of the typhoid shot has worn away.

I am not doing very much around here at the present time. I spent most of the day playing ball, with the exception of an hour of school this afternoon.

My crew hasn't flown this month as yet. However, that does not worry me very much as long as I get four hours this month.

Every night I go to the show as there isn't much else to do to pass away the time after chow.

There isn't any more news about leaving floating around

Love To All

Albert

Tinian in the Pacific

Al's Odyssey, from Catonsville to Japan
Edward Albert Aldridge II's World War II Letters

November 7, 1945

Dear Mom & Pop:

There isn't any more news today of the happenings on Tinian.

We flew four and one half hours this morning around the island. There are a lot of ships in the harbor at Saipan. I saw about three aircraft carriers and about fifty other ships. So I can't see why the transportation of troops home is so delayed.

I have to do KP tomorrow. I hope it will be my last time here. I have to get up early tomorrow morning so I will close this letter for tonight.

I will write again tomorrow night.

Love to All

Albert

Tinian in the Pacific

Al's Odyssey, from Catonsville to Japan
Edward Albert Aldridge II's World War II Letters

Congress was receiving petitions from military personnel which simply said, "No Ships, No Votes."[*] President Truman wanted a slow orderly demobilization, but his secrecy about potential threats to the United States, public pressure, and troop riots caused a disorderly downsizing that greatly diminished military effectiveness.[†] Armed forces troop strength plummeted from 12 million in 1945 to 1.5 million in 1947. The problem was amplified by the fact that most of the remaining troops were inexperienced.

---

[*] Dunnigan, J.F., and Macedonia, R. M., Getting It Right . . ., William Morrow and Company, Inc., New York, 1993.
[†] Dallek, R., Harry S. Truman, Henry Holt & Co., Inc., New York, NY, 2008.

Al's Odyssey, from Catonsville to Japan
Edward Albert Aldridge II's World War II Letters

November 10, 1945

Dear Mom & Pop:

Time is passing by just as fast as ever. There doesn't seem to be much of anything happening around here. Today being Saturday I have a half day off as well as all day tomorrow and all day Monday.

There are several ships leaving this squadron for the States sometime in the near future. However, I don't think I will be on one of them. The men going back with the ships will be those with the most missions.

Yesterday I finally got promoted to Staff Sergeant; it certainly was a long time coming. I haven't been thinking of getting promoted, since all I want is to get out of the army.

As long as I stay here now, I will get getting about $160.00 a month. That is about $30.00 more dollars then I have been getting.

I haven't sent any money home for the last two months as I have been saving it in case I leave here. However, if I am still here for payday this month I will send home then, as I have about all I need now.

Speaking about pay day, I haven't signed the month's pay roll yet and today is the last day I can sign it. It is 11:30 PM now so I will close until tomorrow and go sign the payroll now.

Love to All

Albert

Tinian in the Pacific

Al's Odyssey, from Catonsville to Japan
Edward Albert Aldridge II's World War II Letters

S/Sgt. E. A. Aldridge 33552323
9th B.G. – 99th B. Sq.
APO 336 - c/o PM
San Francisco, Calif.

    Via Air Mail

November 13, 1945

Dear Mom & Pop:

    This morning we flew around the island for about five and one half hours. I haven't been doing too much flying this month as yet, I have only flown twice so far.

    There are quite a few rumors floating here at the present time. I believe that things are going to happen around here very soon. Several ships are being flown from this Squadron to the states in a week or so, but I don't think I will be fortunate enough to fly one of them.

    The fifty pointers here will leave as soon as the ships leave here. So I should be on my way sometime this month. There hasn't been anyone leaving here in some time, and there are quite a few fellows that are ready to be discharged.

    I do hope that I get a chance to fly home as I wouldn't care much for a boat trip for almost three weeks. But if it is the only way I can get home, I will have to sweat it out.

    I am mailing some more pictures of the island tonight. I will explain them when I get home. I think there a few nice shots of different parts of the island among them. Also, a lot of pictures of B-29's.

    I want to go to the show tonight so I will close for now.
        Love To All
        Albert

Tinian in the Pacific

Al's Odyssey, from Catonsville to Japan
Edward Albert Aldridge II's World War II Letters

November 16, 1945

Dear Mom & Pop:

I haven't written in several days as I was hoping that I would have some good news to write

All of the 53 to 59 point men here have cleared and are ready to leave. Tomorrow the list is supposed to come out for those flying home in the next week. As yet I don't' know whether I will be on the list to fly home, but I hope that I am. However, if I don't get to fly I will leave here soon, as the rest of the 50 point men will probably clear next week.

Don't expect me home any day, for if I do go by boat, it will take over a month to get back to the states. And if I have to go to Saipan, there are 12,000 soldiers there waiting there for transportation.

Everything else here is just about the same as usual. Most of the time, everyone is talking about going home.

Yesterday five months ago, I left the states to come overseas. Taking every thing into consideration, I think I have been very lucky ever since I have been in the Army. Although I have been overseas for awhile now, I got here where the missions were very easy and the war was almost over.

Has Aunt Florence ever heard any word of Edward lately? It doesn't look very good at all. I think she would have had word sometime ago, if he was alright.

Hoping I will have better news to write tomorrow.

Love To All

Albert

Tinian in the Pacific

Al's Odyssey, from Catonsville to Japan
Edward Albert Aldridge II's World War II Letters

33552323

S/Sgt. E. A. Aldridge
9th B.G. – 99th B. Sq.
APO 336 - c/o PM
San Francisco, Calif.

Air Mail

November 25, 1945

Dear Mom & Pop:

    I had hoped that I had written my last letter here. As I haven't written for several days I suppose you were thinking I was on my way home, according to my last letter.

    Yes, I was ready to leave here tomorrow, but it seems as if there was some mistake in figuring my points. Therefore I was taken off of the shipment.

    Now, I will have to wait around until the next one. It was really a disappointment to get all ready to leave and then be taken off of the shipment.

    At the present time I won't be able to say just when I am leaving here. However, if any more ships leave this Group, I should be on the first. As now, I am the gunner with the most points and missions here.

    The mail has been very slow getting here lately. Several days each week there isn't any at all and then a lot comes in one day.

Tinian in the Pacific

Al's Odyssey, from Catonsville to Japan
Edward Albert Aldridge II's World War II Letters

I have been looking for the Christmas Package that you sent, however, I don't think it has had time to get here yet.

The weather here is very nice and it doesn't rain too often. Usually it manages to rain late each night.

I will write again tomorrow.

Love To All

Albert

Tinian in the Pacific

Al's Odyssey, from Catonsville to Japan
Edward Albert Aldridge II's World War II Letters

November 27, 1945

Dear Mom & Pop:

Today being Wednesday, I had a half day off. But the day passed very fast as all days off, as all of the Bomber Crews now have details every day but Wednesday, and Saturday afternoons plus of day Sunday. Yesterday and the day before I did painting around the area; and this morning, I had to shovel coral for cement. I don't know exactly why, but we get all of the lousy jobs in the Group to do.

I don't think anyone of the Combat Crews think very much of our Commanding Officer, he seems to be mad at all of us, even though he is a Combat Crew man himself.

There hasn't been any news of leaving as yet, but I hope something will develop in the near future.

The personnel Officer here told me that I should be able to get out of the Army about February 1st. However, first I have to get back to the states.

It is getting late and I have to get up fairly early in the morning.

Love To All

Albert

Tinian in the Pacific

Al's Odyssey, from Catonsville to Japan
Edward Albert Aldridge II's World War II Letters

December 1, 1945

Dear Mom & Pop:

I received a letter from you this morning that was written on the 10th of November. It took quite a while getting here as you forgot to put my APO number on it.

Tomorrow I am flying the first time in a long while. We are going to fly up to Iwo Jima on some kind of a Radar attack. It seems as if they want to keep the crews practicing. At the present time there are enough men here to make two complete crews for every Pilot that is left. Therefore the pilots will have to fly twice as much as the rest of the men.

The weather here is very nice now; it doesn't get too hot in the daytime. And it gets nice and cool in the evenings. It doesn't rain very often here now. It rained this afternoon the first time in several days in the daytime.

I will write again tomorrow when I get back from flying.

Love To All

Albert

Tinian in the Pacific

Al's Odyssey, from Catonsville to Japan
Edward Albert Aldridge II's World War II Letters

December 3, 1945

Dear Mom & Pop:

The mail situation is very slow here now. I have only received one letter in the last few days.

There isn't much to write about, as lately nothing new seems to happen here. I supposed I might just as well forget about coming home for awhile as it looks as if I will be here for at least another month. I suppose I had been not better write any more rumors of my coming home soon, however, I did think I was as good as back in the states two weeks ago. For about a week after I was scratched off of the shipment, I was pretty disappointed, but I can't complain too much as all of the fellows that did leave had more missions and ten more points than I have. At the present time men are leaving here with forty-two months more in the Army. But it will be next month before I could possibly qualify by service in the Army.[*]

Tomorrow I am spending all day at the line; I suppose we will have to do a little work on the plane. I want to pick up some kind of a pipe for the exhaust on my scooter tomorrow, also. Now, the exhaust makes more noise then a motorcycle.

Love To All

Albert

---

[*] Congress and President Truman were being deluged with letters to let the "boys" come home.

Tinian in the Pacific

Al's Odyssey, from Catonsville to Japan
Edward Albert Aldridge II's World War II Letters

S/Sgt. E. A. Aldridge 33552323
9th B.G. - 9947 B. Sq.
APO 336 - c/o PM
San Francisco, Calif.

December 4, 1945

Dear Mom & Pop

    Everything is just about the same here on Tinian. The days just come and go, without much meaning to anyone. Except for the days that I get off, I usually cannot identify one from another.

    I received your letter this afternoon. Tell Elwin I am proud of him getting such good grades in school. I have quite a few small pictures of airplanes for him. They were used for Aircraft Recognition instruction here. If I get a chance I will mail them, otherwise I will carry them with me.

    New crews are being formed here again. It looks as if we will have to go to ground school again. I am on my Co-Pilots crew now as he has been made Airplane Commander. We probably will have to do a little more flying then we did last month. As I only flew about twelve hours. That isn't very much compared with the months that I flew around eighty hours.

    Things must be picking up some in the States as Pop has been working overtime. I was a little surprised to hear that Uncle Johnny was out to see you. I guess that he realizes his bond to his brothers and sisters more since Pop's father died.

Tinian in the Pacific

Al's Odyssey, from Catonsville to Japan
Edward Albert Aldridge II's World War II Letters

    I got a motor scooter the other day from a fellow that shipped out. It is a lot of fun riding around the island. It would be fine for Elwin, if I could just bring it home when I come. But that is impossible, for it weighs about two hundred and fifty pounds.

    There is a pretty good show here tonight, the first good one in sometime. Lately we have been having the same shows over again.

    Love To All

Tinian in the Pacific

Al's Odyssey, from Catonsville to Japan
Edward Albert Aldridge II's World War II Letters

December 5, 1945

Dear Mom & Pop:

I received three letters from you yesterday. It seems as if all of the mail always comes at once.

The last few days I spent down at the line, working around the airplane. It is a little better doing that then pulling details around the squadron. This morning I painted the Group insignia on the vertical stabilizer. The tail is twenty nine feet high, so I had to get a special stand so I could reach near the top.

There isn't much news around the Group now, especially about going back to the states. So I think that I will have to stick it out a little longer.

Tomorrow we are having a practice parade. The 313 wing was given a Presidential Citation, so we are going to practice for the presentation. However, there aren't too many fellows left that were here when it was earned. In fact, what is left of my crew are the only combat crew enlisted men that were here during the mining operations that it is being given for. That is the mining that was done by the B29's around Japan.

I think it was the Navy that recommended the 313th wing for the citation, as the mining was in aid to them.

I saw the picture *Brewster's Millions* that you mentioned seeing. I thought it was very funny too.

Tinian in the Pacific

Al's Odyssey, from Catonsville to Japan
Edward Albert Aldridge II's World War II Letters

    I would like to get all of you presents for Christmas, but it is impossible. It seems as if every Christmas for the last three years all I could do was ask you (Mom) to buy presents for Pop and Elwin. I had hoped to be home before Christmas this year. But I will have to wait until another year, before I will be able to spend a Christmas with those that I wish to be with most of all. I am not complaining as I consider myself very lucky, to be able to look into the future, after this terrible war, considering all of the people that have suffered and lost loved ones.

    I am praying that it won't be too long before I am back with you.

                         Love To All

                            Albert

Tinian in the Pacific

Al's Odyssey, from Catonsville to Japan
Edward Albert Aldridge II's World War II Letters

December 7, 1945

Dear Mom & Pop:

Received your letter of the 30th today. The mail seems to be getting a little faster.

Tomorrow morning we are flying to Okinawa, and am going to stay there for a day or so. It seems it is some new idea to acquaint us with different parts of the Pacific. It is supposed to be more or less a pleasure trip, but I don't care too much about going there.

We are also to go to Manila, sometime, which I think I will enjoy much more, as there is at least some kind of civilization there.

You mentioned in your letter that you were not sure of what to get me for Christmas. I would appreciate you getting me some clothing that I could use when I get back. I think I will need a belt and perhaps a new wallet as I have worn the one I bought over here out. I think it would be better if you didn't send anything else over here though as I have just about everything I need here. It also takes packages such a long time to get here.

I had intended to send some money home this month, however do to the shipment I was on I didn't get paid this month. So if I am here until the end of the month, I will get paid for two months.

It is very late so I will close until I get back from Okinawa.

Love To All

Albert

Tinian in the Pacific

Al's Odyssey, from Catonsville to Japan
Edward Albert Aldridge II's World War II Letters

December 12, 1945

Dear Mom & Pop:

I got back from Okinawa last night. We had a nice time traveling around the island, and seeing what there is to see. The whole island is just a mass of hills, covered with trees or other types of foliage. There isn't much left of the villages, and the town of Naha, formerly 65,000, was completely destroyed.

The nights were very cold, to us. The first night all of us were very cold. I got four blankets and a sleeping bag for the rest of the time. The temperature only went down to about forty-five or fifty, but being used to Tinian weather it seemed very cold.

I received your package today, and also an unexpected one from Mrs. Ridgely. The fruit cake was very good, I certainly did enjoy it.

I am going to close this letter for the present, for I just got off of guard duty, and I will have to turn the lights off.

Love To All

Albert

Tinian in the Pacific

Al's Odyssey, from Catonsville to Japan
Edward Albert Aldridge II's World War II Letters

Are the following two pictures are from Okinawa or Tinian?

344

Tinian in the Pacific

Al's Odyssey, from Catonsville to Japan
Edward Albert Aldridge II's World War II Letters

December 13, 1945

Dear Mom & Pop:

Time here seems to be passing very fast. Today I didn't do very much, for a change. I spent the morning down at the line cleaning the ship and I had the afternoon off. Yesterday we flew formation for about two hours. It was cloudy all around here so the flying wasn't too good.

It will be six months overseas for me on the fourteenth. But I must say it wasn't too bad. I am sure that I won't spend my seventh month here. All men with three and one half years service left here several days ago. I understand that men with 3 yrs. service will leave here around the first of next month. This group will include me, and I am sure that I won't get scratched this time. However, I don't think I will be back to Baltimore before sometime in February. It seems quite a ways off, but I am sure the time will fly by.

I hardly realized that you and Pop have been married for fifteen years this month.

Love To All

Albert

Tinian in the Pacific

Al's Odyssey, from Catonsville to Japan
Edward Albert Aldridge II's World War II Letters

December 17, 1945

Dear Mom & Pop:

Received your letter today that was mailed on the tenth. Mail still is slow getting over here.

There isn't much news to write about, as things are about the same as usual. I just mark up the days as they go by, as one less that remains to be spent on Tinian.

I haven't heard any word of Joe coming home from Guam. I imagine he will get home on the same deal that I will.

As I understand the situation all three year men will be ready for discharge February 1. So I am sure that I will be in the states by that time, if not a little sooner. It will take around two weeks by boat, and if nothing unforeseen happens I should leave here the early part of next month. At least I am sure I will be on the shipment this time. Men with forty-five or more points will leave the same time, so I will go on both service and points.

Rank doesn't mean too much around here, as far as being put on details. The only thing I get out of is KP, however, the first three grades have to pull guard duty, and charge-of-Quarters. I always get my chance to do all of these things first, as everything is taken alphabetically.

It is very warm here during the daytime, but as usual the nights aren't too bad. It is just right for sleeping.

I don't ever seem to get a chance to get to bed very early here, so I am always the last one up in the mornings. I guess that it is just habit but I always wake up 10 minutes to seven, and rush

Tinian in the Pacific

Al's Odyssey, from Catonsville to Japan
Edward Albert Aldridge II's World War II Letters

around trying to eat and straighten everything up by twenty minutes of eight.

There is always something to do here, and it seems that I can never find time to do everything I want to.

We got a watermelon from Okinawa. One of the fellows on my crew found them growing there. But when it was cut open it was rotten on the inside, even thought he outside of it looked good.

Nothing is rationed here at the PX now. I can get all of the candy and chewing gum that I want. But I guess now that I can get whatever I want, I don't eat as much. In fact except to get a few magazines I wouldn't go to the PX at all.

One of the fellows that I met here from Baltimore said that he might stop and see you, when he got back. He seemed to be a pretty good Joe, and I was wondering if he did visit you. I imagine he must be out of the Army by this time.

If I don't stop writing, I won't have much to say in my next letter.

Love To All

Albert

It must be after 12:00 PM so I should get some sleep.

Tinian in the Pacific

Al's Odyssey, from Catonsville to Japan
Edward Albert Aldridge II's World War II Letters

December 18, 1945

Dear Mom & Pop:

Today is Sunday here and everything is OK. There hasn't been too much news here today. I don't want you to depend on what I say too much. However, I may be in California before this letter reaches you. I think I have very good chances of flying home sometime next week. The first ships are getting ready to leave in a few days. According to Capt Waddell I should be on the next group out.

It is also rumored that some of the ships are going to fly to Washington D.C. If I got on one of them it would be great. It is very late, so I will write again if I do not leave soon.

Hoping to see you very soon.

Love To All

Albert

Tinian in the Pacific

Al's Odyssey, from Catonsville to Japan
Edward Albert Aldridge II's World War II Letters

December 19, 1945

Dear Mom & Pop:

I haven't received a letter in several days. Today a notice was posted that we would not receive mail for about ten days due to transportation.

We just got finished popping pop corn that one of the fellows received from home. Once in awhile we cook our own meals in the barracks, when the food in the mess hall isn't too good. We got a lot of canned turkey and chicken, from the mess hall. We use a blow torch to heat it, and make sandwiches.

My writing isn't too good as I have a blister on my finger and it is a little difficult hold a pen.

I have been taken off of the crew that I was on, because I am on the next shipment out. I don't mind though as I don't care too much about flying anymore. If I leave this month I don't think I will ever do anymore flying in the army. However, if I don't leave until next month, I will have to fly four hours then.

I don't think it will be too long before I leave here; however, I am disappointed that I wasn't able to get home for Christmas.

Love to All

Albert

Tinian in the Pacific

Al's Odyssey, from Catonsville to Japan
Edward Albert Aldridge II's World War II Letters

December 25, 1945

Dear Mom & Pop:

Today, being Christmas, we all had the day off. I certainly would have liked to spend today with you, and Pop and Elwin.

We had a very good meal today for a change. I think it was about the best meal that I ever had in the Army. We had turkey and every thing that goes with it plus mince pie[*] and fruit cake. But it would of tasted a thousand times better if you would of cooked it Mom and I could of eaten with all of you.

I haven't written for several days as the mail situation is bad, and I understood that mail would be held up for some time. However, I think that it is all getting through again.

It seems that every time I turn around here lately, I am doing something different. They have me working at the motor pool now. Monday, I was greasing trucks and so forth. I guess I will be working there until I leave. However, that is better then pulling all kinds of details around the squadron.

We haven't received any word as yet, about when the next shipment is leaving here for sure. But I am certain it won't be too long before I get to see you.

This afternoon several of the fellows and me practiced a little basketball. We have a game tomorrow afternoon.

---

[*] Mincemeat pie was a pie crust filled with dried fruit, spices, distilled spirits, beef suet and beef.

Tinian in the Pacific

Al's Odyssey, from Catonsville to Japan
Edward Albert Aldridge II's World War II Letters

I can hardly realize that it snowed in Baltimore, because of the hot weather we are having here. But it usually snows around this time every year there.

Love To All

Albert

Tinian in the Pacific

Al's Odyssey, from Catonsville to Japan
Edward Albert Aldridge II's World War II Letters

Wishing you a Merry Christmas and Happy New Year 1945

Best wishes to Mom, Pop, Elwin
love Albert

Tinian in the Pacific

Al's Odyssey, from Catonsville to Japan
Edward Albert Aldridge II's World War II Letters

December 27, 1945

Dear Mom & Pop:

Mail here finally came through here, as I received a lot of letters today, including Christmas cards from all of you and also Aunt Rolly.

Mom, I did mean for you to get yourself a nice Christmas present for me. I had thought that I asked you to in the letter also. You know I wouldn't forget you.

Yes, I know Elwin would like the motor scooter that I have, but I suppose I will have to give it to one of the other fellows when I leave.

I got it from one of my friends when he left. It didn't cost me any thing, but several fellows have offered to buy it from me.

Due to the shortage of men here now the Headquarters just announced tonight, that men here will not be able to leave until they are eligible for discharge. So I guess that no one will leave here before Feb 1. Usually, as to the past men were shipped about a month before they could be discharged. But when it came to be my turn, they changed the system. However, there is at least a definite set date that I will leave here.

I have done just about everything since I have been here, but I guess I will spend the rest of my time working in the motor pool. I don't mind the work as it isn't hard and the time passes fast.

Tinian in the Pacific

Al's Odyssey, from Catonsville to Japan
Edward Albert Aldridge II's World War II Letters

You mentioned that Joe did not have enough points to get home. But he will be eligible for discharge the same time as I am. So I suppose I will be discharged about the same time as he will.

The weather is certainly nasty there now, but when I get back to Baltimore it should be getting warmer.

Love To All

Albert

Tinian in the Pacific

Al's Odyssey, from Catonsville to Japan
Edward Albert Aldridge II's World War II Letters

January 1, 1946

Dear Mom & Pop:

Today being the first we had it easy with nothing to do all day. I played a little basketball this afternoon. There wasn't much of the morning as I didn't get up until almost twelve. We had a nice dinner, turkey again, just about the same as we had for Christmas.

Everything here is just about the same, just one day passing and another tomorrow. It seems a shame that so much time passes by, while everybody here should be back in the states doing what they want.

There isn't any news at all of leaving so I guess I will have to wait until the first of the month, I mean February.

It has been pretty good here the last week as we have had quite a few days off. There isn't much to do, however, to pass the time, when there is a day off.

I just keep marking the days off of the calendar, wanting for this month to end.

There isn't much to write about, so I will close.

Love To All

Albert

Tinian in the Pacific

Al's Odyssey, from Catonsville to Japan
Edward Albert Aldridge II's World War II Letters

S/Sgt. E. A. Aldridge 38552323
9th B. 6 – 99th H.S.
APO – 336 - c/o P.M.
San Francisco, Calif

January 4, 1946

Dear Mom & Pop:

Mail is coming here in spurts, at the present time yesterday. I received five letters from you. I didn't write yesterday as I made a flight and didn't get back until very late.

I have my time in this month, so I won't have to fly again. I hope that I have made my last flight in the Army.

I thought that I mentioned before, that when my points were refigured I had only forty-nine. I don't know how the mistake, was made but they claimed I needed two more days of service for fifty points.

If I am not mistaken I received four Christmas cards from all of you. I received first one from Mom then one from Pop, and another from Elwin. Yesterday I received another one.

I am going to send a money order for $100^{00} as soon as I can get to the Post Office, so you can keep on the watch for it. This month I got paid for two months. I drew about $176.00, but I am keeping the rest in case I leave before I get paid again.

Tinian in the Pacific

Al's Odyssey, from Catonsville to Japan
Edward Albert Aldridge II's World War II Letters

Tomorrow is Saturday and we are having a basketball game in the afternoon. Also the Squadron is forming a new softball team tomorrow afternoon. They want me to play softball tomorrow, but I told the fellows I would play basketball first. Now I don't know what to do, as I would rather play softball.

There wasn't any mail today, but I will write again tomorrow.

    Love To All

        Albert

Tinian in the Pacific

Al's Odyssey, from Catonsville to Japan
Edward Albert Aldridge II's World War II Letters

S/Sgt. E. A. Aldridge 38552323
9th B. G. – 99th H.S.
APO – 336 – c/o P.M.
San Francisco, Calif

January 6, 1946

Dear Mom & Pop:

    Tonight is Sunday night. I worked this afternoon so the day didn't seem too much like Sunday.

    I can't seem to find my pen tonight. I have my good one packed away, but my other one is around here somewhere, I hope.

    There seems to be quite a bit of news now, concerning the discharging of men from the Armed Forces. I don't know exactly what it's all about, but every news report on the radio, has something to say about it. Today one mentioned that men will be held until three months after they are eligible for discharge. I hope that won't happen here.[*]

    I haven't had a chance to get a money order as yet. But I will try to get it tomorrow so I won't have the money around here too long.

    I can't seem to write very much in my letters lately.

                    Love to All

                      Albert

---

[*] On January 6, 1946, soldiers throughout the world demonstrated and protested a slowdown of demobilization.

Tinian in the Pacific

Al's Odyssey, from Catonsville to Japan
Edward Albert Aldridge II's World War II Letters

January 8, 1945

Dear Mom & Pop:

Today is Wednesday and we all had the afternoon off. That is we get every Wednesday afternoon off.

I played ball most of the afternoon. We had a good game with the Fifth Squadron; it was tied four all until the twelfth inning when the fifth scored a run. I caught[*] the whole game, and now I am so tired I am going to be early tonight.

There has been quite a bit of excitement lately about getting the men back from overseas.

As I understand it there were several meetings of the men on the different islands around here. I think that most of the soldiers complaints are, that men are being discharged back in the states with very low point scores while so many of us here have more points and service. Then they claim that there isn't anyone to replace the men overseas.[†]

I think that the fellows overseas now are getting the worst part of it all, now. I heard of many getting discharges with as few at ten to fifteen points.

It was announced here again that all men will leave when they are eligible for discharge. In my case I think it will be February 1, 1946.

Time passes fairly fast here so I'll just have to wait a few weeks yet.
      Love to All
      Albert

---

[*] He probably meant he played in the catcher position.
[†] The Army Chief of Staff, George Marshall was released from duty by President Truman on January 1, 1946.

Tinian in the Pacific

Al's Odyssey, from Catonsville to Japan
Edward Albert Aldridge II's World War II Letters

Tinian in the Pacific

Al's Odyssey, from Catonsville to Japan
Edward Albert Aldridge II's World War II Letters

Tinian in the Pacific

Al's Odyssey, from Catonsville to Japan
Edward Albert Aldridge II's World War II Letters

Coming Home:
Saipan and Camp Stoneman

33552323
S/Sgt. E. A. Aldridge
9th B.G. 99 B. Sq
APO – 336 - ℅ P.M.
San Francisco, California

January 23, 1946

Dear Mom & Pop:

    Received two letters from you two days before I left Tinian. I haven't written sooner because I didn't want to tell you that I was coming home and then not make it. Monday morning I left Tinian for Saipan, where I am now. I processed all Monday afternoon until ten o'clock that night. Then yesterday morning they woke me up at 7:30 AM and told me I was on KP. I haven't had any time off until this morning.

    Before I left Tinian I waited for another letter from you, but none came. I have been thinking all of the time about Pop being sick.[*] I prayed to God that it would be nothing serious. I suppose I should have written when I last heard from you, but during that time I was clearing Tinian and I could not write and not tell you that I was coming until I was positive.

---

[*] Al is probably referring to Pop having his appendix removed. The only illnesses that Little Elwin recalls that Pop had was appendicitis.

Al's Odyssey, from Catonsville to Japan
Edward Albert Aldridge II's World War II Letters

Sunday before I left, I checked the Post Office all day, but there wasn't any mail at all. This will probably be the last time I will be able to write, and I will not receive any more mail.

I should leave here tonight or tomorrow sometime. If I stay longer, I will write again. The trip by boat should take about fifteen days.

I will call you when I get to California if I can, but for sure I will send a telegram when I get there.

From California I will be sent to Fort Meade for separation from the service. I don't know exactly how long this will take, but it will probably be at least a month before I get out.

I trust in the Lord that everyone be well until I get home.

Love to All

Albert

Traveling across the Pacific Ocean in mid winter could not have been pleasant, but he never said anything about the trip. Camp Stoneman was adjacent to the town of Pittsburgh, California. It was a staging area that housed as many as 21,000 troops. In January 1946, 2250 German prisoners of war were housed there while waiting transportation back to Germany.

Coming Home

Al's Odyssey, from Catonsville to Japan
Edward Albert Aldridge II's World War II Letters

Camp Stoneman February 8, 1946

Arrived in California yesterday. Expect to be at Fort Meade[*] in a week.

All is fine.

Will see you soon.

                Love to all

                Albert

---

[*] Fort Meade, Maryland

Al's Odyssey, from Catonsville to Japan
Edward Albert Aldridge II's World War II Letters

Back to Baseball

Al came back home to live with Mom, Pop, and Little Elwin until he married. He drove his old Ford convertible which Pop had kept in good condition. He considered taking advantage of the GI Bill to go to college. The GI Bill provided all tuition, books, fees and living expenses, and many young men greatly benefited from it; but Al decided he wanted to play baseball more than anything. He returned to the Donut Corporation of America to work and started teaching baseball to little Elwin. Al said that he never wanted to fly again.

Little Elwin tagged along when Al went to see games of the Baltimore Orioles International League AAA baseball team and the Bullets basketball team before there was an NBA.[*] Elwin watched while Al played sandlot baseball around Maryland. Al played with the Oella Grays[†] which had some retired professional players at times. The Grays picked up some active professional players late in the season when the professional leagues ended. Al played left field and third base because he had a good arm. He was also fast and a good hitter. Little Elwin participated by shagging balls in the outfield, chasing balls in the woods, and warming up players. Al taught Elwin to pitch, hit, and field. His rules for baseball and life were simple: Always throw as hard as you can. Run as fast as you can. Hit as hard as you can. Get a score of a 100% correct on every test.

Little Elwin started to grow and it was obvious that he was going to be tall. As a result, Al talked Pop into putting a homemade

---

[*] Little Elwin recalls premier backcourt player and player coach, Harry "Buddy" Jeannette who used to shoot long shots going away from the basket off the wrong foot.. He was inducted into the Basketball Hall of Fame in 1994.

[†] The old Oella Grays Baseball Field is now the site of the Trinity United Methodist Church, 2100 Westchester Ave, Catonsville, MD 21228.

Al's Odyssey, from Catonsville to Japan
Edward Albert Aldridge II's World War II Letters

backboard and basket in the back yard under the trees. Boys came from miles around to play basketball and talk between games there in the shade. When Al came home from work, he frequently joined the boys, but Pop never did. It was a neighborhood gathering point for boys and young men for several years until they got sidetracked by girls. No women or girls joined us when we were playing basketball except Al's cousin Marie, daughter of Uncle Ben and Aunt Kate.

Al participated in sports in some way for the rest of his life and was a great fan of the Baltimore Orioles.

Pop had taught many people to drive. During the war Pop tried to teach Mom to drive, but he gave up saying, "She'll never learn." When Al came home, Mom asked him to teach her, but both Al and Mom came to Pop's conclusion when Mom collided with the house and demolished his old Ford which Pop had worked so hard to preserve.

Al then bought a gorgeous convertible — a beautiful shade of blue, the likes of which had not been seen before or since. During the war and depression one rarely saw a shiny, clean, bright colored or beautiful car. The neighbors came and gathered around to gape in awe. Postwar cars were not coming off the production lines yet. That car was the symbol that the war, black cars, the Great Depression, and extreme war time scarcity were finished. It had the small words "blue eyes" painted under the front side windows. As Al took Elwin to ball games, Elwin often heard the words "Hi blue eyes" coming from other cars.

Back to Baseball

Al's Odyssey, from Catonsville to Japan
Edward Albert Aldridge II's World War II Letters

Al and "Blues Eyes

Back to Baseball

Al's Odyssey, from Catonsville to Japan
Edward Albert Aldridge II's World War II Letters

Elwin Carl Penski
Al's Little Brother

    Elwin Carl Penski (El) received his education at Catonsville High School, Philadelphia Textile Institute (now Philadelphia University), MIT, and the University of Utah. All of his tuition was paid for by scholarships. Nearly all of his other expenses were paid by various jobs that he held. El was a carpenter's helper, and a floor man in an very large A&P bakery in the summers where he belonged to the AFL. In the bakery one of his many tasks was dumping 100 lb bags of donut mix into a automatic donut machine.

    He held various scientific jobs at Philadelphia University and was a teaching assistant at MIT and the University of Utah. He worked as a research chemist at Wright-Patterson Air Force Base while serving as an officer in the Air Force. El was a research chemist at the University of Dayton Research Institute and Aberdeen Proving Ground. He was an expert in an unusually large number of areas of applied and basic research. His publications provided a major resource for the defense of the forces of the U.S. and U.S. allies. He worked with many university faculty members, government scientists from many agencies, and scientists affiliated with contractors on Army supported research. After 35 years of government service, El retired in 1995.

    In the 1960s, El tutored students in trigonometry at Dunbar High School in Baltimore. He also judged science fairs at local high schools and at Towson and Morgan State Universities. El has been a member of the American Chemical Society from 1963 to the present, Chairman of the Maryland Section in 1981, Congressional Science Councilor from 1981 to 1986, Chairman of the Maryland Chemist Award Committee from 1990 to 1998, and holder of many other positions. El held similar positions in Sigma Xi, the Scientific Research Society. He was President of the Chesapeake Chapter during the 1979-1980 period. As part of his work for various groups, he tried to promote science and physical activity in the high schools. El was one of the founders and an active worker for the

Al's Odyssey, from Catonsville to Japan
Edward Albert Aldridge II's World War II Letters

Sharing Table (a soup kitchen in Edgewood) for 12 years. He helped found the Betty Penski Memorial Scholarship Fund, Essex Community College.

El coached soccer, basketball, and baseball in Joppatowne and baseball and soccer in Fallston for the Recreation Councils. He played tennis and basketball in Bel Air, Edgewood, and Joppatowne in County Recreation Programs.

El has always been involved in environmental work. For example, in 1973 in the face of much skepticism, he and his wife, Betty Wright, proposed to the State of Maryland that a large part of Cunningham Falls State Park be set aside as a wildland. In 1981, the Maryland Legislature set aside the proposed area, 3500 acres. He and Betty maintained a few miles of the Appalachian Trail and regional trails for many years. He was President of the Otter Point Creek Alliance.

He is or has been a member of many such groups and of many historical societies. He has been the Webmaster for the Historical Society of Harford County since 1996 and served on the Board of Directors for four years. He served as a Director, Treasurer, and Webmaster of the Baltimore County Historical Society. He is the founder of the Junius B. Booth Society, Inc. El has received numerous awards for his Equal Employment Opportunity, scientific, leadership, historical, and charitable contributions.

Al's Odyssey, from Catonsville to Japan
Edward Albert Aldridge II's World War II Letters

INDEX

313th Bomb Wing, 248, 283
313th Bomb Wing, Presidential Citation, 318, 340
3701 Base Unit, 132
58th Wing, 310
902nd Training Group, 105
9th Bomb Group, 302
Aberdeen Proving Ground, 368
aerial embarkation, 239
Aguigaun Island, 244
Air Force, 12
Air Medal 198, 298
Aldrich, Edward A.; Edward A. Aldridge II; 232
Aldridge family, 18
Aldridge, Edward Albert I; "Ed", **18**
Aldridge, Edward Albert II; "Al", **31**
Aldridge, Frank, 19
Aldridge, Nelson, 19
Aldridge, Samuel, 20
Allotments, 101, 124, 126
Alrewic, 18
altitude chamber, 161
Amarillo Army Air Field, 87
Amarillo, Texas, 87
Appendicitis, 250, 362
atomic bomb, 14, 242, 267, 272-274
Aunt Martha, 24-25
Aunt Rolly; Roseline Shearer, 15,   120, 193, 259, 290, 291, 353
Aunt Sophie; Sophie Smith, 15, 119, 193, 231
Autry, Gene, 256
B-17, 13, 145, 150, 200,
B-24, 150, 157, 171, 177
B-26, 145, 157
B-29, 14, 72, 87, 145, 161, 178, 203, 205, 212, 217. 228, 235-236, 241-244, 262-277, 286, 293, 304, 310, 331
Baltic Fleet, Russia, 7
Baltimore County, Maryland, 31-45, 147, 264, 315
Baltimore Municipal Stadium, 146
Baltimore, Maryland, 26, 28, 31, 35
Baseball, 28, 37-42, 64, 129, 131, 141, 145, 279, 289, 319, 365
Bay Shore, Maryland, 264
Ben; Benjamin Henry Neher "Uncle Ben", 19, 31, 107, 120, 366
Birmingham Congregational Cemetery, 20
blister gunner, 236
blue eyes, 366
Boeing, 72, 200, 228
Brigadoon, 32
Buckingham Army Air Field Flexible Gunnery School, 150
Buffalo Lake, 133
Cadillac Hotel, 59, 77,

370

Al's Odyssey, from Catonsville to Japan
Edward Albert Aldridge II's World War II Letters

Carpenter, 27
Catonsville Democratic Club, 40
Catonsville Elementary School, 40
Catonsville High School, 40-41
Catonsville Manor, 31
Catonsville Public Library, 33
Catonsville, Maryland, 37
change of address form, 234
Cherbourgh, France, 140
China, 7, 14, 148, 276, 304
Cigarettes, 37, 231, 260
class A uniform, 66
Clovis, New Mexico, 203
cord wood, 27
coup in Japan, 276
CQ, Charge of Quarters, 100, 132
Crullers, 45
Cunningham Falls State Park, 369
Dalkiewicz, Edward B., 232
Dallas, Texas, 140-142, 152
Darwin, Charles, 9
DCA, see Donut Corporation of America
Delawders, 220
Deller, Bud, 75
Delmar, Col., 150
Depression, Great, 3, 10, 27, 31, 46, 107, 366
Discharge, 71, 143, 146, 271, 284, 289, 302, 313, 331, 346, 353-354, 358-359
Dolores Smith, 258, 306
Donut Corporation of America, 44, 81, 123, 365
Donuts, 44
Downsizing, 329
Draft, 15, 47
Dunckelman, Lonnie V., 232
Edmondson Heights Park, 32
Edgewood Arsenal, 40
Ellicott City, 35, 41, 44, 50, 81, 166, 183, 220, 262
Emperor of Japan, 7, 273, 274, 278
English Field, 87
Eureka, South Dakota, 15, 24,
Flamingo Park, 64
Florida 46, 149, 176
fly over 69, 286
Flying Fortress, 13, 72, 200,
Fort George Meade, 212, 363-364
Fort Meyers, 150-175
G.I. shoes, 179
gasoline ration, 251, 280, 294,
Geer, Ferel, 52, 61,
Genocide, 9,
German United Evangelical Cemetery, 20
Germany, 5-9, 12-15, 24, 140, 146, 149, 183, 200, 216, 242, 319, 363
GHQ Air Force, 13
GI Bill, 365

Al's Odyssey, from Catonsville to Japan
Edward Albert Aldridge II's World War II Letters

Gonzales, Claudio S., 232
Grandma, 31, 40, 43, 45, 64, 80, 102, 134, 197, 213, 219, 233, 246, 249, 257, 263, 269, 275, 281, 289, 321, 322
Grandpa, 21, 168,
Griel, Martha, 21
Ground Moving Target Range, 150
Guam, 242, 259, 264, 267, 292, 295, 310, 346
Gunner, 13, 150-152, 161, 168, 177, 183, 236, 242, 272, 281
Gunnery simulators, 150, 177
Healey, Bunk, 102, 115, 117
Healey, Dick, 67, 115, 117
Heavy Cruiser Indianapolis, 267
Hershmann, Charley, 220
Hialeah, 78
Hiroshima, Japan, 14, 268, 273
Hitler, 6-8
Hooper, Gene, 50
Hutchens, Wallace J., 307, 232
Income tax, 53, 59, 101, 123
Individual A.A.F. Issue Record
influenza epidemic, great, 10, 23-24
Ingleside Avenue, 31
Ingleside Shopping Center, 32
Iwo Jima, 205, 268
Japan, 5, 7, 9-11, 14, 46-47, 146- 148, 205, 239, 241-245, 252, 262, 265-280, 286, 288, 298, 303, 318, 340
Japanese 1st Naval Air Fleet, 242
Japanese I-58 submarine, 267
Jerkwater, 35
Jero, John P., 230, 257,
Joe, Joseph Shearer, 51, 75, 209, 259, 264, 269, 291, 321, 346-347, 354
Joseph Horne Company, 15-16
Judik's Field, 41, 269
Kamikaze, 14, 241, 245, 266
Kampel, Edward Joseph, 31-32, 43, 102, 197-200, 216, 271, 290, 332
Kampel, Florence "aunt", 15, 31, 64, 112-114, 197, 216, 271, 289-290, 332
Kampel, Larry, 31, 43, 112, 216, 221, 259, 271, 289-290
Kate, see Neher, Kate
Kay Hotel, 229
King, John R., 232
knights of the air, 12
Kokura, Japan, 268
Kumagava, Japan, 277
Kuwana, Japan, 262
Kyushu, Japan, 241, 244
League of Nations, 242
LeMay, General Curtis, 262
Lincoln, Nebraska, 169, 196, 203-204
Little Elwin, Elwin Carl Penski, 368
Lord Tarleton Hotel, 60-62
Los Angeles 224
lost B-29s, 266
Maebashi, Japan, 272

372

Al's Odyssey, from Catonsville to Japan
Edward Albert Aldridge II's World War II Letters

Major Bowman, 108
Manchuria 7
Mariana Islands, 14, 197, 205, 242-243, 248-
Marianas Campaign, 243
Marshall, George C., 14, 359
Mather Field, California, 239
Meadows Industrial Park, 32
Mellor, Roger, 132, 183, 207, 216, 220
Miami, 46-85
Miami Beach, 46-85
Miami Beach Schools, 46-85
Miami Hotels, 46-85
Mincemeat, 350
Mining, 18, 340
MIT, 368
Mom, **15**
model airplane, 39
Mory, Robert M., 232
motor scooter, 337, 339, 353
Nagaoka, Japan, 272
Nagasaki, Japan, 14, 268, 272
Naples Municipal Airport, 175
Naples, Florida, 175-195
Napoleon, 5
National Life and Accident Insurance Co. of Nashville, Tennessee, 15, 19
Nazi, 9-10, 47, 72,
Neher, 15
Neher, Benjamin Henry, "Uncle Ben," 15, 19, 31, 107, 120, 366
Neher, Edward James, "Buddy", 24
Neher, Kate, 80, 290, 366
Neher, Maria; see "Grandma"
New Orleans, 152
Nigata, Japan, 268
Nippon Oil Company, 277
Nylon, 290
Occupation of Japan, 225, 278
Oella Grays, 365
Okinawa, Japan, 244, 310, 314, 342-344, 347
Oriole Park, Baltimore, 146, 148
P-38, 145
P-52, 145
Pacifism, 6
Palo Duro Canyon, 132
Parry, Ann Elizabeth, 20
peace ultimatum, 268
Pearl Harbor, 7, 11, 46
Peggy, 18
Penski, Carl August, 24
Penski, Elsie, 22
Penski, Elwin "Pop", 21
Penski, Elwin Carl "Little Elwin" "El", 16, 30, 32, 43, 83, 109, 368
Penski, Freda, 22
Penski, Herman, 22, 122

Al's Odyssey, from Catonsville to Japan
Edward Albert Aldridge II's World War II Letters

Penski, John (see Grandpa)
Penski, John (Johnny), 22, 338
Penski, Lillian; Lillian Rice, "Aunt   Lilly", 113-114, 116,
Penski, Margaret Elizabeth (Neher   Aldridge), "Mom", **15**
Penski, Roland, 22
Pentagon, 13
Pets, 43, 103
Pettit, Alvin E., 232
Philadelphia University, 368
Pilots, 6, 12-13, 72, 203, 215, 233, 264, 266, 272, 281, 312, 321, 336, 338
Pinar del Rio Hurricane, 173
ping pong balls, 41, 121-122, 250
Pittsburgh, Pennsylvania, 15, 19-20, 31-32, 40-41, 64, 107-108, 112, 197, 199, 222, 226, 275, 281, 289
Pneumonia, 84
point system, 289, 292, 302, 304, 307, 312-313, 315-318,   321-324, 326, 331-333, 337, 346, 354, 356, 359
Poland, 6, 8
Po**p,** 21
Potsdam Conference, 268
pressurized area, 161
property List, 361
punch card tabulating machine, 44-45
Puschmann, Martha, 21
Queen Victoria, 18
Quonset huts, 248, 293, 302, 304, 309, 317-318
Racism, 9
Radio, 2, 21, 49, 81, 140, 147, 172, 214, 217, 278, 358
Rationing, 34, 46, 48, 54, 57, 61, 63, 83, 103, 116, 145, 204, 251, 280, 294, 347
Religion, 9, 39-40
Rice, Vernon, 246, 248, 259
Rice's Bakery, 36, 104
Ridgely, Emerson M. "Emery", 166, 183, 216,
Ridgely, Mrs., 183, 207, 223, 262, 343
Ridgely, Russell, 262
Roger Mellor, see Mellor
Roosevelt, President Franklin D., 46,148, 225
Roosevelt, President Theodore, 12,
Route 1 in about 1910, 24
RP-63, 150
Russia, 5-9, 145, 147, 245, 276
Sacramento, 237
sail boat, 69, 280, 282-283, 300
Saint Agnes Lane, 33
Saipan, 197, 242, 248, 284, 306-307, 313, 328, 332, 362
San Francisco, 67, 224, 239, 248,   267, 298
Seabees, 244
Shearer, Joesph, see "Joe"
Shearer, Roseline, see "Aunt Rolly"
Shell Road, Ingleside Avenue, 35
Shot Tower, Baltimore, 27
show of force, 286

Al's Odyssey, from Catonsville to Japan
Edward Albert Aldridge II's World War II Letters

slowdown of demobilization, 329
Smith, Dolores, 258, 306
Smith, Neil C., 232
Social Security Administration, 32
Socialism, 6, 8,
Stalin, Joseph, 6, 9, 268
Stearman Aircraft Company, 228
Strauss, 110
Streetcar, 25, 35
Submarines, 48, 69, 267
Suicide Cliff, 243
sulfa drugs, 84
Super Fortress, see B-29
Surrender, 226, 242-243, 268, 273-274, 276, 278, 286, 288
T-6, 150,
Tail Gunner, 236, 238, 272
Taiwan, 7
Tax, see Victory Tax
Texas Panhandle, 87, 104
Tibbets, Paul Warfield Jr, 72, 272
Tinian, 14, **242**-244, 248, 255, 267-268, 231-272, 274-275, 281, 284, 290, 292, 302, 307, 310-313, 315, 318, 321, 323, 328, 338, 343- 344, 346, 362
Tokuyama, Japan, 268
Tolchester, Maryland, 264
Topeka Army Air Field, 226, 228, 230
Topeka, Kansas, 226, **228**-229, 233, 239-240, 252, 269
Total war, 47
Treaty of Versailles, 7-8
Trolley, 25
troop strength, 329
Truman, Harry; President and Vice President, 148, 225 244, 329
Tsu, Japan, 266
Tsuchizakiminato, 277
Tucson, Arizona, 222 224
Twentieth Air Force, 14, 268 270, 272 298
Typhoid, 19-20, 326
Typhoon at Okinawa, 314
Uji-Yamada, Japan, 270
Uncle Ben, see Ben
Uncle Carl, 15, 275
United States Army Air Force, 12
Ushi Airdrome, 242
V-E Day, 226
Veterans of World War II, 2
Victory Tax, 123
V-J Day, Victory over Japan, 286
WAAC, Women's Army Auxiliary Corp, 76
Waddell, Charles R., 313 320, 325, 348
Walden Circle, 32
Wallace, Henry; Vice President, 46, 225
Walsall, 18
Walther League, 141

375

Al's Odyssey, from Catonsville to Japan
Edward Albert Aldridge II's World War II Letters

War time, 315
Warnings, 273-274
West Baltimore Baptist Church, 40
West Edmondale, 33, 41
Westinghouse, 28
Westview Park, 32-33
Westview Shopping Center, 32-33
Westway Theater, 36
Whitlock, A.J., 232
Wichita, Kansas, 228
Wiedenhoeft, John, 38
Winchell, Walter, 145
Witt, Byron, 98
Wood business, 26-27
World War I, 12-13, 23,
World War II, 5-13
Wright, Wilbur and Orville, 12
Wright-Patterson Air Force Base, 368
Yawata, Japan, 286
Zimmerman Cemetery, 20